आ नो भद्राः क्रतवो यन्तु विश्वतः ।

ā no bhadrāḥ kratavo yantu viśvataḥ

Let noble thoughts come to us from every side

- Rig Veda I - 89-i

BHAVAN'S BOOK UNIVERSITY

MODERN SCIENCES IN VEDAS

by

Justice Dhananjay Deshpande

BHAVAN'S BOOK UNIVERSITY

MODERN SCIENCES IN VEDAS

Justice Dhananjay Deshpande

Translation
by
G. N. Kamat, Advocate

2007
BHARATIYA VIDYA BHAVAN
Kulapati Munshi Marg
Mumbai - 400 007

First Edition, 1000 copies : 2007

Price : Rs. 270.00
$. 11.00
£. 7.00

PRINTED IN INDIA by Nilesh Parekh, at Paras Prints, 34, Cowasji Patel Street, 17, Lakhani Terrace, Fort, Mumbai - 400001 and Published by P. V. Sankarankutty, Deputy Registrar (Publications), Bharatiya Vidya Bhavan, K.M. Munshi Marg, Mumbai - 400007.
E-mail : brbhavan@bom7.vsnl.net.in
Web-site : http://www.bhavans.info

DEDICATED

to

All the great scientists Rishis of Vedas

Who, by their boundless intuitions,

discovered, revealed and explained

the secrets of the Universe

in most scientific terms and concepts,

in a language shrouded in mystery,

waiting for generations

to decipher their language

and

find in Vedas

the ocean of modern scientific knowledge

Dr. A. P. J. Abdul Kalam
ISRO Distinguished Professor

833, Asiad Village Complex
Siri Fort
New Delhi –110 049

2nd December, 2001

Dear Justice Deshpande,

May I refer to your letter of 19th November, 2001, I am delighted to see such an intellectual and powerful hobby. I am just setting up my tasks. For the next few months, I may please be excused on publication because it may get delayed. The book on Science in Vedas indeed will be a great addition. I always feel, such enriched information have to be researched and added to the growth of modern science as a unique Indian contribution.

My friend Dr. Anil Kakodkar, Chairman, Atomic Energy Commission is an excellent scientist. You may request him for the publication of this very important book.

With regards,

Yours sincerely,

Justice Dhananjay Deshpande
12, Rocky Hills
N. D. Road, Malabar Hill
Mumbai –400 006
Maharashtra

PREFACE

It is a moment of great pleasure and pride for me to present my research in Vedas to the intellectual community world over.

My study of Vedas and the research was accidental or you may say that it was destiny. For three months before I opened Atharva Veda I went into deep meditation or Dhyanyoga just to find out what is the correlation between Gayatri Mantra and the Sun. After about three months I accidentally opened the Marathi translation of Atharva-Veda by the great Vedic Scholar, late Siddheshwar Shastri Chitrav of Pune, and found a Vedic hymn - 'one who contemplates easily on the real, basic and true form of the Sun can grasp and understand the ultimate truth of all deities.'

This gave me further inspiration to study Vedas and very soon I came across certain Vedic hymns or Ruchas which described the entire theory of magnetism.

Six months of my study thereafter was most amazing and astonishing. The very index of this book will show what I discovered and found in Vedas. They include everything from atom to cosmology.

This research was first published in Marathi by Popular Prakashan of Shri Ramdas Bhatkal. For the publication ceremony of this book I invited Hon'ble Dr. A.P.J. Abdul Kalam, who was then Chairman of ISRO. I had sent to him translation of seven chapters of my research. He appreciated my work very much and suggested that I should approach Dr. Anil Kakodkar, Chairman of Atomic Energy Commission. The letter of Dr. Kalam appears just before this preface.

The book was then published at the hands of Dr.Kakodkar and Dr.Siddhartha Wakankar of Vadodara, a well known Vedic Scholar.

The book then received an award from the Govt. of Maharashtra and another award from Parle Tilak Vidyalay, Vile Parle, Mumbai.

The Marathi book was very much appreciated by readers and scholars and its second edition is now published.

The English translation is the outcome of tremendous interest and enthusiasm shown by Shri. G. N. Kamat, Advocate and one-time public prosecutor in City Civil & Sessions Court, Mumbai. He was amazed by my research and took upon himself the enormous task of translation. Mr. Kamat apart from being a keen student of science, is an original thinker and is deeply rooted in meditation and kundalini yoga. He has, however, not translated the Marathi thesis word by word. That was his style. But I have seen that his style does not affect the flow of logic and thinking adopted by me.

However I must clarify that English cannot carry cent percent of what I found in my research. This is not because English does not possess adequate words or vocabulary. But every language carries with it, all its culture, tradition and philosophy. The concept, a language expresses are special to that language and they cannot be properly transliterated. I can give many illustrations here but one is sufficient.

Ayurveda uses three terminology Waat, Pitta and Kapha. These are three types in which all the human beings are classified for the purpose of grouping and diagnosis. Unless one gets some basic knowledge of Ayurveda he cannot understand the significance and meaning of these terms. But not knowing these special characteristics, they are translated in English as Air for Waat, Fire for Pitta and Water for Kapha.

Now, air, fire and water as known to English knowing people are totally different from Waat, Pitta and Kapha. There is not even five percent similarity in these words in English and Ayurveda. Therefore those readers who know only English will form totally distorted opinion about these concepts of Ayurveda leading to misunderstanding and misinterpretation of Ayurveda.

Same thing has happened with all the Vedas when English knowing scholars embarked upon the study of the Vedas and this resulted in total misunderstanding of the Vedas.

This misunderstanding is not only among the English knowing scholars but also among the Indian scholars. The reason was that the Vedic Sanskrit is totally and basically different from literary Sanskrit. Vedic grammer is totally and basically different from other grammer. Not considering this basic difference, the scholars and researchers tried to give most common meaning to Vedic terminologies and came to wrong conclusions. For example Dhenu as in literary Sanskrit was regarded as cow, Ashwa as horse, Odan mean cooked rice and Brahmodan means rice cooked for sacrificial fire, all such translations and interpretations of Vedas therefore resulted in misunderstanding and misconceptions.

Another reason for this confusion was that the Vedas are more than five thousand years old. The material things referred in Vedas or described therein are not available for comparison. In the excavation of Mohenjodaro and Harappa we have come across many articles used by those people but their language is still unknown to us. Therefore, we do not know what was the name for a pot, a cow, and idol, a city or a village in their language. Therefore we have only fifty percent knowledge of those cultures. On the other hand, we have Vedas with us but no means to know which articles, things or objects are referred to as Dhenu, Ashwa and so on.

In fact a word carries with it the simple meaning, the hidden or secret meaning, the meaning with reference to context, the literary meaning, the traditional meaning, the scientific meaning etc. There are about fifteen ways a word can be used and interpreted.

But even then, most of the attempts to interpret Vedas were by ascribing the meanings by literary standard. I found that this approach was not correct.

Luckily for me I was not a Vedic scholar and hence not bound by traditions. My mind was totally free, unbiased or without any prejudices or convictions. I delved into Vedas without any preconceived ideas. And this proved to be great asset in itself.

If you look upon Vedas by literary standard then Vedas are, as they are, understood and studied in all the 44000 books published on Vedas all over the world. But if we look at Vedas from my mind of approach then Vedas are nothing but an encyclopedia of all modern sciences.

My approach is not to take the literary meaning of Vedas but try to find out the concepts explained in them. My approach is to find out the hidden meaning, the causes for expressing things in such obscure way or manner.

One illustration in this regard is sufficient. Vratya is a terminology used in Atharva Veda. Literary or traditional meaning of Vratya is a man without any kind of *sanskars*. If you accept this meaning then the whole chapter does not give you any clear and concrete idea of what a Vratya is. But when

I studied this chapter again and again I realized what Vratya actually is.

A hymn or Rucha described Vratya as under:-

अहा प्रत्यंग व्रात्यो रात्र्या
प्रांग नमो व्रात्याय !!

meaning: I salute or do Pranam to Vratya who faces east in the morning and west in the evening.

This hymn or Rucha made me think again and again. I realised that if I can properly decipher this hymn, then the whole concept of Vratya will be unfolded before me.

While concentrating on this hymn I suddenly remembered about comets. I got excited by this intuition and opened encyclopaedia. Britanica about comets and to my astonishment I found the following sentence 'comets are often seen near the western horizon after sunset and near eastern horizon before sunrise.'

After this revelation the entire chapter on Vratya was found to be devoted to Comets. And from that I learnt that Vedic Rishis were knowing everything about comets what we know in this twenty first century with the help of all the spacecrafts and telescopes.

My research is therefore of such kind. I have ample proof to show that Vedas contain all knowledge of modern sciences including atoms, astronomy, chemistry, physics, cosmology and what not.

My study of Vedas have given me a new insight for looking at Vedas. And that is - do not take the words of Vedas as per their traditional and literary meaning. Do not treat Dhenu as cow, Ashwa as Horse, Udaka or Jala as water which we drink, milk as cow's milk or she buffalo's milk, Indra as a deity with human like form, Asuras as Demons or Rakshas, rivers as flowing water.

With all the humility I must admit that I do not proclaim that every word of my research is true and correct. Some theories may not be cent percent correct, some may be fifty percent near truth. But there are many theories and interpretations which are cent percent true and scientific. And therefore with pride I can say that change your approach towards Vedas, try to find the hidden meaning and you will be amazed, astonished and surprised to know the depth of knowledge the Vedic Rishis possessed.

How did the Vedic Rishis know about all such things ? This will be another aspect requiring deep and sincere research. Let somebody embark upon such study.

In the end I must thank all readers who appreciated my research. I also thank my stenos Mr.Chandan and Ms.Chandka for the valuable help they rendered in typing the English version and preparing the manuscript and also successfully completing the onerous task of proof correction.

My special thanks to Bharatiya Vidya Bhavan for selecting this work for publication. The reputation of Bhavan, I am confident, will take this book all over the world benefiting thereby the study and understanding of Vedas in proper perspective and with a totally new approach. That is the need of this age.

I must also mention the valuable assistance given to me by my daughters, Madhavi, Mrinal and Chetana in taking down the notes of my research. My brother Hrishikesh, who is a good critic with sound background of scientific approach also rendered valuable help in making me understand different branches of science.

Many well wishers who do not want to be acknowledged have not only inspired me but also gave valuable suggestions and assistance in this research. I must sincerely thank them.

Last but not the least, the entire credit for this intutional research goes to my Goddess Bhagawati Durga. She is behind each of my creation. I owe everything to her.

— Justice Dhananjay Deshpande
Bombay

10 Vidhi
Jagannath Bhosale Marg
Nariman Point
Mumbai 400 021
Tele. 22 810 642

CONTENTS

Chapter 1
OBJECTIVE

Objective - The objective of this book is to show that some conclusions reached by modern science through intensive research in 19th and 20th Centuries, compare well with conclusions reached in the holy texts of ancient India, written some hundreds of years B.C.

Areas which are subject matter of comparison are as follows:

1. Creation of the Universe
2. Atom and its construction
3. Hydrogen its qualities and its three types
4. Lithium as an element
5. Carbon and some statistics and its evolution
6. Nitrogen
7. Oxygen
8. Sodium
9. Phosphorous

10. Concern of matter and anti-matter
11. Configuration of shape of the Universe
12. Power that creates .... starts
13. Our galaxy and knowledge of its construction
14. Comets
15. Sun its orbit and other details, sun spots.
16. Black-holes and some details
17. Storms in the sun
18. Magnetism
19. Photo synthesis and other details.
20. Some beams and Corpses
21. Dissection of Corpses and details
22. Description of live volcanoes

Holy Texts:-

The word Vedas is broadly used to include above research. The word Vedas for the purposes of this book is deemed to include the following:-

(A) Vedas:- They are four :-

1. Rig Veda
2. Yajur Veda
3. Atharva Veda
4. Sam Veda

Word "Veda", means "Knowledge". They were written between 2500 years to 5000 years B.C. These calculations differ according each scholars.

(B) Upanishadas:- They are in hundreds and they were written some what later. "Upanishads" means that which is gained by the disciple by sitting (meaning listening) near his teacher.

(C) Shad (six) Darshanas (intuitive knowledge)
They are:-

1. Mimansa
2. Vedant
3. Nyaya
4. Vaisheshika
5. Sankhya
6. Yoga

Although each of the "Upanishads" and each of the "Darshanas" were authored by a separate sage, that does not hold good about Vedas. Each of the Vedas had "Mandalas" (chapter) and each chapter was authored by separate sage.

Roughly wisdom of about 1000 sages had gone into erection of aforementioned three varieties of texts and for convenience is called Vedas, but more precisely so because "Upanishadas" and "Darshanas" drew inspiration from Vedas.

During the British rule various British Scholars including Edward Gott, while appraising the contents and quality of Vedas, made observations which denigrated them. This was the result of their failure to understand the symbolism, and secretiveness contained therein. Their ignorance to interprete is to be litied.

About Vedic Sages :-

We will soon discover that without the aid of sophisticated

modern equipment, olden sages reached conclusions in area of science, which is indeed awe-inspiring.

It is therefore necessary to assess their qualifications.

These sages were gifted with highest degree of intellectual capacity. Their love for truth was peerless. What then was the methodology adopted by them would need explanation. But explanation has to be elaborated a little.

Science of Yoga tells us that within our gross body, there is a subtle body, (of various layers, but we need not go into them) and within the subtle body is spirit.

Subtle body+spirit can delink itself from gross body and externalise itself and go out in the physical Universe. Limitation of speed of light does not apply to this sortie undertaken by the Duo viz. spirit+subtle body.

One such translator (a keen student of yoga) without having any capacity for externalisation, by accident (or gift one does not know) went to Saturn, touched one of its outer rings, found that it was of ice, and returned in seconds. Even at the speed of light it would have taken hours to go from earth and return.

Sages doubtlessly had this capacity and one of them actually trust have seen "Black Hole" (Krishna-Vivar). Krishna means Black and Vivar means hole, a shocking similarity in the use of phrases.

This capacity to go freely in the universe was first qualification. This is attainable during highest flights of meditation.

Second gift that highest type of meditation confers is intuitive knowledge. It just flows into you. Plato called it the realm of Archetypal Ideas.

Benefit of sophisticated modern equipment, the two ways known to Yogic science, through which scientific knowledge could nonetheless descend into an individual are set out above.

But after gaining this knowledge, either through one of the methods described above or through a method not known to us, being part of highest meditational flights: the problem still remains as to how and why its expression appears to us as disguised.

We must know that the sages, after acquiring knowledge, had to express it in language, knowledge had to filter through his personality before being shaped in words. This knowledge was meant for outsiders whose range of intellect, and mannerism of understanding had also to be looked to.

The Sage's personality, need of outsiders, and perhaps the sage's anxiety not to openly lay down truth, lest it is abused; all this partly or wholly went into the words expressed.

As we go on deciphering the words used, we will slowly get to know that the use of the words were capable of being explained by no other hypothesis than the one suggested by the author.

It is humbly stated that the writer is not interested in making mountain out of a mole-hill, nor is he motivated by slightest chauvinism to glorify ancient Indian sages, only because he happens to be a Hindu by birth.

Chapter 2

MODERN ATTITUDE TOWARDS VEDAS

In 1878 when India was under British Rule, a British Writer by name Edward Gog wrote several articles in "Calcutta Review". Later in 1979 they were published in book form entitled "Philosophy of Upanishadas."

He summarised it by saying that India had nothing to contribute at highest intellectual level.

Following are some of the excerpts from his book:-

> "While considering Indian Philosophy the writer is confronted with undeveloped thought trends of lower level. Cultural level of Europeans is of a higher level than those of Indian both in respect of language and intellect."
>
> "Indian philosophy is undeveloped, wild, devoid of subtilty, delicacy and is artless. It is an attempt to express in lofty language thoughts which are of an extremely low order."
>
> "To study Indian Philosophy amounts to stepping down from high cultural heights of Europeans, and attempt to

reach union with undeveloped & Wild society and their thoughts."

"To see deities in principles of nature such as sun, fire, rain, lightening is outcome of childish mentality."

"Customs and other set modes of living of Aryans, such as human sacrifice, Sati, ritualistic sacrifice, and pouring of milk and butter in fire, were customs of highly undeveloped, primitive men living at the level of lower instincts."

The above critical appreciation reached by a Britisher about 125 years back, appears to click with the view point of modern Indian Scholars. These Indian Scholars appear also to think that Vedas are no better than prayers offered to powers in nature, which (out of fear) were saddled with Godliness.

When Edward Gog offered his critical comments, India was a slave nation. The superiority complex which is natural with those who rule was present. This complex naturally seems to have affected British thinkers also.

The attitude that there is nothing worthy of being learnt from slaves prevailed among British Scholars, and therefore their study of Vedas etc. was prejudiced by this attitude. This prejudice was therefore reflected in the observations of Edward Gog.

Even scholar of the level of Maxmuller who studied Vedas etc. in depth, did not escape from this prejudice. In the book "The Upanishads" Maxmuller sought "Preface" from a Christian Priest. The Priest observed in the preface to this book that "Rulers must always study the religion of those whom they rule".

Indian scholars were affected by British Rulers, not only in respect of critical appreciation of the Vedas etc. but also by their culture, civilisation, mode of living, and more obviously by the progress that they had made in science and technology. The dynamic effect resulted in wholesale acceptance of foreign ideas and culture, including designation of Vedas, Upanishadas and Shad-darshanas.

The net result was that Four points of view emerged in respect of this old store-house of knowledge (viz. Vedas etc.)

The first view point was of those who traditionally were conditioned to look upon Vedas etc. as source of all knowledge, spiritual or scientific, and that vedas were supreme.

The second was of those who were influenced by modern ways of thought, like Edward Gog.

The third was that vedas formed excellent examples of literature built in the form of poetic verses, but were otherwise unrelated to life.

The fourth was that all those deities referred to in the Vedas were utterly fictitious. If they did exist, their existence ought to be empirically proved, and if their existence could not be empirically proved, best thing was to totally forget them.

All these four view-points are proper in their own way at their own level. In view of this there is no need to demolish each of these one by one.

The charitable Indian outlook that each one has a right to go about in this own way, warrants that no attempt is intended to convert anybody's view point. Freedom is first and last of the values (Vivekanand).

One thing however is certain. It is possible to look to Vedas (including Upanishadas and Shad-darshanas) from altogether different angle. Elaboration of this view point is the main burden of the present book. This view point is based on theism. This view point is scientifically oriented. And last but not the least, it is down with transparent honesty and without any kind of chauvinism.

All the four Vedas and Shad-darshanas are available in the form of books. Ved-Santhitas are available in original Sanskrit. Similarly, translations of verses (sutras) and Mantras (verses that are intended to be repeated inwardly for spiritual progress) are also available. Similarly original Shad-darshanas with critical appreciation are also available. On the basis of the material which is available and is referred to above, it appears, that all the authors in their own way, had attempted research on the subject of cause of this universe with great concentration, honesty, subtlety of intellect, observation, analysis and presented their view point in respective books reciting the causality link, in Sutras, Mantras, and Suktas (i.e. various types of verses).

The fifth view point to look at the Vedas is followed by me and this view point is scientifically oriented. In tracing the cause of the universe the causality chain and order which Vedas set out, is attempted to be tested by me scientifically in this book, in my humble way.

Scientific attitude does not accept anything blindly, nor does it reject anything at the thresh hold without tresting it scientifically. What passes scientific tests is truth, and what fails to pass such test is rejected.

Despite the above, Albert Einstein observed that science does not have any final truth, or has not reached any final formula.

Author refers to the following observations as explanation of "Scientific Attitude".

> "Science is a self correcting enterprise to be accepted. All new ideas must survive rigorous standards of evidence. Science is generated by and devoted to face inquiry, the idea that any hypothesis no matter how strange, deserves to be considered on its merits. We do not know who will discover fundamental new sights."

Progress of science is based on proved hypothesis which are tested scientifically. However there are certain assumptions even in area in science e.g. that every atom is spherical in shape, or Ether occupies the whole space.

In next chapter I have explained what is meant by scientific attitude towards Vedas and its study.

Chapter 3

EXPLANATION OF SCIENTIFIC ATTITUDE TO VEDAS

Studying Vedas with scientific attitude does not mean, to accept the text as it is. Conclusions which Vedas reached are not to be accepted as they are set out. Some fundamental conclusions are to be kept aside. Concepts referred to in Vedas in respect of "Deities" and Godliness" are to be reviewed for codified information. Thereafter, without accepting prima-facie meanings of the words used, to look for some concealed concepts behind the words.

Since the subject of our study is a creation of the Universe, construction of the universe, and the Vedas: it is necessary to divide Vedic concepts under two heads. First head would be Society, and second head would be Universe. When we come to society, we naturally come to the study of individual who is part of society, his life-style, family, their life, society and its nation and its aspirations, their expectations and desires, and their happiness and woes. Since this aspect is unrelated to science we would eliminate it from our study. Similarly other worldly life of an individual, liberation (Moksha), his duties, his worldly activities (Karma) are also eliminated from our study.

Similarly study of deities, their existence, nature, position, their powers etc. are also to be reviewed for scientific truths, principles or laws. Because these areas are incapable of scientific probe.

But we are certainly going to undertake a scientific probe to find out, whether, behind these concepts, any scientific truth exists or not, or whether through some kind of symbolism an attempt was made to set out practically or fully some scientific theses.

Third meaning of scientific attitude is to reject things which Vedas take for granted, for example Vedas assume that creation pervades whole reality (Isha Vasyam Jagat). Similarly the thesis that Brahma, Vishnu, Mahesh created the universe. We are also rejecting the thesis of Para-Brahma.

There are two reasons for this rejection. Firstly, the answer given by Vedas, on creation of universe does not pass scientific test. Secondly, if we proceed on the hypothesis that God created the universe, then our research orientation ends, and our curiosity is thwarted. To take things for granted that God created the universe and stop there, is attitude of the devout and is symptom of ignorance.

If Vedas stopped by just making a solitary observation that God created the universe, there would have been no need to subject Vedas to any scientific probe. We would have rejected Vedas "ab-initio". But Vedas did something more besides telling that universe was created by God. Vedas told us the nature of this God (Creator or Ishavar), and also told us how this whole universe was born, and this elaboration was characterised by subtle, deep and all embracing study. And therefore even if we eliminate the study of concept of God, the all embracing elaboration of "How? and Why?," as explained by Vedas, still becomes an area worthy of scientific probe. This residue of How? and Why? that survives in the Vedas, is the object of scientific probe of this book.

During the last 150 years, science progressed by leaps and bounds. Many fresh offshoots of sciences sprung up and got enlarged. Physics, Chemistry, Biology, Zoology, Atomic Science, Astronomy, Cosmology, Anthropology, etc. which developed, had some link with the problem of creation of this universe. This development was simultaneously accompanied by development of most modern instrument of detection, verification and proof.

We intend to make use of aforementioned development, in our probe of Vedas.

We also intend to find out whether the most modern scientific conclusions reached so far either click with the conclusions reached in the Vedas, and or whether there is some kind of reciprocity between these conclusions.

On point of fact I must confess that it is as a result of reciprocity which I found in conclusions reached in Atharva Veda and conclusions of modern science, that I decided to embark on comparative study.

Such a comparative study postulated having at least elementary knowledge about conclusions reached by various modern sciences, particularly physics, chemistry, astronomy and science dealing with energy. It also postulated knowledge of Sanskrit and Concepts of Vedas.

Such a comparative study was not possible 100 or 150 years ago. Because the entire human race was frisking in area of scientific ignorance. Such of modern science had yet to dawn. The result was that those who studied Vedas upto the stage of first world war, could not have and did not study Vedas with necessary scientific orientation. For this they can not be held guilty. Their study was based on contemporary assessments, mixed with certain prejudices born out of unrealistic superiority complex.

But during the present time, when all embracing research development had taken place in all branches of science, including cosmology and on to the topic of construction of the Universe, scientific probe in the Vedas under the light of this research is apt to be useful.

It naturally follows that this probe is a step in the direction recently discovered. Whether this probe would result in fruitlessness, or would result in some kind of astounding discovery remains unpredictable. Nevertheless author is certain that his labour would not be wasted. Reasons for this confidence is that conclusions reached by modern research are before us, and the disinterested, objective, subtle and deep probe which Vedas made in respect of cause of this universe is also before us.

There is no a-priori thesis to warrant, that scientific research cannot be conducted without the aid of modern instruments or equipment. In fact the famous equation of Einstein $E = MC^2$ is a product of pure inspiration. The whole superstructure of subsequent scientific calculations which aided and aids practical technology is based on it.

Instruments are means and there are limitations on it, no matter how ultra modern they could be. At the base of scientific research following faculties are involved.

1. Close observation
2. Analysis
3. Study
4. Concentration

5. Logic

6. An intense curiosity to know the unknown combined with theism (as defined earlier).

Since there is no evidence to show existence of scientific equipment during Vedic period, we have necessarily to proceed upon the hypothesis that they did not exist.

However sages of vedic period were possessed of all the six qualities mentioned above in intense form. Therefore their thoughts, theories, conclusions, cannot be rejected as threshold, instead, they should be studied in the light of modern research. In fact such study would be a step in the right direction.

Vedas are formulated both in poetic verses as well prose. Shad-Darshanas are phrased in terse formulas (Sutras). Their language is Sanskrit. However there is difference in the grammer of Sanskrit language in Shad-Darshanas and that of Vedas.

Our study of Vedas is going to be based on the words used, construction of the words, and the meaning of those words.

Despite the above words have various types of meaning viz. plain meaning, symbolic meaning, research meaning, concealed meaning, contextual meaning, scientific meaning, etc. We have to delve into all these types of meaning.

But before we go into it, (comparative study) it is necessary to take stock of conclusions reached by modern sciences regarding creation of universe.

Chapter 4

NASADIYA SUKTA

Although modern science advanced by leaps and bounds during last 150 years, and came out with various theories regarding creation of universe, it is universally admitted that there is no finality about them. Even Einstein admits this limitation in following words.

"Search for truth is never completely final but always subject to question and doubt."

Why was the Universe born, what was the motivation, when will it wind up, are problems still not answered by modern science. Of course this does not amount to defeat to modern science. These answers are hidden in infinity.

It is wrongly held that Indian Philosophers having reached God as the creator, stopped probing scientifically into the problem. This is held to be the cause of absence of scientific research in India. This wrong conclusion is traceable to negative attitude taken by westerners towards Indian efforts.

Westerners like Maxmuller and Edward Gog were not able to decipher Sanskrit words properly with the result that wrong conclusions were reached.

To take a simple example the word "Tej" is interpreted to mean "Fire" which was wrong. This word was used both by "Sankhya" and "Vasishashika" Darshanas.

Similarly to understand three words "Satva", "Rajas" and "Tamas" and "Panch-mahabhutas" used in "Sankhya" to denote cause of the birth of universe, these words needed correct understanding. They interpreted these words as follows :-

Satva	=	Purity, Chastity
Rajas	=	Passions or Foulness
Tamas	=	Ignorance, Darkness

Having misinterpreted the words, wrong conclusions were used.

Any number of such misinterpretations can be cited. It is therefore clear that their whole thesis went wrong.

Nasadiya Sukta from Rig Veda is in the Tenth Chapter (Mandal). It contains seven verses. Knowledge reflected in these 7 verses compares well with modern scientific conclusions in some respects about the creation of Universe.

In this "Sukta" there are certain statements of facts: Some fundamental questions raised and answered, and certain hypothesis laid down. No claim is made that answers are final. All in all, "Open-mindedness" a trait of modern science is reflected in this "Sukta".

In "Nasadiya Sukta" following problems are raised:-

1. At the beginning (Birth) of the Universe neither "Sat", "Asat", nor space in any form was present.
2. For whose benefit was all this done?

3. Was limitless water "i.e. Salil" present at the time?
4. When nothing existed, who imposed limitations?
5. This universal spreading out of Sat (existence) was born out of what?

Having raised these problems "Nasadiya Sukta" made certain statements of facts as follows :-

1. At the beginning of the Universe, perishable universe was not present. Nor was any imperishable matter in existence.
2. During whole night, there was no divisible means.
3. At that time the unperceivable universe was pulsating on its own and was breathing without any gases (i.e. Oxygen).
4. Beyond the above Salil nothing existed.
5. Entire (storehouse) of water i.e. Salil was impregnated by quality of "Tamas" and non-differentiable.
6. All encompassing "Brahma" (Aabhu) which was manifested out of "Tapas" (Great Effort) was covered by illusory Maya which "Tutchha" (contemptible).
7. The thread between "Sat" and "Asat" (existence and non-existence) spread from below upwards.
8. Part of this thread, turned into a seed and grew.
9. Power of this thread spread closer and its effect spreads beyond Prayati?

Above nine statements of facts were laid down by author of Nasadiya Sukta, after raising problems first. Who would explain better as to how "Sat" (existence) spread?

By raising the following question, author of Nasadiya Sukta showed their scientific attitude. If spreading of universe is unknown to Gods, how would they know as to who created the universe?

By raising the above problem, author of Nasadiya Sukta not only exhibited modesty and humility, but showed loyalty to scientific disposition of mind. No scientist can say that his conclusions are 100% right. Same insight and attitude was adopted by the said author.

Author further adds "The place from where universe was born may or may not be known to the powers that reside in space (Hiranya Garbha). Hiranya Garbha is a word used to describe all powerful God. By raising doubts cited above the author has shown scientific attitude of mind.

We will try to see as to what theories Nasadiya Sukta set out about creation of Universe and we will be shocked to learn that those theories are similar to modern scientific theory about creation of Universe.

Chapter 5

THEORIES ABOUT CREATION OF UNIVERSE IN VEDICS AND UPANISHDAS

Let us first embark upon discussion of certain statements of facts in "Nasadiya Sukta".

"At the beginning of the Universe, perishable Universe was not present, nor was any imperishable matter in existence:-

The Universe is made of organic, and inorganic material. Organic matter is perishable. But there is no death for inorganic matter. It is scientifically admitted fact that both organic and inorganic matter were not in existence at the beginning of the Universe. The "Big Bang" theory says the same thing. Whatever matter or energy or space that is in existence today was condensed into a Cosmic egg having unbelievable density. Whatever existed was neither organic nor inorganic, nor were elements born, nor were there any gases, nor was there any solidity, nor any energy. Because all the aforementioned varieties were born after "Big Bang".

We have seen that in the first verse itself author has stated that in the beginning of the Universe even space was absent.

This observation compares well with the observations made by modern scientists which is as follows:-

> "It was not that all the matter and energy was squeezed into a minor corner of the present Universe. Rather the entire Universe, matter, energy and space they filled occupied a very small volume. There was not much room for the events to happen in........... then there was exposition......... space began to stretch....."

Next observation in Nasadiya Sukta is as follows:

> "During whole night there was no means of divisions."

It means that there was nothing but darkness, and there was no means to dispel this darkness. It means that stars, light, fire, were born after the "Big Bang".

Next observation of the "Sukta" has to be examined carefully.

> "At that time 'ABODHA SRISHTI' (UNCONSCIOUS OR IGNORANT + INNOCENT, UNIVERSE) was pulsating on its own and was breathing without any gases (Oxygen). Nothing existed beyond this."

In this "Sukta" every word is million-dollar worth, and deserves independent treatment.

1. Abodha Srishti (unperceivable universe)
2. Swabalane (on its own)
3. Breathing without gases (oxygen)
4. Was Pulsating

The state of the universe prior to "Big Bang" where Elements, Energy and Space were mixed, was described as Abodha which here means not perceivable. It is un-perceivable in the sense that defies classification. That state was beyond perception and understanding.

Although it was unperceivable there was the feature which the author nonetheless could describe and that feature was "It was pulsating of its own accord and was breathing without gases."

What was signified was the state of universe prior to Big Bang although unperceivable had its own intrinsic capacity and with this capacity it could breath without gases. Breathing without gases means it was pulsating on its own.

This pulsation had kept the universe operational.

This pulsation was Super-Huge and universe was full of energy.

This pulsations had resulted in huge internal commotions. Perhaps in the process, elements, energy and space was born. An old Sanskrit phrase "Samudra Manthan" (Internal rolling of oceans) is an apt phrase applicable. This universe is then described as "difference-less" and pervaded by Tamas. "Difference-less" means unidentifiable, undistinguishable, "unclassifiable".

When one becomes divided into two or more, resultant pieces are comparable. But when it is just one it remains a mystery.

This universe was called "Salil" (made of water). But this meaning as water is inapplicable there. Because "water" is one of the Panchamahabhutas according to "Vasishashikas", hence water is born after the "Big-Bang" and not before it. This description is pre-Big-Bang description. Hence cannot cannote "Watery" here.

Water is traced on earth and to comets, but otherwise there is no evidence of water being traced anywhere else.

Use of the words "Salil" to unperceivable universe is therefore used to signify "softness". Perhaps element, energy and space and their combination resulted in or required "softness". Pulsation also require softness or pregnability.

Thereafter comes a "Sutra" having reference to "TAP". "BRAHMA" and "MAYA".

Out of the above, "Brahma" and "Maya" which we will give up. Because they have traditional philosophic connotation which, it would be un-scientific to adopt.

However we will consider the aspect of "That which was manifested out of "TAP" (Tapas)".

Pulsation is "Spandan". We know pulsation of heart. But heart pulses because of the electrical current or it requires an external energy source. But the pulsation or spand referred above before Big-Bang was without any external source of energy. It was automatic pulsation. Pulsation is the source and origin of all kinds of energy.

Pulsation is obviously a kind of power & science approves this. When unperceivable universe started pulsating in manner described earlier, its result was tremendous heat and the outcome of that heat is described as "TAP-MAHATMYA".

This resulted in establishment of relationship between "Sat" and "Asat". Having stated this in the 4th verse, the author referred to "Big Bang" in the 5th verse saying that this thread between Sat (existence) and Asat (non-existence) spread itself from down below and thereafter vertically. The original hymn has used the word "RET". Ret is Sprem. Sprem is different from Semen. It is the sperm that creates progeny. Therefore the use of the word Ret or Sperm for that ray of light it most apt and scientific. The Universe came into existence from out of that potent light. And the power of this thread remained on one side and effect spread elsewhere (or every where).

The word "Rashmi" means light or a ray of light. A ray is like a thread. Two adjectives have been used here in respect of Rashmi or ray of light. They are "SWA-SHAKTI" and "PRABHAV". Swa-shakti means "Potency" and Prabhav means "Energy" of "Effect of Energy". Effect of energy is mostly visible and, therefore, the potent ray with energy inside was the first stage of creation of Universe.

Energy, elements and space contained in unperceivable universe spread everywhere.

In "Cosmos" Karl Sagan says that as space stretched matter and energy in the Universe expanded. The radiation of the cosmic fire-ball (Rashmi) filled the Universe.

It is clear that Cause of the Big-Bang or creation of Universe, as stressed by the Rishi of Nasadiya Sukta was the original huge, immeasurable and unfathomable pulsation or spand.

We must bow our heads in reverence to the great Rishi of Nasadiya Sukta, who, without any external means or instrument discovered, how the Universe was born? This discovery is thousands of years old than the Big-Bang theory.

What Karl Sagan described as fiber of space was described by Chitrav Shastri as thread and what Vedas described as Rashmi is described by Karl Sagan as fire-ball. The resemblance in description in spite of the gap of thousands of years is astonishing.

But even then the Vedic Rishis do not take or claim the credit for this discovery. With humbleness they say, "How Sat spread? And, how the Universe came into existence? may not be known even to the Gods." But they have revealed this secrete in five/ six verses only.

Vedas do not say nor admit that Universe is created by the God, Brahma or Vishnu. Those are all concepts from mythology and Puranas. Vedas go for thruth and not mythology.

Chapter 6

INDRA, ADITYA, USHA AND SCIENTIFIC PROBE

After considering the scientific thought in "Nasadiya Sukta (Chapter V) many words, terms and concepts conceal mysterious scientific thoughts in the Vedas would be the correct conclusion. But the traditional concept of God and Deities that is mixed up in those terms must first be given up. That is the first step of understanding Vedas in proper Scientific perspective.

Indra, Aditya, Marut, Usha, Vayu, Agni, Rudra are some of the many terms or concepts, the Vedas move and describe their characteristics and praise them. In the eulogies these terms appear to be elaborated. To be able to indulge in eulogies the features, specialities, achievements, properties, action, and their distinction from others requires to be known. Even exaggeration has to have some foundation. In the result, if we closely examine, text of the eulogies such as Indra, and Aditya, with rational zeal, we reach some astonishing Scientific truths.

In Rigveda there are many chapters on "Usha". In them Usha is praised and described. "Usha" means the period of early dawn, which is very pleasant and delightful. In these chapters it appears as if Sage's and their inspirational talents had blossomed. Many Commentators wrote about the love which Sages had about nature as well as their poetic talent to describe it.

It is on the basis of chapters on "Usha" that Mr.Lokmanya Tilak laid down the thesis that the origin of Vedas was North Polar region.

However the Scientific orientation through which we are looking to the Verses, leads us to the conclusion which is entirely different. This chapter seeks to discuss that view point in respect of those terms like Usha, Aditya, Indra, Marut etc.

In Nasadiya Sukta (Chapter No. 5) we saw as to how the mystery of creation of universe is stated, and how it tallies with modern conclusions. In the 72nd chapter of 10th Tome, Aditi has set out the order in which universe was created. If those and other chapters are considered, Scientific concepts of Usha, Aditya etc. get cleared.

Sun has 12 names. According to Rigveda there were 8 Suns. Thereafter concept of 12 Adityas (Sun) was accepted. These 12 Suns are different or there are 12 different names given to one Sun (our Sun) has got be probed. When such a probe is undertaken we must note that there is difference in the idioms in use in common language, and idioms in Sanskrit. "Naming" in Sanskrit has relationship with properties, religion, shape, appearance, construction of an entity. Same entity has different names, then either they are indicative of its different properties or common properties of different entities are grouped under one head.

Therefore, when Vedas used different names for Sun, then as per common notion they were supposed to denote the same entity. But this is not invariably true, we forget that those various names could stand for entities which have common properties.

The result is that the terms Surya, Savita, Aditya etc., do not necessarily designate the same entity even according to Vedas.

Twelve names used by Vedas to designate the Sun, really was intended to stand for 12 different Suns or no, deserved to be probed. During this probe we are not going to merely depend on difference in name, or what that name connotes, but we are going to consider appearance, properties, place, characteristic and other features that are available by way of description.

12 names of Sun in Rigveda are as follows:-

1. Aditya	5. Surya	9. Anshu
2. Martand	6. Mitra	10.
3. Bhag	7. Savita	11.
4. Aryama	8. Varuna	12.

(Vedas have described only 8 Suns at least this is what I found. The concept of 12 Suns might be from Puranas or mythology.)

The limited knowledge in society then or thereafter created a traditional attitude of looking to these 12 names to stand for our Sun, (centre of solar system) which was fallacious.

Since the birth of human race for a very long period no star bigger than Sun was visible despite open skies cluttered with stars. And nothing more powerful than Sun could be conceived.

Due to the leap of modern science during last 50 to 100 years, we have realised that all stars in heaven are sun, and they are in millions, and often bigger than our sun.

Therefore to think that Vedas by giving 12 different names actually sought to describe only one entity, was an unjustifiable conclusion per-se.

Under the light of modern discoveries the text of Vedas relating to 12 sun requires a probe.

Out of 12 Sun, Aditya is first. This Sun is different from our sun, and this has been stated in 72nd chapter of 10th Manual of Rigveda.

The 6th, 7th and 8th verse are as follows:

यदेवा अदः सलिले सुसरब्धा अतिष्ठत
अत्रा वो नृत्यातामिव तीव्रो रेणूरपायत ६.

यद्देवा यततो यथा भुवन्यानपिन्वत
अत्रा समुद्र आ गुळह मा सूर्यमजभर्तन ७.

अष्टौ पुत्रासो अदिते यें जातास्तन्व स्परि
देवाँ उप प्रेत सप्तभिः परा मार्तण्ड मास्यत ८.

Oh Gods, who are inhabiting in water, when you were dancing in water from your area Hot Aditya came up.

Oh! Gods of water, after you spread out like clouds Jalagohya sun came up.

Aditi who created 8 sons from her body, went with 7 sons to God. Her 8th son martand she released in space, and established him there.

We have already seen that as per Nasadiya Sukta after the Big Bang, in the Universe in the non-differential world energy and space had been united. Its description after 1/1000th of second, after one second, and after one lakh of years has been done at page 1008 in Encl.Britannica.

After going back we find that universe at that time was extremely dense and hot. When universe was one lakh years old the temperature was 1000^0. Density & radiation of matter was same. Earlier to that, intense heat was in existence. This period was soon after Big-Bang.

(It is called primordial fire ball). When universe was one second old, radiation had stopped. The heat was $5x10^9$c.

Positron, revetrions which were born out of protons were present. When universe was 1/10,0000th second old heat was $5x10^9$cx1000 times and in universe there were particles and antiparticle."

After the Big-Bang the state is described as "Primordial Fire Ball". Karl Sagan calls it primeval fire ball. Both are synonyms.

This "Primeval Fire Ball" is also called "Adim" by scientists. Vedas called it "Aditi" means first. The first fire ball or sun. Aadi means which came into existence first.

12 suns described by Vedas do not describe the same entity. "Aditya" does not describe our "Sun" but describes "Primordial Fire Ball", in which whole universe was contained and of which, our sun is just one most negligible particle like speck of dust.

3 verses cited above support this view. All 3 verses together read as follows:-

1. Hot Aditya came out of water.
2. After cloud like God pervaded, sun came up.
3. In all 8 suns were born.
4. Out of them 7 went to God.
5. 8th Martand got established in sky.

As per "Nasadiya Sukta" before Big-Bang the egg was watery (salil). That is why it is stated that whole universe was born out of water. Abodha Srishti (Unperceivable universe) was in watery condition before Big Bang. (It may be steam that caused it or whatever) and first fire ball that came out of it was "Aditya", who was terribly hot.

Then 7th verse described birth of Aditya "Oh water Gods after you spread like clouds, water-born sun came out."

After "Big-Bang" element, energy and space were equally thrown all around. After Big-Bang was over, every where clouds of matter & energy spread all over.

This truth is told by Karl Sagan in his book "Cosmos" as follows:-

> "Then little pockets of gas, small uniformities, began to grow: Tendmills of vast gossamer gas clouds formed, colonies of great lumberings slowly spinning things."

From these clouds, or cloud like state many galaxies were born. Our "milky way" was also born, and with it "Our Sun" came into existence.

From the Scientific disenssion that emerges from 6th & 7th verse, it follows that "Aditya" and "Our Sun" were two different entities, one is the cause of the universe and second is born much later (perhaps millions of years) out of elements, energy and gas clouds that "Aditya" spurted.

As per 8th verse after the Big-Bang 8 "Aditya" like suns were born, Sun, Bhag, Martand, Mitra, Savita, Aryama, Anshu and Varun.

We have examined 2 out of them viz. Aditya and "our sun". As per 8th verse "Martand" (3rd sun or fireball) is described as different from "Our Sun" & "Aditya". Because in the 9th verse it is stated "Aditi" established "Martand" in sky for creation and destruction of universe. Birth of living beings and their destruction takes place only on our earth. Therefore earth's life giver is "Martand" (Two Maharashtriyan Saints have referred to "Martand". Saint Ramdas & Saint Dynaneshwar).

After noting that 8 suns referred to in Vedas are different from our sun, let us see whether the Common dawn "Usha" refereed to in the Vedas, has some special Scientific significance.

Out of four Vedas "Usha" is more frequently referred to in chapters of "Rigveda" and Atharva Veda. In it there is poetic and delightful description of Usha (Dawn).

"After completion of night, entire life wakes up, it is fresh having rested, every where there is a pleasant atmosphere. Cool breeze is blowing. The chirping of birds, and movements (pleasant) of leaves, have made the atmosphere musical. East is painted with reddish tongue. The tempting light enlivens nature. And this interlude before rising of the sun, is called "Usha" (Dawn).

Usha is as if a beautiful maiden. Her mother having bathed her, her skin has become lustrous. She has worn reddish or whitish apparels, and the sun is chasing her." Such types of descriptions abound.

We are not concerned with these poetic descriptions. But we want to probe into Scientific truths behind these words.

Late Lokmanya Tilak relied on 3rd verse of 76th chapter of 7th Manual of Rigveda, and other evidence to propound that Aryans originally came from area near the north pole.

That verse is as follows:

"एते ते भानवो दर्शताया श्चित्रा उषसो अमृतास आगुः ।
जनयन्तो दैव्यानि व्रतान्या पृणन्तो अन्तरिक्षा व्यस्थुः ॥

Oh! Goddess Usha! You (who are honourable well behaved maiden) give us the pleasure of experiencing "Prolonged period of Dawn" before sun-rise.

Mr.Tilak relied on the phrase "prolonged period of dawn", and laid the thesis that near the north pole night lasts for 6 months and so also the day, and hence the prayer reflects the state which in existence only in that region.

However we are concerned with something else, to which we will apply our mind. Some verses are as follows:

आदह स्वाधामनु पुनर्गर्भत्वमेरिरे ।
दधाना नाम यज्ञियम ॥ Rigveda (1.6.4)

Oh! Human Beings, Indra who destroys darkness and creates light, and who makes indistinct things distinct, is getting born along with Usha.

युन्जन्ति बन्धमरुषं चरन्तं परि तस्थुषः ।
रोचन्ते रोचना दिवि ॥ १.६.१

Indra, who like clouds revolves round the earth, and who is kind and (Adityarupi) formed like Aditya, such Indra is made to work by people, and then the sun starts shining.

अप द्वेषो मघोनी दुहिता दिव उषा उच्छदप स्रियः ।
द्युलोकीची ही धनसंपन्न कन्या. १.४८.८.

This affluent (extremely rich) daughter of Dyu-lok

उष आ भाहि भानुना चन्द्रेण दुहितर्दिवः ॥
देवयजनकाळी प्रकाशमान होणारी. १.४८.९

One who becomes illuminated during Dev-Yajan period

उषा भद्रेभिरा गहि दिवश्चिद् रोचनादधि ।
वहन्त्व वरुणप्सव उप्रत्वा सोमिनोगृहम् ॥ १.४९.१

Riding on Reddish vehicles or cows. Come from shining Dyu-lok

माता देवानामदितेरनीकं यज्ञस्य केतुर्बुहती वि भाहि ।
देवमाता अदितीचे साक्षात मुख १.११३.१९

You are the mouth of Dev-mata (mother of Gods) Aditi.

भगस्य स्वसा वरुणस्य नामि रुषः सूनृते प्रथमा जरस्व ।
भग नामक आदित्याची आणि वरुणाची भगिनी १.१२३.५

Sister of "Bhag" named "Sun" and of "Varun".

उषा उच्छन्ति समिधाने अग्ना उद्यन्तसूर्य उर्विया ज्योतिरश्चेत ।
१.१२४.१

After Fire is illuminated, Usha assumes light like rising sun.

अभ्रातेव पुंस एति प्रतीची गर्नारुगिव सनये धनानाम्
जायेव पत्य उगसी सुवासा उषा हस्रेव निरिणिते अप्स १.१२४.७

Like a widow who after death of her husband approaches court for money.

ऋतस्य पन्थामन्वेति साधु प्रजाततीव न दिशो मिनाति

1.124.3

She follows the path of Aditya.

(As regards verse 1.124.7 scholars Mr.Shideshwara Shastri had opined that this verse is controversial in view of absence of knowledge regarding vedic period establishments.

उषसा पूर्वा अश्व यद् व्यूषुर्महद् वि जज्ञे अक्षरं पदे गोः ।
व्रता देवानामुप नु प्रभूषन महद् देवानामसूरत्वमेकम् ॥ 3.55.1

Rising Ushas established sun in the skies.

एते त्ये भानवो दर्शतायाश्चित्ता उषसो अमृतास आगुः ।
जनयन्तो दैव्यानि व्रतान्यापृणन्तो अन्तरिक्षा व्यस्थुः ॥

7.75.3

Usha, who is space-pervading, Divine, executive, Earthly, wonderful, and well established is coming.

तानीदहानि बहुलान्यासन् या प्राचीनमुदिता सूर्यस्य ।
अनेक दीर्घ उषःकालांचे दर्शन तू आम्हास घडव. ७.७६.३

Give the pleasure of experiencing many prolonged day-lights.

तावद्दुषो राधो अस्मभ्यं रास्व यावत् स्तोतृभ्यो अरदोगृणाना
यां त्वा जज्ञुर्वृषभस्या रवेण विदृळ्हस्य दुरो अद्रेरौर्णो ॥ ७.७१.४

Oh Goddess Usha, who roars like ox, attractive, and manifesting light which breaks the barrier of mountains.

"तावद्दुषो राधो अस्मभ्यं रास्व
यावत् स्तोतृभ्यो अरदोगृणाना ।
यां त्वा जज्ञुर्वृषभस्या रवे वि दृळ्हस्य दुरो उद्रेरौर्णोः ॥ ३६७

White coloured Usha

After going through above descriptive verses let us try to understand true nature of "Usha".

Out of above verses, two verses from 1st Tome of Rigveda appear to be important. This chapter is named "Indra-Chapter". After calling Indra kind and Adityarupi (who is like Aditya, it is added that people cause him to work with the result that Sun starts shining out of its own illumination.

According to "Nasadiya Sukta" Aditya means "fire ball that first emerges out of Big Bang". Then 8 suns were born out of it.

Authors of Veda in the 3rd verse have connected Usha with Aditya.

Chapter 7

VEDIC ASHVA & URJA TARANG (VEDIC HORSE & ENERGY WAVE)

Every vedic deity has its own vehicle; and majority of the Deities have chariots with horses. The number of horses and wheels of chariot of every Deity is fixed.

Name	Vehicle	Wheels	Puller
Sun	Chariot	One	7 Green Horses
Aditya	do		
Ashwini Kumar	do	3 Triangular	Ass
Indra	do	--	Two horses
Varuna	do	--	--
Rudra	do	--	Swine
Marut	do	--	Spotted Deer

Vedas are full of fire, light, illumination. Every Deity in Veda is fire like, sun-like, lustrous. Creation of universe is from fire, light and Tej (illumination). Veda is a graph of universe creation. Every deity in Vedas and every thing, whether it is atom, Big star or supernova is full of light and is Dyutiman. And Vedas have referred to these powerful sources of light as Deities, and then set out their shape, factum specialities, functions, limitations, achievement in contemporary language, but symbolically without compromising with truth.

Deity means a centre of light, heat, energy. Every Deity has a vehicle. They are linked with speedy horses or allied animals. Deities are not invisible but they are visible like any other matter. But visibility is a word to be used broadly. Just as scientists use the word light broadly. White light is visible, but X rays, Alpha, Beta, Gama, Radio magnetic waves are not visible although they exist. Visibility or invisibility is dependent on its production process, producing agents + light of visible matter is visible, and light of invisible matter is invisible.

Every matter Radiates Energy. This is theory of science. Every particle whether stationary or moving, charged or uncharged, has it's potential field. This is field, either pull of gravity or electro-magnetic field, or magnetic field.

Time-based electric field, or magnetic field is created at one and the same time, and electro magnetic waves are created. It is called transverse electro magnetic mode.

Radiation means light of atomic or subatomic particles, or current of waves. Like heat rays, light rays, X rays, there are following types of radiation.

1. Electro-magnetic waves, having speed of light.
2. Other all types of radiation whose speed is less than speed of light.
3. Radio waves (long Electro magnetic waves)

4. Infra red & Ultra Violate waves.
5. X ray waves
6. Gama rays waves.
7. Waves between x rays & Gama rays, which are product of enormous power.
8. In Beta rays there are wave-like properties.

After energy or power is created in space, from all sides in all directions it gets thrown. And the medium through which it happens is waves. There are two ways in which these waves are assessed, (a) wave length (b) other yardstick is the number of cycle per second.

The table about those 2 methods is as follows:

Name of Wave	**Length**
Radio	exceeding 900 Cms
Subtle Waves	3 x 10^{-4} mtr – 900 Cms
Infra Red	8 x 10^{-7} mtr – 3 x 10^{-4}
Visible light	4 x 10^{-7} mtr – 8 x 10^{-7}
Ultra violet	3 x 10^{-10} mtr – 4 x 10^{-7}
X Rays	3 x 10^{-12} mtr – 3 x 10^{-10}
Gama Rays	3 x 10^{-12} mtr less than m tr.

(Ref.N. Brita Volume 15 Page 402

These figures are approximate And the border line between the two nearer waves are not Well defined.

(Ref. No.2

"Khago-Shastrache Vishva"

Dr. Jayant Naralikar)

Lighted Deities from Vedas means stars and their chariots means medium of light and horses means light waves, and having noted this equation, we have to see how Vedas have considered this.

In the 1st Mandal of Rigveda there are 2 chapters called Ashvamedh Sukta. Out of this chapter 163 is symbolic and mysterious. And in this two yardsticks of measuring light waves, are discussed. It is advisable to set out the whole chapter and then consider its meaning, and thereafter the comparative study.

Sanskrit verses 1 to 11

यदक्रन्दः प्रथम जायमान उद्यन्त्समुद्रादुत वा पुरीषात ।
श्येनस्य पक्षा हरिणस्य बाहू उपस्तुत्यं महि जातं ते अर्वन ॥१॥
यमेन दत्तं त्रित एनमायुनगिन्द्र एव प्रथमो अध्यतिष्ठत ।
गंधर्वो अस्य रशनामगृभ्णात्ससूरादश्व वसवो निरतिष्ट ॥२॥
असि यमो अस्यादित्यो अर्वन्नसि त्रितो गुह्येन व्रतेन ।
असि सोमेन समया विपृक्त आहुस्ते त्रीणि दिवि बन्धनानि ॥३॥
त्रीणि त आहुदिवि बन्धनानि त्रीण्यप्सु त्रीप्यन्तः समुद्रे।
उतेव मे वरुणश्छत्यसर्वन्यत्रा त आहुः परमंजनित्रम् ॥४॥
इमा ते वाजिन्नवमार्जना नीमा शफानां सनितुर्निधाना ।
अत्रा ते भद्रा रशना अपश्यमृतस्य या अभिरक्षन्ति गोपाः ॥५॥
आत्मानं ते मनसारादजानामवो दिवा पतयन्तं पतंङ्गम ।
शिरो अपश्यं पथिभिः सुगेभिररेणुभिर्जेहमानं पतत्रि ॥६॥
अत्रा ते रुपमुत्तममपश्यं जिगीषमाणमिष आ पदे गोः ।
यदा ते मर्तो अतु भोगमानळादिद्ग्रसिष्ठ ओषधीरजीगः ॥७॥
अनु त्वा रथो अनु मर्यो अर्वन्ननु गावोऽनु भगः कनीनाम ।
अनु व्रातासस्तव सख्यमीयुरनु देव ममिरे वीर्य्यं ते ॥८॥

हिरण्यश्रृंङ्गऽयो अस्य पादा मनोजवा अवर इन्द्र आसीन
देवा इदस्य हविरद्यमायन्यो अर्वन्त प्रथमो अध्यतिष्ठत ॥९॥
ईर्मान्तासः सिलिक मध्यमासः सं शूरणासो दिव्यासो अल्याः ।
हंसाईव श्रेणिशो यतन्ते यदाक्षिषुर्दिव्यमज्ममश्वाः ॥१०॥

(Essence of these verses, without sequence is: -

Horses are born from the sun. Yama and fire gave birth to Horses. Wind who travel 3 world joined them. Horse is gaseous of nature. 3 limitation of horses are in Dyu-lok, 3 on earth, 3 in space. Horse in Dyu-lok at its lower heights (that are good) flies like birds. Horse is on Yadhya Vedi (limits) and is also seen there. Horse is stronger than ox. Chariot follows him. It flies in space with its body.

Type of Horses

Having golden horns, having golden clothes, having Iron hoops, having mind like speed, having good omens.

Description of Pratyavarti and Punaravarti.

The motion or speed of horse:

Like wings of the bird sheyn

Like speed of legs of deer.

Faster than Indra

Fast like wind.

Description in terms of wave lengths (2nd yardstick):-

1. Initially and towards the end wider.
2. Short in the middle
3. Like the white egrets who fly in order

Medium of Horse-speed:-

1. Space
2. Water
3. Dyu-lok

The description of these horses and their speed and medium, and classification fits in with classification of energy waves by modern science. Although mathematical figures were not given, still they have revealed their basic and fundamental knowledge of the transmission or transfer of energy in the forms of waves.

All types of energy is born from sun and fire. Energy spreads like wind every where. Yadnya vedi also is birth of fire. And fire and light is born from sun. Horse is stronger than ox. The metaphor of ox is used by Vedas to symbolise power. Energy in any form is cause of the universe. Horse and chariot are inseparable, horse stands for energy and chariot for waves.

If the energy waves are unobstructed, they travel with tremendous speed. Space with dust particles so also space charged with Electro Magnetic force affect the speed of energy and therefore Vedas have stated above that the horse i.e. Energy travels with a great speed from the space which is charged with Electro Magnetic and where the space is dust less.

In science the motion of energy is shown by frequency yardstick. Vedas have used the word punravarti i.e. for frequency and it is i.e. frequency is compared or explained by 3 metaphors like the speed of Shyen i.e. Eagle or Garud, speed of deer and speed of wind.

The fact that energy can travel in space, water, electro magnetic field, is reflected in saying that horses move in space, water and Dyulok.

The concept of wave length in science viz. short and long was expressed by saying:

Brihadhakar (long)

Laghukar (short)

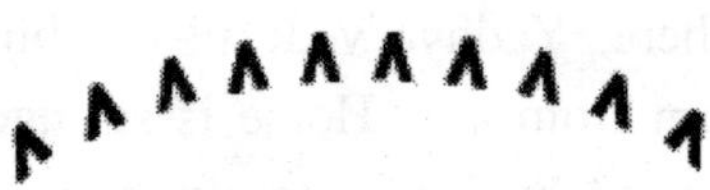

Laghutam (shortest like orderly egret birds flock)

There are five types of energies i.e. Horse. a. Hiranyashrung (like antlers), 2. Hiranya Kesh (like hair) 3. Lohapad (like iron hoofs) 4. Manojav (speed of mind) 5. Subhalakshani (of good women). No further explanation is given. But from plain meaning following comments can be made.

Hiranyashrung means one who has golden antlers (Horns). Horn is sharp pointed, and golden would be finest. If simile is applied to light it would mean light which has the capacity to pierce. Such light would be x ray. "Hiranyakes" means golden hair. When horse is in motion his hair fly, spread, and hence "Hiranyakesh" would mean "Radio" waves.

Shubhalakshni (of good women) light would be white light. Because white light is of good women.

"Lohapad" is indicative of heaviness and power. And word "Manojay" is broad and not precise. It is difficult to assess what they stand for.

Horse = Light ray

There are verses in Shukla - Yajurved which indicate that Horse means light waves and chariot means light.

Kandika 5/2 Sanskrit

हे रथ वाजसाः त्वम्

Oh chariot you are food giver, and you are strong like "Vajra" of "Indra". (इंद्रस्थ वज्राः अति)

Oh horse! Space travelling gases, mind, 27 stars (Nakshatras) and Gandharva, first fixed you to the chariot, and created speed in them.

The speed of light is stored in the cavity of heart. That speed is present in the bird shyen or Garud and also in wind.

स्कंभुवन्तः योजना मिमाना यूयम् काष्ठाम् गच्छत ।

Oh speedy Horses! You who cover miles after miles with great speed, go upto the limit set by us.

Oh horses! You, as per need go at medium speed, or fast, or who like a bird of Prey (Bahiri - Sasand), cross high mountains with same speed without getting exhausted.

Oh you horses, who have a complex speed or wicked speed with which you bring sufficient food and wealth for thousands of people from the side of enemies.

अप्सु अन्नः अमृतम् अप्सु भेषजम् अत्तः हे अश्वाः ।

Necter is stored in the stomach of water, and so also medicine. Hence Oh Horses, effect an entry in the area of water, and enjoy yourselves.

Let us see the meaning of all these verses in their proper perspective.

Chariot means light is provider of food, and he destroys enemies (meaning darkness) and after removing all obstacles in his ways reaches the universe and supplies sufficient food to all. All forms of light are life-sustainers, food and power givers, and out of two types of light if we leave invisible light viz. X rays, radio waves, Alpha, Beta, Gama; these lights tend to penetrate matter and hence are compared to the Vajra (weapon) of Indra. Mountains means obstacles, which light & their waves easily over come.

The speed of light meaning those of light waves, are described in various terms like medium, fast, like bird of prey, like wind etc. But even to light there is a limitation. The limitation on light depends on the intensity of its origin and power. Similarly it depends on distance also. It is for this reason that some stars and galaxies are not visible. Some are faintly visible, and some are clearly visible.

In Kandika 6 reference to " Garbha or core of water" etc. is made which stands for fluidity. Before reaching earth from sun light has to travel through many fluids and clouds including water.

On this point let us see what science has to say.

"Light energy is propagated through space in the form of a wavy motion, some what like ripples in a pond at the drop of a pebble."

Similarly verses that show the Horses born from Agni (Fire) are listed below:-

Intelligent devotees worship Fire who creates horses. 10.5.2

Oh God of Fire, Ensure, good days for us by giving us Horses (light) and food.10.7.4.

Sukla Yajurved Kandika 16 : Oh horses (Light) that destroys all wolves and demons.

As per Vedas light (horses) has a limitation in Dyu-lok space, and on earth. But these limitations are not defined. As per modern science no such limitations are clearly set out.

But it would not be futile to try to find out these, under the fundamental principles of creation of energy.

Light is a product of fire. This process is as follows. Element Attraction repulsion pressure speed heat fire light: (This process is related to universal phenomena and not to fire on earth).

At the time of creation of universe all elements were in gaseous form. Pull of gravity brought the gases together. It resulted in great speed. The pressure was created at the centre of density. Process of attraction and repulsion created heat. When heat become enormous it exploded and process of fire creation started, it became a fire creating plant and that created light and radiation and spread every where in space.

In this process Vedas saw 3 limitations. First is in the element which is the cause of heat. It has relation with number of atoms in elements. If they (Atoms) are less it will catch fire soon, if more, fire will be delayed. It is easier to explode helium than iron. Hence nature of element and its construction in terms of atoms is the 1st limitation.

All the stars in the universe are not capable of all kinds of radiation. It has relationship with construction of star. From light, the composition of stars and their elements are identified.

The second limitation arises out of ratio of attraction and repulsion. That depends on density and its size: Where density and size is enormous their process of explosion and fire begins early. But if both these properties are weak, then prospect of self-propelled explosion is less.

If size comprises of rarified gases, possibility of explosion is less. Because action and reaction is equal and opposite.

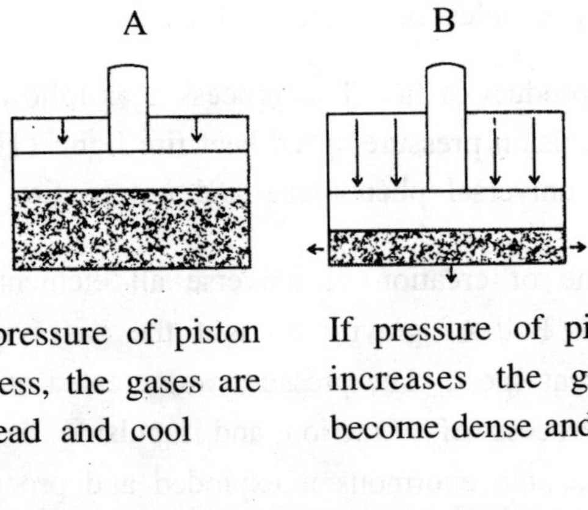

A: If pressure of piston is less, the gases are spread and cool

B: If pressure of piston increases the gases become dense and hot

In the first figure, the size of gas is more in the chamber, but density and pressure is less. In the second figure, pressure is more, size is less, but density has increased. When this density increases enormously, its action will be on the outer side of the chamber, with the result that the chamber will either break, or get extremely heated. If this heat is controled inside itself, then gas can explode inside. In a chamber in which the size of stored gas is enormous, and pressure also is equally enormous, and resultant heat has no exit, there, internal explosion is inevitable, and if the gas is hydrogen it will catch fire. Hence pressure is the second limitation.

Space, Dyu-lok and Earth, are shown as the field of Light's spreading capacity. Process of production of light is same everywhere and the two limitations apply to all 3 world referred fires. If the element because of its inherent quality of attraction and repulsion, is in Dyu-lok (i.e.. in a field charged with electro magnetism) then explosion will be expedited. But in space where this kind of area is not in existence, explosion will not take place.

Element and Pressure are common but for spreading of light, the third limitation in each world is different.

After light is created it spreads in all directions. Those three worlds are technically different but they interpenetrate. There are no hard and fast lines separating the three. Nevertheless these three worlds in respect of properties and degrees are different.

Dyu-lok means interstellar space between galaxies, which is charged with tremendous electro magnetic field, acting from various sides. It is here that we find the 3rd limitation on light. Light ordinarily travels straight, but when it enters this field it becomes curved. And if the gravity is more can disappear also. Stars that absorb light of other stars are in existence. This is the limitation on light in Dyu-lok.

The space where effect of electro magnetic field does not exist and affect light (i.e. total and absolute vacuum) does not exist. Because dust, clouds of dust, meteors, comets are always in existence in space. All these affect both speed, motion, and direction of light. The result is that light becomes obstructed is blocked, reflects, turns, or weakens. That is why matter distributed in space is the third limitation.

The layer of Ozone obstructs Ultra violet rays and other energy also weakens.

The three limitations of "Horses" (Light) referred to in Vedas but not explained, are attempted to be explained here.

Chapter 8

MARUTA - AN UNIVERSAL PHENOMENA

Marut is an important deity of Vedas. In Rigveda alone 33 tomes are devoted to Marutas and while praising them, their qualities, characteristics, speciality, place, action, effect of action all are also considered.

The commentators of Vedas have considered the Marutas as cyclones, typhoons or stormy-wind, accompanied by stormy-rain and lightening. Same view is taken by the modern students of Vedas.

This is not at all a wrong approach. But it is in incomplete approach. Because the concept of Marutas is considered with reference to earth only. Secondly, while doing so, the thinkers or students have disregarded certain special characteristics of Marutas. And thirdly, they have not considered Marutas with reference to the Modern Science. But if we adopt the independent attitude and consider all the characteristics of Marutas in a broader sense and proper sense, then we come across astonishing result and we have to surrender to the deep knowledge of Vedic Rishis.

We had found that Vedas have considered creation of universe at length. But because the Marutas were never linked with that creation we are deprived of real knowledge of Vedas. After the Big-Bang that occurred in Aditya a huge continuous process started. That process of creation never comes to an end. It is still going on. That process includes creation of elements, particles, gases, energy, their combination at different level and in different proportion.

The universe is unlimited. Our milkyway galaxy is one of the thousands of galaxies in the universe. In milky way galaxy there are about four billion stars and to every minute, new stars are born and old stars are becoming dead. Therefore, this process of creation is unending. But the stages of creation are going to be same or similar wherever they occur.

The Big-Bang took place in Aditya. Then in the 2nd stage of creation Sun was born and million of years thereafter planetary system was born including earth. If we get this sequence in mind, then Sun is the centre of our planetary system and Aditya is the creator of Sun.

Therefore while studying Marutas, we will have to consider all these three stages viz. 1) Big-Bang in Aditya; 2) creation of Sun from Aditya and; 3) creation of earth from sun.

When the Modern Science studied Sun in detail, they found that Sun emits not only visible light but also all sorts of energy from X-Rays to Radio Waves. Almost all the 92 elements are found in sun. The activities on sun include some of the following:

CORONA: Corona is a luminous high temperature rarefied gas envelope of the Sun. Its temperature is about 3,60,000F. It spreads out to several solar raddi (a raddi is double the radius of the circumference). This high temperature produces an outward flow of electrically charged particles which extend beyond the vicinity of the earth. The corona owes its beauty to its form which is made of streamers, filaments and rays of pearly white light.

SOLAR WIND: It was predicted in 1958 that the high temperature of the corona would cause some of it to boil off the Sun and the coronal particles would appear in the neighbourhood of the earth as a solar wind moving with speeds of 300 to 1000 Km. per second. This was confirmed in 1962 and it was found that solar wind reaches the Earth with the stream of protons and electrons along with magnetic field. Consequently, interplanetary space is filled with a fully ionized hot plasma of coronal origin.

PROMINENCES, FILAMENTS: Prominences are among the most beautiful of solar phenomena. A typical fully developed P is a thin fish tailed or ribbon like gaseous structure standing above the Sun surface. It may have the size of two lakh Kms. length, 40,000 Kms height and 6000 Km thick. Against the dark sky they are seen as bright clouds composed of myriad of fine threads. Generally P are connected by appendages to the Sun surface or rest upon it. They have fanciful forms like clouds. The large scale structure of such P is fairly constant.

FLARES: In plage area sudden and distinct brightening occur from time to time. They are called flares. They are very violent. After the onset of a flare a surge of gas is ejected with a velocity of about 1000Km. per second and they go up to the distance of five lakh Kms.

Flares cause many geophysical phenomena. There is a fade out of short wave radio communication caused by a flash

X-ray penetrating to the ionosphere of the Earth. Plasma clouds at the speed of 2000 Km. per second appear followed by geomagnetic storms. Cosmic ray particles from very large flares penetrate to the ground level. There is burst of short wave length (hard non-thermal X-rays).

If all these activities on Sun are compared with the description of Marutas, we are wonder struck by similarities we find in them. The similarities are almost to the extent of 100%.

Rigveda has noted the following speciality or characteristics of sun.

- Marutas are destructive of all. (1.19.4)
- They are very very bright, they are frightening in appearance and very very powerful. (5)
- They are ever shining (6)
- By their own power of shining, they take sun rays through out the Universe (7)
- Marutas, if compare to birds, then their birth place is stable or firmly attached. (1.37.9)
- Where Marutas are going with long steps like Sun rays or long waves of sun rays? (1.39)
- To the chariot of Marutas spotted deer are attached and it is headed by a reddish deer (1.39.6)
- Marutas are born from Dyu-loka (1.64.2)
- Marutas are hissing like snakes, they roar, they are stable, but they can move every animate and inanimate objects. (1.64.9, 10, 11)

- Marutas are decorated like a woman. Their weapons are shining bright (1.85.2)
- Marutas spread like waterflow which have become red due to electric fire (1.85.19)
- Oh! Marutas destroy all the demons or asuras with the help of lightening.
- Marutas are shining like gold. Their chariot is reddish yellowish (1.87.2)
- The wheels of the Marutas have small axis (short wave radiation) (1.166.9)
- White or bright coloured terrible Marutas are fast going, got united with lightening like a man united with his wife (1.167.3)
- Vibrating Marutas (2) Marutas originating from numerous places, Marutas coming down from Dyu-loka (4)
- Marutas disintegrating or breaking clouds with the help of lightening (1.168)
- Prushni (Pakhal, explained in the Chapter on Rudras) produced Marutas and created Marutas which all look alike; with the help of clouds and those Marutas were in group and very shining. (1.168.9)
- Marutas are great worriers. They are terrifying and their ways are complicated. (1. 169.7)
- The Tej (Brightness) of Marutas goes beyond nights and nights of darkness (5.52.3)
- Marutas are looking like an ocean of electricity and their light has scattered everywhere. (6)

- Marutas throw their shining spears in the space and in the roaring rivers (7)
- Marutas are like invisible thieves (12)
- The group of Maruta is like Aditya. (14)
- The seven members group of Sapta Marutas (7x7=49)

In the earlier tomes the Sun has splitted Marutas into 49. In fact, from all the four Vedas we can get more detail of characteristics of Marutas. But we cannot consider them all because of the limitation of the book. Now we will find out resemblance between Marutas and different eruption on the Sun described above.

It is said, as above, that the chariot of Marutas is being pulled by spotted deers. This poetic description tallies with the description of Corona where it is said "Corona is shining like white pearls".

The Vedas described Marutas, as above, that their birth place or place of origin is stable, whereas about prominences it is said "Prominences are connected by appendages to the sun surface or rest upon it."

Marutas are described as going by long long steps and their chariot has small or short outraged (Find English word for "Aasal"). These two concepts are found in description of Corona, flares and prominences where in it is said that they include all types of energy in Shortwaves and long waves.

The Vedas described Marutas as looking identical or similar and going fast where as about prominences it is said "large scale structure of prominences is fairly constant".

Apart from these four important similarities, the description of Marutas that they are destructive, very much shining, bright, terrifying in appearance, hissing like snakes, born from bright Dyu-lok, roraring, holding sharp shining weapons, golden coloured and taking help of lightening, tallies 100% with the description of Corona, flares and prominences.

There is one more strong resemblance. Vedas say, Marutas spread like waterflow which have become red due to electric fire. This tallies with the description of Corona which is as "because of its high temperature, it evaporates continuously producing outer wind flow of electricity charged particles, called solar winds which extended beyond vicinity of the earth.

Further the Rudra is said to be the father and the Prushni as the mother of Marutas. Similarities between the two will be discussed in the Chapter of Rudra.

Therefore, in the background confining concept of Marutas to the storms on the earth is one side and incomplete.

Chapter 9

WHO STABILISED SUN IN SPACE?

Every person after reaching a certain stage of maturity becomes curious to know, or at least ought to be curious to know, as to why Sun and moon keep on floating in space and don't fall down, and as to How our earth, remains afloat in space.

Till modern science gave final answers to these questions, various civilisations gave various answers. All these answers were invariably wrong. In Indian Legendary books (Puranas) it was stated that the earth was situated on the backs of four elephants, who are on the back of a Turtle, and Turtle is floating on the sea. Obviously the answer is absurd.

But legends and science are poles apart. And attempt to find truth in legends (Puran) is futile and meaningless. But that is not our subject.

Fundamental knowledge about magnetism was known to Vedas. Similarly sun or other stars floating in the sky and its casue was also known very clearly.

Reasons as to why and how sun is stabilised in space is a problem that rocked common-man's curiosity as much as that of scientists, with this difference that a layman does not probe deep to find its cause, whereas scientist does.

Vedas and its authors probed into it with the same zeal of scientists, and the answers they got tally with conclusions of modern science.

In Tome 4 chapter 15 of Rigveda there are 5 verses, which have raised the same problem and answered to it.

अनायतो अनिबद्धः कथायं न्यङ्ङुत्तानोव पद्यतेत
कया याति स्वधया को ददर्श दिवः स्कंभः समृतः पाति नाकम् ॥
ऋ.४.१३.५.

1. Why does the supportless and uncontrollably moving sun in space does not fall down?
2. Which is the power impelling sun to rotate?
3. Who has the knowledge of his real nature?

Three questions cited above, reflect scientific curiosity of Vedas. First two questions apparently appear separate but they are two parts of the same question. Answer of both these question is one. Science knows the answer which is "Gravitational pull".

This answer was also given by Vedas in the same chapter, which is as follows:

दिवः स्कंभः समृतः नाकम् पाति कः ददर्श ।

Sun is protected by Stambh (Bar or Beam or Pillar) who is Swarlokgami (spreading in space), and Dyulokrupi (electro magnetic).

In this answer all four words have meaning. Protects means stablises, and does not allow him to fall.

This function of protection of the sun is made by "Swarlokgami" (Spreading in space), Dyulokrupi (electrico magnetic) Stambha (Bar). These words reveal scientific truth viz. pull of gravity.

Every matter having mass and shape has gravitional pull. This power lies in the core of the matter. Gravitational pull or gravity works in all directions. But it is connecting North and South Poles of the Mars and, therefore, the stretch of the gravitional power is like a Bar or Beam or Pillar connecting North and South.

This magnetic power obviously is in the sun also, and hence it is stabilised in space and is moving. Sun's gravitational pull is many many times the magnetic power of earth. Sun's north and south poles are operational and effective for thousands of miles Urdhav (Up) and Adhah (Down), and we are going to see it in our discussion on chapter on Rudra. In the midst of this background let us examine as to how answer given by Vedas is scientific.

"Swarlokgami (Spreading in space), Dyulokrupi (Electrico magnetic) Stambh (Bar), are 3 words used to denote pull of gravity of the sun, its North and South poles, and electro-magnetic field which joins these two poles. This description is scientific.

Mass rotation or revolution and electricity perhaps creates the gravitional pull. The sun has all the three. The magnetic power is present in the Sun in the form of Bar, Beam or Pillar between the North South Poles i.e. Stambh. It spreads thousands of miles on both the directions North and South. Therefore, all these areas under the force of Sun's magnetic power is called Dyulok in Vedas and because the power extends into space thousands of miles on either side hence it is called Swarlokgami (Operational Space).

By using the word Stambh (Bar) Vedas have indicated existence of poles of a Bar magnet and the field which arises as a result of joining of the Poles. Word "Swarlokgami-Stamb" denotes the spreading magnetic field resulting from joining of two poles.

The sun does not merely protect himself, but keeps all planets in the solar system in their orbits. This scientific truth is stated in the following verse from Shukla Yajurveda.

तत्सूर्यस्य देवत्वं तन्महित्वं मध्याकर्तोर्विततं संजभार ।
यदेवयुक्त हरितः सधस्थादाद्रात्री वासस्तनुते सिमस्मै ॥

The godliness of sun who remains at the centre consists in attracting members of solar system and keeping them in their orbits.

Chapter 10

VEDAS AND MAGNETISM

The modern scientific theory lists four causes for creation, construction, shaping, and evolution of the universe. They are 1. Heat 2. Gravity 3. Electro magnetic power 4. and Magnetic power. All these powers are self-existent, which means they are in existence since birth of the universe. Magnetic power can be created by coiling iron with electricity for along time. But gravity can't be created.

Every solid has gravitational pull. It has a relationship with its mass, shape and density. It exists in centre of that entity and spreads from its surface in space. Its extension depends upon its capacity.

Among elements, magnetism exists in iron and in Maganese. Greeks knew about it in 8th century. It exists intrinsically and its power is felt externally. And in the presence of another magnet can experience a tarque.

Magnet is bi-polar.

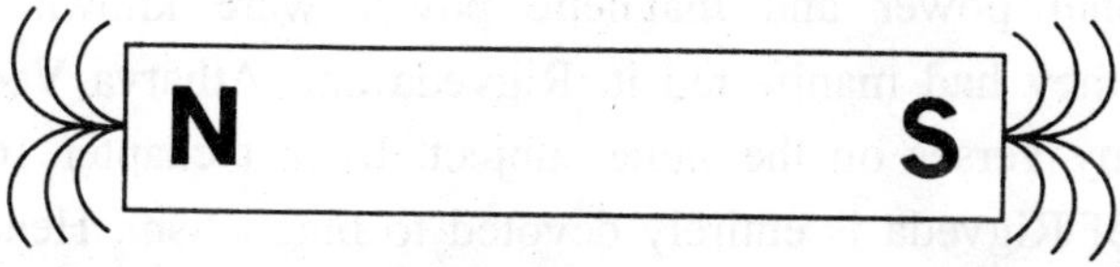

If bar magnet is broken in any number of pieces, each piece acquires two poles.

Scientists have not so far come across magnet with just one pole. Even if a magnet is divided into atoms, each atom will acquire 2 poles. The electrons have a specific motion called spin angular momentum.

Magnets are ordinarily of 2 types. Bar magnet and horse-shoe magnet. Both have north and south poles. North pole always emits energy and south pole always attracts that energy.

Following figure of Bar magnet is self-explanatory.

If small particles or dust of iron is spread on a piece of paper kept on a Bar magnet, it will show above type of waves.

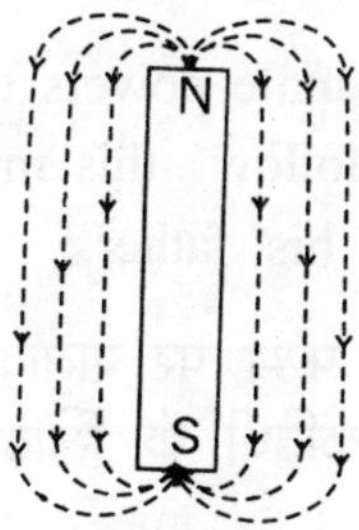

Bi-Polar Magnet

Gravitational power and magnetic power were known to Vedas, and they had manifested it. Rigveda and Atharva Veda contains many verses on the same subject. In fact chapter 164 of Tome 1 of Rigveda is entirely devoted to magnetism. Hence present chapter deals with that portion. There are in all 52 verses in this chapter. Hence only selected verses are quoted here and explained. Although others are summarised. Translation of verses is bodily lifted from Shri Chitrav's Commentary.

इह ब्रवीत या इमङ्ग वेदास्य वामस्य निहितं पदंवेः
शीर्ष्णः क्षीर दुहुते गावो अस्य व व्रि वसानां उदकं प्रदातुः ॥
ऋ.१.१६४.७

If anybody knows, he should tell me about the form of that beautiful mysterious bird, whose cows spurt milk through their heads and which they drink by their own shining feet. (7).

The mother earth is conjoined to the axis i.e. to the South and she got conceived.

स्रीयः सतीस्ताँ उ मे पुंस आहुः
कवीर्यः पुत्रः स ईमा चिकेत ॥१६॥ अपूर्ण ऋचा

I gave male powers to my wives, only my highly intelligent son will follow this mystery and he will become great grand father of his father.

अवः परेण पर रानावरेण पदा वासं बिभ्रति गौरुदस्था न
सा कद्रिची कं स्विदर्ध परागात् सित सूतेन हि यूथे अन्तः
॥१७॥

A cow has awakened or arisen. She has two legs. By one leg she holds the earth below and by other leg she holds the upward universe. At present where in the sphere of Aditya she is wondering. She lives in solitude and not a part of cattle heard, where does she reside and deliver.

अवः तरेण पितरं यो अस्यानुदेन पर एनावरेण ।
कवीयमानः क इह प्र वोचद् देवं मनः कुतो अभिप्रजातम् ॥१८॥

Who has the knowledge of the creator of space above, and the creator being Dyue?

ये आवाञ्चस्ताँ उ पराच आहुर्ये पराञ्चस्ताँ उ अर्वाच आहु ।
इन्द्रश्च या चक्रथुः सोमतानि धुरा नयुक्ता रजसोवहन्ति ॥१९॥

Oh! wandering Indra Somas like horses attached to a vehicle you support the world. And in this world the oriented people are looked upon as disoriented and vice versa.

अस्य वामस्य पलितस्य होतुस्तस्य भ्राता मध्यमो अस्त्यश्नः ।
तृतीयो भ्राता घृतपृष्ठो अस्या त्रापस्यं विश्यति सप्तपुत्रम् ॥१॥

Elderly and fully white-haired and good looking Hotu fire, has twelve brothers. Out of them one is "All-Eater", and the other is a conductor of electricity (Ghritwahak). This king has in all seven sons.

Oceans flow from Dhenu (cow). All directions and their sub-divisions survive and sustain because of her and the milk flowing constantly and continuously from her udder sustains the universe.

The cow or Dhenu described above is very mysterious. The mystery is obviously hidden. We cannot dream that such a cow or Dhenu or animal can ever exist. Therefore we are compelled to find the secret meaning lying behind this concept.

The cows from this chapter are strange. None can dream of existence of such cows.

This cow is of two legs. Her legs are of strange type. One leg faces the sky. The other faces the earth.

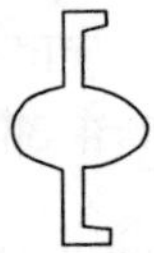

Two legged animal

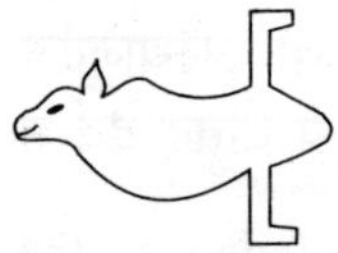

Two legged Dhenu holding sky above & earth below

Besides this milk erupts from its head and the same is consumed by its legs.

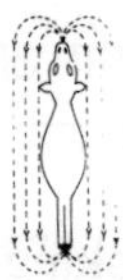

Dhenu spurting milk from head & consuming it through Legs.

It is obvious that this is metaphorical description of magnetism. We will once again draw a bar magnet and compare it with above description.

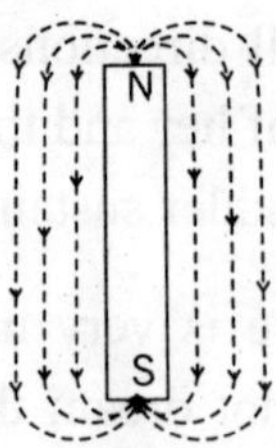

Bar Magnet with North South Poles

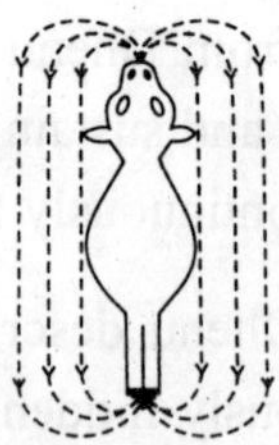

Flow of Magnetic Energy consuming energy emitted from North Pole

This two legged cow with one leg supports the space above universe, and with other leg holds earth below.

Two legged cow and earth are synonymous. In universal creation world is mother, and Dyue is father. Mother and father have joined together. Universal mother is joined with south direction shaped Dhura. She conceived.

To conceive a woman needs to have capacity to accept sperm. Out of two magnetic fields, the south attracts. Hence the south represents female. North spurts milk. South drinks it.

The all eater brother of Hotu Agni is South pole and conductor of electricity is north pole.

Universal magnetic north pole is an udder giving milk, and south absorbs it sustaining the universe.

In the 19th verse Vedas tell us that even poles repeal and opposite poles attract. But this is said in mysterious fashion.

North pole is called Abhimukh and south pole is called Parangmukh. Poles of magnets are like two horses pulling a vehicle. How this mixing up takes place is best explained by a figure.

Opposite Poles attract

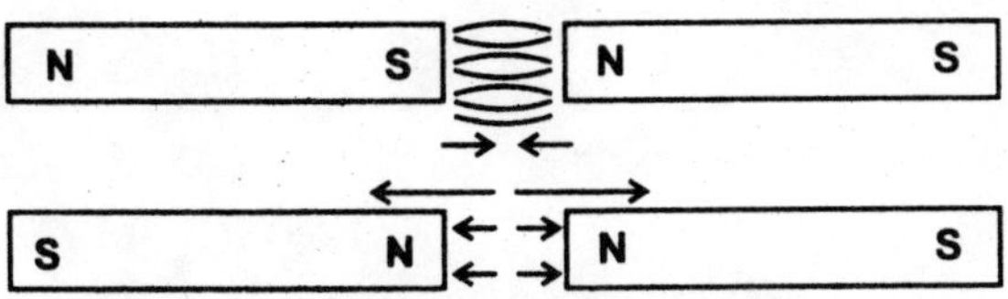

Even Poles repel

In the first sketch above North and South attract each other. In the second sketch they repel each other.

"I gave male power to my wife" etc. is another mysterious verse. It is also scientific, Prithvi (Earth) stands for Atom, it also stands for positive electricity and also earth. In the context of Earth Dyue means electro magnetic power, which is father and earth is mother. Earth is attracted towards Dyue. Around the magnet interstellar dust collects with + positive charge. But once mass formation takes pace, then it creates its own universe. Just as Earth created its own independent entity and her husband viz. electro magnetic field concealed himself in her. Hence this situation was described as "I gave my wife all male powers."

Even today despite modern science and its progress, this gravity and magnetism and its creation are unsolved riddle.

And hence Vedas say modestly "Who knows Dyue, who is father of space and nature?"

Chapter 11

ATHARVA-VEDA AND SECRETS OF ATOM

Atharva-Veda is a Veda which deals, among other subjects, with activities such as hypnosis black Magic and allied topics of various types. It is for this reason that this Veda does not enjoy the same status as other Vedas.

Strangely enough it is this Veda which deals with the problem of creation of universe minutely. This study enabled this Veda to deal with an explain forces behind.

Many secret and complicated theories in respect of knowledge, philosophy and science are dealt with here. There was an all embracing study of almost all forces working in nature. We will deal with only that part which is relevant for our purposes.

In the 9th Tome at chapter 10. Some important problems were raised and answered.

१३. – पृच्छामि त्वा परमन्तं पृथिव्याः पृच्छामि वृष्णो अश्वस्य रेतः
– पृच्छामि विश्वस्य भुवनस्य नाभिंपृच्छामि वाचः परमं व्योऽम

Where is the end and centre of Earth? Where is the elevated position of speech? Where is the elevated position of sperm of a male horse (un-castrated bull)?

१४. उत्तर - इयं वेदिः परो अन्तः पृथिव्या अयं सोमो वृष्णो अश्वस्यरेतः - अयं यज्ञो विश्वस्य भुवनस्य नाभिर्ब्रम्हायं वाचः परमं व्योम ॥

Yadnya-vedi is a small structure created for performing Yadnya i.e. sacrificial fire. The border of Yadnya-vedi is the limit of earth and Yadnya is the center of world.

This answer be followed only when right interpretation is put on Sanskrit words, and the symbolism that is used.

Apparently the answer will strike one as absurd.

If we closely examine the question we will realise that the question that is raised relates to universe.

The word "Pruthvi" (Earth) is used here in the sense in which it was used by "Sankhya" and "Vaisheshika" Darshan, to mean an "Atom". If this symbolism is understood, we can reframe the question to mean where is the end (meaning "final limit") of an atom?

Once we know that the question relates to universe, we have to give up any interpretation which could have reference to "Yadnya-Kund" or four walled fire place.

The centre of Earth and its final limit, are problems raised by treating earth as an atom.

We must realise that at the centre of atom, is positively charged electricity Protons - and also neutrons which have no charge. Electrons move around this nucleus.

In the reply that Yadnya is the centre of earth, the symbolism is that fire (positively charged electricity) is at the centre of an atom.

Parametre of "Yadna Kunda" is given as final limit of earth. This symbolism means that the orbit of electrons which move around protons is the final limit, because electrons have a fixed orbit.

In the 11th tome at Chapter No. 8, similar fundamental problems are raised and answered. Since they relate to creation of universe its consideration is necessary.

Question raised in the first verse is as follows:

पहिल्या ऋचेमधला प्रश्न असा -

यन्मन्युर्जायामावहत् संकल्पस्य गृहावधि ।
क आसं जन्याः के वराः क ऊ जेष्ठवरोऽभवत् ।

When God got married in "House of concepts of Will" and brought home his wife, who were the guests on either side (i.e. Bridegroom and Bride)?

तपश्चैवास्तां कर्म चान्तर्महत्यर्णवे ।
त आसं जन्यास्ते वरा ब्रह्म ज्येष्ठवरोऽभवत् ।

In the Universe as Ocean Tapa and Karma were the guests from the side of "Bridegroom" and "Bride". And Brahma was the Bridegroom.

In this answer reference to "Brahma" is to be disregarded as this word has traditional connotation.

In the first part of the answer guests of Bride are termed as "Tapa" and "Karma" as the Bridegroom's guests.

In this answer is concealed the secret of creation of Universe which was considered in "Nasadiya Sukta". Even in Manduka Upanishad it is observed that as result of "Tapa", "Brahma" expands. (The word "Brahma" arises out of the root word

"Briha" which means to grow, expand, develop). The fact that universe is expanding is the latest scientific discovery, and it was reached through "Doppler effect". Taking this into consideration, we find that the observation that Brahma develops as a result of "Tap", means that universe developes out of "Tap". Thus the expanding universe concept is rooted in this observation.

In the answer given in this Veda, "Tap" is called bride, "Brahma" as Bridegroom and "Karma" is called guests of bridegroom. In this symbolism this Vedas has shown not only scientific attitude but literary excellence.

Tap is bride because the bride is always connected with fire (kitchen). Fire generates heat. Bride cooks with aid of fire. Hence Veda authors saw resemblance between Bride and "Tap".

Similarly "Karma" is called guests of bridegroom because "Deeds - and achievement" is part of area where bridegroom functions. During marriage those who are on the side of bridegroom have upperhand, because in human life "Deeds - and achievements" are considered superior. It is achievement that decides who would be in driver's seat. That is why authors of Veda by, calling "Karma" as belonging to bridegrooms side, manifested their close observation of reality.

In the creation of universe it is necessary to see the role of "Tap" and "Karma". Even here we must know that terms which appear to have been applied to individual relations are also meant to be applied to Universal relationships.

"Tap" means Heat or to heat. Creation of heat can range from 10 celsius to crores of degrees of celsius: or can run into limitless extent of degrees.

Pulsation of Abodh (unperceivable) universe prior to the "Big Bang" resulted in creation of unimaginable degrees of heat. And when Abodha-Srishti (Unperceivable universe) could not endure this heat is resulted in what is now termed as Big-Bang".

The word Karma has specific and special meaning in this verse. Cause of heat is Karma, without Karma heat is not generated. Heat is the first manifestation of energy or its seed. Connecting Tap and Karma by the Rishis together is most scientific. If we understand the real meaning of words Tap and Karma i.e. Heat and Action.

Following passage from Encyclopedia Britannica page 849 will endorse the above: "Energy is normally and most simply defined as the equivalent of or capacity for doing work. The word itself is derived from the word "Energees" in Greek. Energy can be associated with material body or it can be independent of matter."

Hence action and heat (Karma and Tap) are two sides of the same coin. Karma (Action) is the basis of "Tap" (Heat) and Tap is the result of Karma.

The heat that was generated in "Abodhsrishti" (Un perceivable Universe) worked in five ways: 1. Ut-Prekshan (Throwing up) 2. Awakshepan (Throwing down) 3. Akunchan (contraction) 4. Prasaran (Expansion) and 5. Gaman (movement or going). (All activities otherwise than above four.)

The entire process can be set out in following order:-

Result of pulsation: 1. Karma (Activity) and its result 2. Tap (Heat) and its effect 3. Big-Bang, and resultant process of birth of elements, Energy, space, independently.

NOTE: Karma is action or work

After the Big-Bang elements started emerging separately. It began with Hydrogen first, different kinds of energy was born.

Karl Sagan in his book "Cosmos" says, "the early universe was filled with radiation and plenum of matter. Originally hydrogen and helium were formed from elementary particles in the dense fire ball."

After the Big-Bag "Tap" (Heat) manifested itself in the form of energy. If we examine all kinds of energy, we find that barring gravity and magnetic-field all other variety of energies possess heat. It means that the heat that caused creation of universe is still operational.

Similarly the five types of Karmas (Motions) mentioned above which caused heat: resulted in increased activity. The elements, energy and space and its mixture which was in abodha-Srishti (Unperceivable Universe) separated themselves after the Big-Bang, and universe started acquiring shape. This process of universe taking shape was due to the five-fold action or Karma as stated above.

Matter that was spread in space, (had not acquired their identity. Panch-maha-Bhutas Pre-elemental five kinds of substances) and their subtlest particles, were acted upon by five types of motions (Karma) and the process of building up of atoms of elements commenced. Element is a union of certain kinds of properties. The union taking place on account of five types of Karma.

Here, it is necessary to understand modern concept of electro-magnetic field. Electro-magnetic field means a kind of property of space, which is created due to motion of electrical charges. Positive electricity creates electric field in space. But if positive charge is in motion then it creates magnetic field. Electrical charge and magnetic charge together create Electro-magnetic field, which is considered as having its own existence in space apart from the charge.

Pancha-Karmas (five properties of Motion) which caused "Tap" (Heạt), and electrical charges and magnetic charges (and their results) have a remarkable resemblance.

Chapter 12

EXTREMELY SUBTLE KNOWLEDGE OF ATOM IN THE VEDAS

We have seen, how Vedas, both secreted and expressed, have knowledge of magnetic power. In the earlier chapter on Atharva-Veda we saw that Vedas had knowledge of construction of atom. In this chapter we are going to consider how Atharva-Veda manifested their mysterious knowledge about magnetic power, Electro-magnetic power, and construction of atom.

In 13th Tome, at Chapter 1, verse No.42, there is a reference to "Dwi-Pad Dhenu" which literally means two legged cow, which in fact means "Magnetic Power".

Verses No. 42 to 55 that follow are very important because they throw light on magnetic power and construction of atom.

The substance of mentioned verses is as follows:

Verse 42:- The one leg cow becomes 2, 4, 8, 9 and thousand legs and the Universe expands. This cow is the creator of Udak or water.

Verse 46:- Where expansion is the limit, in such a Rohit both Cold and hot fires are established.

Verse 47:- After erecting an endless or mountain like Yadnya-Stambha, i.e. Pillar, Beam or Vertical structure, cold and heat fire is established which in turn spreads or showers in the sunlight.

Verse 48:- Fire ignited by the Mantra of Sun creates hot and cold fire.

Verse 54:- The sun addressed earth as follows:

All existing creatures, past or present, are dependent upon you and this world has been created from Aditya or Primordial fire.

These verses have repeatedly used the word "Udak" in literary Sanskrit. Udak means water. But that is no proper interpretation. Udak or water is nothing but energy or energy waves.

Hydrogen is the first element with a single proton in its nucleous. This proton is called one leg cow. From this, other elements having different number of protons and electrons are created.

In Yajurveda, 10th Adhyay, word "Aap" has been used. It means wave, vibration, spand (palpitation). It is also said that it is from Aap that the Universe is created.

In 2nd Kandika or Hymn it is said: "Oh, wave of energy! You are small in the begining like a single soldier". And then it is said: "You go ahead and revert back." Further it is said: "that energy or Udak emanates from Sun and spreads everywhere.

Admittedly, there is no water on sun and, therefore, Udak or Aap cannot be translited or taken as water.

There are many orbits around centre of atom. These orbits are called water-waves (Udak-Tarang) emerging out of one legged cow. According to science these orbits around atom are important and they always multiply by doubling themselves e.g. 2, 4, 8, 16 etc.

At the centre of atom there is positive charge of electricity. And electron rotating around the centre is negatively charged. Magnetic power is also divided in terms of North and South poles and North is positively charged and South is negatively charged.

This was stated by Vedas in the above verses. Cold Fire and Hot Fire in the original verses are called "Himam" and "Dhramsam", cold fire means negatively charged electron and Hot Fire means positively charged proton. Similarly positively charged Hot Fire is magnetism in North pole and negatively charged cold fire means south pole.

Verse 47: Means and describes two poled gravitational power among all stars, suns, planets etc. and is described as "Parvatiya-Yadnya-Stambha". The word "Yadnya" is very subtle, expansive and mysterious word.

"Parvatiya-Yadna-Stamba" have North and South Poles, positive and negative electrical charges, positive and negative charged centre, which Atom has, and on these three the construction of universe is based.

While telling this truth sun says "Oh, earth! Everything in nature is based on you and from this initial "Yadhya", everything is born.

Two verses from ninth chapter of ninth Tome of Atnarva-

Veda deserve to be quoted below because they reflect secrets of Atomic and Sub-atom particles.

द्वा सुपर्णा सयुजा सखाया समानं वृक्षं परिषस्वजाते ।
तयोरन्यः पिप्पलं स्वादत्त्यनश्नन्नन्यो अभि चाकशीति ॥२॥
यस्मिन् वृक्षे मध्वदः सुपर्णा निविशन्ते सुवते चाधि विश्वे ।
तस्य यदाहुः पिप्पल स्वाद्वग्रे तन्नोन्नशद्यः पितरं न वेद ॥

Those Birds who are complete on their own have become friends and have come together. They stick to one another and are sitting on a common tree. One eats the fruit while other eats not but watches. But the tree on which nest is built, bears sweet fruits, which is also resting place and birth place.

If we see construction of atom we find that it has a positively charged centre, and negatively charged electron moves around it. This scientific truth was reflected in the above verses. The tree referred to above is immobile and hence it represents the nucleous of atom, out of the two birds one is stable and other is moving. The stable is the proton and the moving is the electron.

In Vedas there is frequent reference to one legged, two legged and four legged as adjective. Till scientific truths were reached the interpretation was, two legged meant human being and four legged meant animals. But after getting to know scientific truth, we realise that one legged meant atom, two legged meant magnetic power, and four legged had reference to protons and electrons and Udak-Tarang (wave of water) meant orbits of atoms.

Rohit which is frequently referred to in the first chapter is the cause of Atoms, magnetism, gravitational forces, and therefore is the prime source of all these powers.

This is deducible from following verses:-

Verse 1:- Oh! Rohit, creator of universe and who is concealed in water.

Verse 2:- Oh, Rohit! make all two legged and four legged animals powerful.

Verse 4:- Rohit, the creator of life, being equipped with several types of energy and by virtue of its creative power, creates treasures in the core of the earth.

Verse 15:- Oh Rohit! Those born out of your power are following you just in the same manner that calf follows the cow and have become your disciples. You combine within you all elemental powers.

Verse 16:- This all pervasive Rohit, inhabits also inside earth Dyue Lok and space.

Verse 35:- Let Rohit cause prosperity of nations by merging with Deities that are revolving around themselves.

Verse 38:- Due to Rohit food is provided to various directions, animals and people.

Verse 40:- Rohit rises in the Sun, he is a giver of knowledge and igniter of fire. Only few realized souls know the real nature and characteristics of Rohit.

The above set of verses will show that Rohit is the main principle behind creation of universe, and that this principle pervades everything including Atom and Space, Electrons, Portons, and all stars which are rotating around themselves, do it due to Rohit. All stars are born out of Rohit's power and Rohit gives power to one legged, two legged and four legged creatures. This will show that Rohit is nothing but electro-magnetic power. Because Rohit is the centre of atom charged with positive protons and negative neutron.

Rohit is called creator of water and seated in water and is cause of several types of energy. Water means orbits of Atom. Rohit creates these orbits, and he stays in the centre of atom. This is a full description of Electro-magnetic power and fields.

All the powers in the world are born out of this Rohit power viz. magnetism, and hence the analogy of calf following cow. Then Vedas go on to say that existence of Rohit is known only to the knowledgeable thereby indicating that Electro-magnetic power is a mysterious secret of nature.

If we check up the history of science, we find that magnetism, gravitational power, Electro-magnetic field, and power at the centre of Atom, are discoveries dating back to within 200 years. Yet these discoveries were known to Vedas not less than 3000 years ago.

Chapter 13

UNIVERSE IS ATOM AND ATOM ONLY

The entire Universe is full of atoms. It has come into existence out of atoms is the basic principle of modern science. Hydrogen having one proton is the first element or the basic element from which all other elements have evolved and all these elements are found in the galaxies, sun and its family and every other existence.

In all elements where there is more than one proton and particularly in all elements coming in the periodic table after Oxygen there are many protons and their electrons are orbiting in different circles. But even then they are entangled in each other like the bricks of a modern house and therefore scientist used the term "Block" for atoms. Block in Sanskrit means Ishtika. The Vedic Rishis have referred to a single atom as Ishtika and a group of atoms also referred to as Ishtikas. Therefore, we have to find out what the Rishis have to say.

Yajurveda Chapter 14:- 1. Ishtika is having a place of origin, which is steady, or stationary. It is remaining stationary and it consumes the fire in the void or vaccum.

Taking forms like a house and having the capacity to hold many Ishtikas.

3/4/5 - Ishtika is consumer of strength. It originates from water i.e. waves. It holds space or vaccum and if functions like waves of water.

11 - Ishtika, You are holding earth, space and the universe by your power and you also promote them. You control them.

14 - Let Vishwakarma - the Creator of Universe, establish you the Ishtika in space as you are having the speed of light.

24 - You are the part of original fire.

12/53-54 - Ishtika You reside in the body steadily. I have put another Ishtika by your side. There is a void or vacant space in between the two. But you see that both of you are attached to each other.

13/34. O void! You are stationary, but have the power and capacity to sustain the weight of the universe. The original fire was born from this void and then in the forest.

From the aforesaid description it is clear that Ishtika or bricks or blocks do not refer to the blocks or bricks used for erecting sacrificial places or houses. Even if such bricks are necessary for sacrificial place i.e. Yagnya-Bhoomi, it was no necessary for the Vedic Rishis to compose such hymns in praise of the bricks. The Vedic Rishis were not masons and no mason would compose such a lengthy poetry of about 60 to 70 stanzas on bricks and therefore we have to go deep to unfathomed the meaning hidden in these stanzas.

Ukha is the word used by the Vedas to denote a pit in the earth. It is in fact a void or vaccum and according to Vedas this void is the birth place of fire. Similarly void also sustains the weight of the universe. These two things clearly show that Ukha refers to the structure of atoms.

According to the theory of Democritus i.e. theory of atomism, void is essential for existence of atom. Without void atoms cannot move and they cannot be separated. In the 17th century, Descrot rejected this theory. But after Newton the existence of void began to be recognized with reference to the atoms.

"Newton's conception of action at a distance was in perfect

harmony with acceptance of void and the drawing of a sharp distinction between occupied and non-occupied space."

En. Brita Vol. II Page 348.

Science therefore has recognized the importance and value of void. It also considers that void is inseparable in the theory of atoms. Vedic Rishis pressed the same thought when they considered Ishtika i.e. blocks as atom Ukha as void.

Now therefore if we interpret the above quotation from Vedas we find that they are perfectly scientific. For example, Ukha is described as bearer of the weight of universe, which means that the void or vaccum in the core of atom sustains the entire weight. We know that the capacity of void or vaccum to sustain pressure and force is unlimited.

In the above Rucha it is said that it is from the vaccum, that Jatvedas Agni i.e. original fire was born. Jatved is the first name of the fire in the Vedas and that is the first fire. In the core of atoms there is a positive charge. It is this positive charge which Vedic Rishis described as hot fire or Jatvedas Agni. The combination of vaccum or void with electro-magnetic force is called by the Vedas in 12th Chapter - 58 Rucha as "Chiti - Ukha Sanyog" meaning thereby it is a combination of vaccum and fire. This Jatvedas Agni i.e. electro-Magnetic fire or force is the elementary basic and first force working in the universe. In the further Rucha it is said "O Fire! i.e. Chiti and vaccum, let Your mind, action and tendencies be one and merged into each other.

Therefore, when the Vedas described Ishtika, they were referring to atoms. The composition of atoms and atom as element are rightly and aptly described by the Vedas and this description is most scientific. Even though, atom is the basic of element, a single atom is never in existence. Element is the composition of millions of atoms. In other words, element is found "in mass". The same process is described by the Vedas in Rucha Nos.53 and 54 as under:-

"For preparing Yagna-Vedi i.e. the place where sacrificial fire is burnt or evoked, every block is to be put systematically with recitation of Mantras. O Block! You remain stationary at the place assigned. I have put another block by your side. Let it be also stationary. Let the vaccum in between the two blocks be filled with some element. Let the two blocks be bound to each other."

This description of Ishtika or Block applies to all elements, all matters and all masses. This is clear from 13th and 14th chapter as under:

"O Block! I establish you in water, in vegetation or medicinal herbs, in land, in sea, in sands, and in food 13.53

"O Block! You are everywhere in the universe. You are in space, on earth, in water, in sun, in moon, in wind, in gases, in gold, in twelve suns, in carbon, in food. You are the one responsible for prosperity, wealth, food and strength.

"O Block! You are 3, 15, 17, 21, 18, 19, 20, 22, 23, 24, 25, 30, 31, 34, 36, 38 and 48."

The figures mentioned above are very significant. More clarification about them is to be found in the Chapter on Viraj or Carbon and also in the Chapter on Suns spots. These figures there represent the elements and it can be said that Vedic Rishis were knowing at least 48 elements.

Therefore, it is clear that Vedic terminology has to be approached from totally different angle. When they say fire or Yagna or Ukha or Ishtika or cold fire or hot fire and vibrations of water, they are not referring to things, which we commonly understand. We have to get rid of this kind of approach for looking to the true meanings of Vedas and then only we can go to the real scientific secrets hidden in the coded Vedic language.

Chapter 14

HYDROGEN AND DEITY *"SKAMBHA"*

Distinctive feature of Power *Skambha* is that out of Four Vedas it is referred to only in Atharva Veda. As per vedic tradition this power is saddled with "Deity" hood. But since all Deities (powers) are supposed to have been concentrated in the Sun, one who knows this property or any power that it is Sun-Born, becomes exceptionally knowledgeable. This guarantee is given by Atharva Veda. That is why lust as Sun is self-luminous, extremely powerful source of energy, and life giving entity, all the Deities originating from or merged in sun, were expected to share that power, and hence Vedas thought that they deserved to be probed, into.

Each of those powers were bound to have some distinct form and place, and it is advisable to look into the scientific probe undertaken by Vedas in respect of one of these powers, otherwise named as a "Deity".

In this chapter an attempt is made to probe into seventh and eighth chapter of 10th Mandal (tome) of Atharva-Veda, which relates to Deity "*Skambha*", and which is treated as self-luminous, powerful, and capable of giving out light.

Barring these two chapters in no other veda is this "*Skambha*" described, nor is this "term" used anywhere.

There is typical practice followed by Vedas to describe any power or Deity, and that is to describe the place of that power in the universe, and further describe status, function, power, achievement and its external effects, subtle and at length. Vedas also adopted the policy of repeating the description, so that a lasting impression was left on the mind.

There are about 88 verses in the seventh and eighth chapter. Out of these about 20 verses are moot and mysterious, and from them it is possible to cull out scientific secret of the power. Other verse emphasize expansiveness of the power as well as on the role played in creation of the universe.

In the 7th chapter principally some subtle problems are raised about the nature of "*Skambha*". From the questions asked and the line of direction taken, we can get to know the nature.

Following are the questions:

1. In which part of the body Deity *Skambha* (i.e. the power) is particularly operational?
2. From which part of the body "*Skambha*" lights fire?
3. In which part of the body *Skambha*a subsists as a form of gas? Who has the yardstick to ad measure *Skambha*?
4. In which part of *Skambha* Body are earth, space and "Dyu" where is the part of *Skambha* Body which exists beyond it?
5. From whose inspiration does sun shine and where does gas go?

6. Amongst the thousands of shapes which *Skambha* assumed, how far did he effect progress?

10. Give us the knowledge of *Skambha*, who is the cause of or storehouse of existence?

12. Give us the knowledge of *Skambha* who is the basis for the existence of earth, space, fire sun and air?

15. Tell us about *Skambha*, who is vast like Ocean?

19. Tell us about *Skambha* in whom resides Viraj i.e. Carbon as explained in the next Chapter?

37. Tell us about *Skambha* why gases are always moving and water is floating?

10.8.35 Tell us about *Skambha* that inspirational element giving motion to air or gases and the creator of five elements?

34. Tell us about *Skambha* which is the basis of all other elements?

It is noteworthy that these questions were not raised to be answered by laymen. These questions were part of the conversation between two or more advanced sages. Because such extremely scientific problems could be raised only by those who had high degree of expertise.

Towards the end of 4th and 6th verse there is a repetitive but extremely cleverly worded request which reads thus:

> "Tell us details about *Skambha* who is as if the cause of union of all universal water. This question itself is worthy of note, because it is going to tell us as to what we are talking about?"

After raising the above problems, Vedas have set out expanding scientifically about *Skambha*. Important part of it is set out below in the language of Vedas.

"Original fire was born out of this *Skambha*. The kingdom of fire spread everywhere. None is greater than *Skambha* in this whole universe. Sun and Moon are his eyes and fire is his mouth. In actuality the whole Pranapan (Life of Life) is Him. Both universe and space is pervaded by Him. It is manifested by effort and Heat (Tapacharan) Original Fire Creator Hiranya Garbha also is created by Him. He is self-luminous, fully pure, and flame-like. He is in space, shinning, and is involved mutually, and is woven. All breathing and moving (Living) entities are full of *Skambha*. 3 types of frequencies viz. Sun frequency, space frequency, and vegetarian frequency and creatures are products of *Skambha*. In a glass which is upside down and whose mouth is curved *Skambha* is pervaded (Note: This refers to Chamas-patra chapter No.24). *Skambha* is in anything that is moving, breathing and non-breathing. In *Skambha* there are trillions of or innumerable principles. A thing could be subtler than air, second would be still subtler, i.e. invisible, to such invisible entity *Skambha* can stick, merge and be one. It is due to protection of *Skambha* that all vegetation remains green. Like the axis which supports a chariot, he supports animate and inanimate entities. I know *Skambha* which is the thread of creation of universe.

Besides the above there are many verse mysterious in nature but throwing light on its scientific nature. But before considering them, we will consider the modern scientific information about hydrogen.

The one element which is found in greatest abundance in space is hydrogen. In the upper stratrosphere of earth it is found at the rate of 0.14%. But it is huge in abundance in oceanic waters, rivers, North and south pole Icy continents etc. As part of innumerable carbon compounds it is present.

Hydrogen is a gas without taste, colour, or smell and it is light and it is a simple chemical entity. At the centre of hydrogen is one proton and in the orbit there is only the electron. In ordinary conditions it is made of rarified, loosed molecules, and in it there is a pair of two molecules. It is called diatomic molecule. If hydrogen is combined with oxygen water is born. Greek meaning of the word hydrogen is water maker. In the periodic table it is listed.

Hydrogen has 3 Isotopes. They are called twins born out of action of Rays. When the numbers of atom is same but its weight is different it is called Isotope. Among 3 kinds of isotopes protons are same but number of neutrons changes. Mass numbers of hydrogen isotopes are 1,2,3. Variety with mass 1 is available abundantly. It is called Protium. Those with Mass 2 are called Dutorium. And those with Mass 3 are called Iritium of 3H. In the centre of this variety there is one Proton and two neutrons.

Hydrogen has a very low dissolution and boiling point. If hydrogen travels from high pressure to low pressure, it expands and its temperature increases. But in respect of other gases this temperature decreases. According to the law of Thermodynamics it means that the power of expulsion is greater than power of attraction.

Power of spreading heat is very great and intensive in hydrogen. That is why hydrogen is the best conductor of heat. Now we will compare hydrogen and *Skambha*.

Hydrogen is plentiful in space, stars and galaxies, and as per Vedas hydrogen is the foundation of earth, Dyu, Space, Fire and Sun. In sun it is primarily hydrogen and Vedas have hinted at it by saying, by whose inspiration does sun exist?

Hydrogen is the main source of creation of water. It is constituent of water, *Skambha* is origin of water and is responsible for the flow of water and *Skambha* holds in itself veins of oceans. Hydrogen and *Skambha* is the support of universe, because in creation of universe it was the first product, and became operational.

Hydrogen is very light, and *Skambha* is externally unstable, and floating. Hydrogen has innumerable compounds. More than carbon compounds *Skambha* has innumerable forms, manifested itself.

Skambha has given speed to wind, and it is original inspiration of Panchmahabhutas. Similarly hydrogen is original element.

Hydrogen, after the Universe was created, formed compound with many elements in the space. Similarly got entangled or woven with many elements in the space.

Even if Hydrogen is found little in the crust of earth, it is in abundance in oceans, rivers, lakes and vegetation. The three offshoots of *Skambha* are in the sun, in the space and in the vegetation. *Skambha* is responsible for the greens in the vegtables and it is now proved by science that the sunlight which is created by the atomic burning of Hydrogen and Helium gives green to the vegetation further and like an axis to the wheel *Skambha* supports all animates and inanimate so also the hydrogen.

The word "tritium" kin of hydrogen referred to earlier, was also discovered by Vedas and was termed as "Trivritta Hans".

In these two words, one used by Modern science and other used by Vedas there is profound similarity in its phonetics.

The relevant Sanskrit verse which refers to "Trivritta-Hans" is as follows:

ये अर्वाङ मध्य उत वा पुराणं वेदं विद्वांसमथितो वदन्ति ।
आदित्यमेव ते परि वदन्ति सर्वे अग्निः द्वितियं त्रिवृत्तं च हंसम् ॥
(१०.८.१७)

Fire that acquired renown during Vedic period, middle ages and modern times and termed as "Aditya Agni" and "Trivritta Hans" is nothing but a kind of hydrogen or *Skambha* otherwise also called "Tritium".

This similarity in names "tritium" and "Tri-hans" is the first link. (In Ency.Brita. volume of page 96 it is said:)

> Tritium is present in minute concentration in water. It is formed continuously in upper atmosphere by cosmic rays induced by nuclear reaction. Cosmic rays consisting mainly of high energy protons react with nitrogen atoms to form neutrons which in turn react with more nitrogen atoms to form tritium. This naturally found tritium ends up in form of water and reaches the surface of the earth in rain.

Having read the above passage, please read the following verse.

महद् यक्षम् भुवनस्य मध्ये तपसि क्रांतम् सलिलस्य पृष्ठे ।
तस्मिञ्छ्रयन्ते य उ के च देवा वृक्षस्य स्कन्धः परितश्व शाखाः ॥
(३८)

The great principle of *Skambha* which gives support to huge trees having branches having been formed in upper atmosphere surfaces in the form of rains.

In molecular hydrogen, there are two types, Ortho hydrogen and Para hydrogen. The difference between the two arises by virtue of the fact that the spinning motion of proton is affected by effects of magnetic interaction. In ortho hydrogen both the protons spin in the same direction parallelly. In para hydrogen the spin is alligened in opposite direction and therefore is parallel.

Above description is ultra modern and subtle because it deals with movements of sub-atomic particles invisible to eyes.

The same however came to be described in apt and delightful words in Vedas in following verse!:

तयोरहं परिनृत्यन्तोरिव न वि जानामि
यतरा परस्तात् ।
पुमानेनद् वयत्युद गृणत्ती पुमानेनद्
वि जभाराधि नाके ॥ (१०.८.४३)

From among the dancing girls, we cannot identify or distinguish between one who is closer to you from the other, similarly we cannot distinguish between two persons who are weaving and undoing the strings of destiny on this earth by their actions:-

From earlier reference to "tri-Hans" we have seen how Vedas knew about "Isotopes" (Hydrogen's two varieties).

First verse from VIIth sukta is itself indicator of this: "The question was, in which part of the body does *Skambha* Deity reside?

The question in the second verse straightaway goes to the root of *Skambha* nature.

Verse 2:- Who knows the variety of body of the great *Skambha*.

In the above two verses there is reference to "Matarishwan" and "Aja". Out of these two references, it is difficult to say whether "Duterium" and "Hydrogen" were intended to be signified by these two words.

Chapter 15

GLORY TO CELIBATE LITHIUM

The order in which elements are listed in the table of elements is based on the number of protons at the centre of an atom element, like one proton hydrogen, 2 protons helium, six protons carbon etc. As per this table lithium is listed at No.3, because there are 3 protons at the centre of lithium, and around this centre 3 electrons revolve in orbit.

Lithium is Alkali metal which means it is a metal with salts. In the periodic table it is listed at No1, followed by Sodium, Potassium, Rubidium, Sesium and Frankium. ·The melting point of these metals is low.

Lithium is white in colour, soft, very active and "Shines" like silver. It is light in weight. It is good conductor of heat and electricity. When Lithium comes into contact with water, that reaction results in emitting hydrogen which burns.

Lithium as salt is available in sea water and mineral springs. In California in Syrele lake Lithium is extracted from crude phosphate or Lithium oxide.

In vegetation Lithium is available on large scale. Therefore it is also found in Animals. On human body it has various effects. If salt is deficient in human body it can have adverse effect.

All kinds of non-metallic elements are scavanged from Lithium like oxygen, Hydrogen, Nitrogen, Carbon, Sulphur etc. In Industry Lithium is used to purify metals; like Iron, Copper, Zinc.

Lithium is an excellent conductor of heat. From Lithium many allies are created. From Lithium hydrate, Hydrogen is extracted. For this heat at 700^0C is necessary. Lithium resembles sodium and potassium to certain extent. It also resembles magnesium.

All Alkali metals are extremely good conductor of heat and electricity because each of Alkali metals has valance of one, i.e. one atom of Alkali combines with one atom of another univalent element.

Reason for this property of Alkali metal is that on its external orbit there is one electron and that electron right from Lithium to Frankium gets progressively less attached.

In Atharva Veda Litium has been given special place and in Tome 11, Chapter 5 its basic description is given.

Atharva Veda has called "Lithium" as Brahmachari (Celibate). This adjective or name is totally unconnected with the word "Lithium" Skambha or hydrogen, viraj or carbon are also unconnected. But the number given to all these elements by science, and the number given by Vedas is the same.

In the Brahmacharya chapter there is reference to No.3

ब्रह्मचारिणं पितरो देवजनाः पृथग् देवा अनुसंयंति सर्वे ।
गन्धर्वा एवमन्वायन् त्रयस्त्रिंशत् त्रिशताः षट्सहस्राः
सर्वान्त्स देवांस्तपसा पिपर्ति ॥२॥

Deities and ancestors and gandharvas approve the Brahmachari and this Brahmachari by his good conduct pleases 3, 30, 300, 6000 Deities.

Verse 3:- Venerated Teacher (Acharya) keeps the celibate for 3 nights and having given him advisory lessons, gives him a new birth.

Verse 4:- This celibate takes form of 1. Earth, 2. Dyulok 3. Space and thereby worships Agni (Fire).

In these 3 verses there is emphasis on No.3. In 2nd verse 3 is basic No. of 3, 30, 300 and 6000. And according to modern science the No. of Litium in the table of elements is 3.

Lithium is found in Sea-water, lakes and mineral springs. This scientific truth finds a place, is laid down in the 6th verse which says "Celibate after socialisation, his influence extended from East sea upto North Sea. (स सद्य एति पूर्वस्मादुत्तरं समुद्रं लोकान्त्संगृभ्य मुहुराचरित्रत)

Lithium is found as per the modern science in vegetation on wide scale and Vedas say that vegetation and medically useful herbs are created by Brahmachari. This is said in 20th verse.

Lithium shines like silver. "Hence celibate shines due to his inner shinning capacity, (Rochmanam) and he is Yellowish". ("स स्नातो बभ्रुः पिङ्गलः") Lithium is found in sea, similarly Brahmachari, "सलिलस्य पृष्ठे तपोतिष्ठम् तष्मानः समुद्रे" meaning:- heats in sea and stays on surface of water. All Alkaline metals of Lithium class, are constantly kept in hydrogen or catch fire. This verse is directly related to this property.

Through vegetation Lithium enters body and stomach of animals, similarly "The celibate protects the knowledge acquired by all living beings". "Animals in villages and in forests and animals with or without wings, were created by action of the celibate." These two observations indicate existence of only one principle. i.e. Lithium is found in them.

In alkaline metals and Lithium the tendency to get in touch with fire and catch fire is an innate property. All metals don't catch fire or do not get dissolved in ordinary heat. But Lithium and alkaline metals are good conductors of heat and electricity. This quality is set out in 11th verse very clearly. That verse is as follows:-

अर्वाग्न्य इतो अन्यः पृथिव्या अग्नी समेतो नभसी अन्तरेमे ।
तयोः श्रयन्ते रश्मयोऽधि दृष्टास्ताना तिष्ठति तपसा ब्रह्मचारी ॥

The fire from earth and beyond earth combine become powerful and the Brahmachari worships those rays.

In this verse fire from earth, and fire from beyond earth are a mystery, and are words of secretive and wider meaning. Earthly fire is a fire which grows out of burning of dead or live substances. Similarly several kinds of matters are hot like fire or are inflammable like Caustic Soda, Sulphur, Phosphorous, Acids, etc. and Fire from Earth-lok means lightning. And the heat generated by explosions of hydrogen and helium on the sun.

Hence fire from Earth and fire from beyond earth means fire and electricity combined in Lithium, and hence Lithium is good conductor of both fire and electricity. And as a result of stored fire within it, it immediately catches fire, and its melting point is low. This scientific fact is clearly explained in the above verse.

Lithium has the capacity to draw atom from other elements like Oxygen and Hydrogen and store them inside itself. The same property is in the celibate (Brahmachari) "Celibate had capacity to include within itself all kinds of Deities and also oxygen."

Chapter 16

DEITY "VIRAJ" MEANS LIFE SUSTAINER "CARBON"

Just as Hydrogen is connected with earth, space, galaxies and universe, similarly carbon is connected with all life on earth. There are innumerable compounds of carbons and they all are necessary and useful for life. Naturally if Vedas exhaustively probed into hydrogen, they could not have probed less into carbon.

Vedas did this probe and starting point of this probe is in 7th chapter of Skambha, (Hydrogen). That verse is as follows:-

"Tell us about "Skambha" whose mouth is wide like universe, whose tongue is "Madhusharupi" (...) and whose udder (source of cow's milk) is Viraj (i.e. Carbon)."

In chapter on Skambha while referring to "Pancha Vayus" (Five Gases) there appears an observation to following effect: "Among horses that inspire cycle of Time, five are important, others follow them. Although the speed of horses is felt, their trotting (movement) is not visible". In all there are eleven gases. Among them Hydrogen, Helium, Oxygen, Carbon-di-oxide, and Nitrogen are important ones. In code from the hydrogen is probed in Skambha Sukta, and carbon is probed in Viraj-Sukta. Carbon-di-oxide is the result of synthesis of carbon and oxygen.

Special feature in Skambha-Sukta and Viraj-Sukta is that in Skambha-Sukta, Dyulok, sun, space and Hiranya Garbha (God or Ishavar) are frequently and principally considered, because Hydrogen (more than the earth) is the support of sun, stars, galaxies etc. and its creator. Whereas Viraj-Sukta (carbon-chapter) principally is related to earth.

Either accidentally or as a consequence of scientific attitude of veda authors, Hydrogen is earlier principle with one proton and one electron i.e. two in all in number, Skambha chapters are also two and since Carbon has six electrons carbon chapters are also six.

Speciality of 9th chapter is this that in it the numbers, and clusters of numbers are given altogether different importance. The principle indicated by numbers and clusters of NDS, I have not found in any other Veda (I have not checked up Yajur Veda). Reference to "Indra's 8, Yamas 6, Dyutas (...) 6 Honey of 7 types, Gold 7 poets, is not found anywhere else.

Nevertheless these Nos. and groups of Nos. are meaningful. There is a secret in it. This secret is connected with carbon. It revolves around carbon. The fact that this number group is stretched upto 8 is also important.

Viraj's 10th chapter and its five sub-divisions describe carbon cycle with great expertise. Carbon cycle and chain and its relation with Time is also manifested in this chapter. The expansion of this cycle and its extension is also described there.

After above introductory remarks let us examine scientifically carbon as an element. It must however be noted that in the word carbon all forms of carbon are included.

In the life on this earth, carbon has a unique role to play. Our daily consumption items, like cereals, pulses, sugar, wood, kerosene, medicines, dyes, scents etc. and innumerable other consumption goods are product of carbon compounds. Similarly in all consumption food items like Protein, Carbohydrates, fats, carbon is present. Similarly in all cells of vegetations and living beings carbon compounds are present.

Speciality of carbon (as distinguished from properties of other elements) is capacity of carbon Atoms to join atoms of other elements in a long chain quickly, or otherwise described as its electacity. Only atoms of carbon have capacity or ability to synthesize with atoms of other elements after preserving its eight electrons. Two or more atoms of carbon, in this fashion, either form a chain or synthesize and create other compounds. In the first orbit of electrons revolving around nucleus of carbon atom, there are 2 electrons and in the second orbit there are 4 electrons. Electrons in the second orbit join with electrons of other elements like hydrogen, Oxygen, Nitrogen, Halogen, Sulphur, Phosphorous, and create a new compound in partnership.

In hydro-carbons only electrons of hydrogen and carbon exist. In such two varieties of combinations, one is called Aromatic in which there is cyclic chain, and all kinds of scents (Fragrances) are included in it.

In carbon group of 5 sets, are included the following 1. Silicone (Si 14), Germanium (G3-32), Tin (Sn-50), Lead (P2-82) and carbon (C6).

If 2, 4 or 6 elements are combined with two carbon items, they get connected, depending upon the number of elements so connected. Three chains are created in carbon items. They are called in Sanskrit as Ekbandha, Dwibandha and Tribandha i.e. synthesis or compounds.

When any other element combines with carbon then it is called Carbide. Carbides of Boron (B-5) and Silicon (Si-14) are crystallized and densed.

Product of carbon and oxygen atoms group is called Carbonil Carbose. Carbonil group >C=O is important, in carbon chemistry. Besides this, Protein, Sugar, Fragrance products, and fats contain carbonil group. In vegetation creation of carbose products, is the result of an extremely complex process called "Photo-synthesis."

In our diet the percentage of carbose varieties is plentiful. Because it is the source of energy. In our diet, 60 to 80% energy comes out of Carbose. Glucose is a form of carbose. Through vegetation sources, carbose energy is made available in the form of cereals, pulses, bananas, vegetable tumerers, chiku, sugar, jaggery. From animal sources, carbose is made available in the form of milk, milk products etc. Carbose is source of energy and hence heat. Carbose means starchy food. Proteins also are products of carbonic compounds. (Carbon is extremely wide subject. Organic chemistry is its from. We are only touching its important aspects.)

Similarly "Carbonic Cycle" is also important. For living beings carbon is extremely necessary. Almost all major constituents of living beings are derived from carbon. They are called live matter. Carbon's principal source is atmosphere. Carbon is plentiful in water. Photo-synthesis and breathing are two principle activities of carbon cycle.

All fuel in the world is made up of carbon. Wood, coal, petrol, gas etc which comes from trees is carbon. (Though petrol and gas are not considered in Vedas.)

Having cited all important information about carbon, now we will turn to "Viraj" chapter (sukta) and try to find out as to how description given in Viraj-Sukta tallies with our knowledge of carbon.

Carbon is listed in periodic table of elements as sixth, because in centre of carbon atom, there are six protons. This number six is given great importance in Ninth chapter (Sukta). "Oh! Sage Kashyap, tell us we six disciple-sages about the scheme of nature and role of Viraj (carbon)." These six sages are friends and disciples of Sage Kashyap. This reference to six disciple Sages of Kashyap (Teacher-Sage), is reflective of six protons in the nucleus.

Similarly "(Oh! Kashyap) the source of five original elements viz. the sixth principle, and its creation, please explain to us".

Even in the above verse the symbols six which stands for sixth element is reflected.

In the 13th verse (Rucha) there is reference to 3 Female Deities out of which one satisfies cravings of people, second gives power (energy) and third protects. There is also reference to 3 kinds of Fire in the same verse. Total of 3 female deities and 3 types of fire works out to six. But the qualities attributed to 3 female Deities throws light on functions of carbon. Carbon gives food, increases power, and protects.

In the twenty fifth verse disciples ask the following question:-

Which are the six original principles (elements) which although separate total six, like ox, house, blessing, deity, season and the giver of answers (i.e. Kashyap sage).

In the 22nd verse Sage Kashyap observes "By giving this knowledge, and for your benefit, I make friendship with you and I mix with you." Because of mixing six don't have independent existence.

Verse No.6 says "As long as there is fire lit on this earth, till then, the sixth major part (element) which causes the beginning of earthly affairs, exists in spread condition in Paradise (space). Home "Fire" referred to includes heat, light, electricity, or fire necessary for sustenance (calories). Verse further says that all earthly affairs dissolve in it. This means that energy necessary for daily chores is product of this sixth part (element) viz. Viraj or carbon. This verse also means that vegetation start creating energy by absorbing carbon-di-oxide, which is also part of worldly affairs. "Vaishwa-nar Fire" referred to in the verse includes fire necessary for digestion, and without digestion there cannot be energy or worldly activity.

The cycle is: Fire in the stomach - Digestive power - consumption of food - creation of energy - sustenance of life - collection of energy - growth of life.

Ninth verse is mysterious. It reads;

"Although it is itself lifeless, it enlivens the whole universe, and Viraj (Carbon) establishes its kingdom all over the earth. It energises all living beings.

(अप्राणैति प्राणेन प्राणतीनां विराट् स्वराज मध्ये ति पश्चात्॥९॥

Oxygen is the giver of life. In comparison with oxygen, Viraj (Carbon) can't be called life giver. Hence it is called "Life-less". For life, oxygen comes first for living beings which is originally absent in carbon. Nevertheless since it is otherwise energy giver it is called enlivener of universe, and energy giver of all living beings, and also life supporter. Carbon or Viraj is called lifeless because excess of Carbon-di-oxide can result in death. Life become lifeless.

Eleventh verse says "Viraj (Carbon) which is original light (Fire) giver and which is all powerful (because of its energy giving capacity) enters all living beings and exists everywhere on the earth."

In the next chapter, we will consider other aspect of Viraj (Carbon).

Chapter 17

SCIENCE OF STATISTICS RELATING TO VIRAJ (CARBON)

In the 9th chapter which includes questions and answers, there is probe into some numbers and group of numbers. This grouping of numbers clearly relates to carbon. These Verses range from 11 to 76 and numbers 1 to 8 or their groupings are considered here. From the grouping of these numbers and their additions, some secrets are revealed.

Verse 11 :- Original light giver in the universe Viraj (No.1)

Verse 12 :- Wings (2) which are huge and which shine in Usha (Dawn), fly around carbon. The shining power of the sun is created out of this. (2)

Verse 13 :- Three female Deities, one which satisfies the people, the other which gives power, and the third which protects. Three kinds of fire Ahavaniya, Garhyapatya, Dakshinagai. (No.3) 3+3=6

Verse 14 :- Double wings of Dev-Yadnya, Agni and Soma (No.2). Fourth part of speech "Gayatri" (No.4) Trishtubha, Jagati, Anushthubha, Brihati Chhanda (No.4) or Gayatri No.5

Verse 15 :-

Panchadasha Hritwij	=	No.15
Pancha Ushakal	=	No.5
Pancha Dohansamay	=	No.5
Pancha Rutu	=	No.5
Pancha Disha	=	No.5
Pancha Dhenu	=	No.5
Total	=	40
Ek Jaga (One world)	=	1
Ek Vichar (One thought)	=	1
Total	=	42

Nos. 15, 5, 40, 42

Verse 16 :-

Adhajanma Ruta	=	7
Six Bhutas	=	6
Six Yadnyharupi Vrishabha	=	6
Six Samrupi Ploughs	=	6
Days for recitations	=	6
Division of Dyava Prithvi	=	6
Total	=	30

Nos. 6, 30, 37

Verse 17 :-

Months of Cold 6

Summer months	6
Adhik Mas	1
(One which can join both)	
Suvarna Kavi	7
Chhand	7
Disha	7
	28

Nos.7,28

Verse 18 :-

Sapta Yadnya	7
Sapta Samidha	7
Honey of 7 types	7
Sapta Rutu	7
Sapta Ghrit	7
	35

Nos. 7, 35

Verse 20 :-

Gayatri Tripad	3
Trishtubha	15
Jagati	33
Anushthubha	21
	72

Nos. 3, 15, 33, 21, 72

Verse 21 :-

Bhutas from Adyajanma Yadnya	8
Ashata Yoni Aditi	8
She delivered sons	8
	24
Havan is done on the eight days from 1st moon If 8th night is counted together	1
	25

24 + 8 = 32

Nos. 8, 24, 25, 32

Verse 23 :-

Kinds of Indra	8
Kinds of Yama	8
Kinds of Sages	7
	23
Jal Lok	1
Medicine	1
Panchabhutas	5
	7
Total	28

Nos. 8, 6, 7, 21, 28

Verse 25 :-

Ox	= 1
One Sage	= 1
One Place	= 1
One Blessing	= 1
One Deity Pervading Earth	= 1
One Season	= 1
Which	6
No.6	

Verse 26 :-

Ox, Place, Blessing, Deity, Season,	= 5
+ Kashyap	= 1
	6

If we consider all these Verses and the grouping of numbers, we find that they range from No.1 to No.8. We have seen that Carbon Atoms have the capacity to combine upto 8.

In these Verses the Nos. and group of numbers that frequently come is dropped. And if the total of numbers in each Verse is considered, we find as follows:-

1, 2, 3, 4, 5, 6, 7, 8

Verse 15:- 40, 42, 15

Verse 16:- 30, 31

Verse 17:- 28

Verse 18:- 35

Verse 20:- 33, 21, 72

Verse 21:- 24, 25, 32

All these numbers if set out in order, they read as follows:

1, 2, 3, 4, 5, 6, 7, 8, 15, 21, 24, 25, 28, 30, 31, 32, 33, 35, 40, 42, 72.

As per the periodic table of science of chemistry dealing with Atoms and their Time following order and numbers are laid down.

As per this table following order is noticeable:-

1. Hydrogen
2. Helium
3. Lithium
4. Beriliyan
5. Boron
6. Carbon
7. Nitrogen
8. Oxygen
15. Phosphorous
21. Skandium
24. Chromium
25. Mangneese
28. Nickel
30. Zinc
31. Galium
32. Germanium
33. Arsenic
35. Bromine

40. Zirconium

42. Molindayam

72. Hafnium

Out of the above, most of the elements are found in the upper crust of the earth like, in granite, Basalt rocks, Shells, conch, stone of sand, Metamorphis rocks, and sea water. From their Nos. as well as from periodic table, it appears that from 21 to 30 comprise of transition metals, otherwise also called Iron transition metals. All these elements are directly or indirectly connected with Carbon. The elements are certainly connected with human life.

Hydrogen and helium are original constituents of sun and this is set out in Verses 12 by saying "that the shining power of the sun is created by two huge wings etc." Wings are always two. Hydrogen has one proton and helium has two protons.

If we consider only the numbers in this chapter we find that they range from 1 to 8 and No.6 is their central point. The fact that electrons of carbon can absorb electrons of other elements upto 8 and can remain together, appears to be related and reflected in the number 8 cited in this chapter.

Therefore if we consider the numbers 1 to 8 individually we find that life sustaining entity are gaseous. Group Nos. also appear to have laid emphasis on figures ranging from 1 to 8, like for instance, Five Rithus, Six Bhutas, Seven Yadnyas. We have seen the result arising out of adding Nos. in a Verse and traced the relevant element. All this leads us to the conclusion, that the elements so traced is some way linked to carbon in one of its thousands of forms.

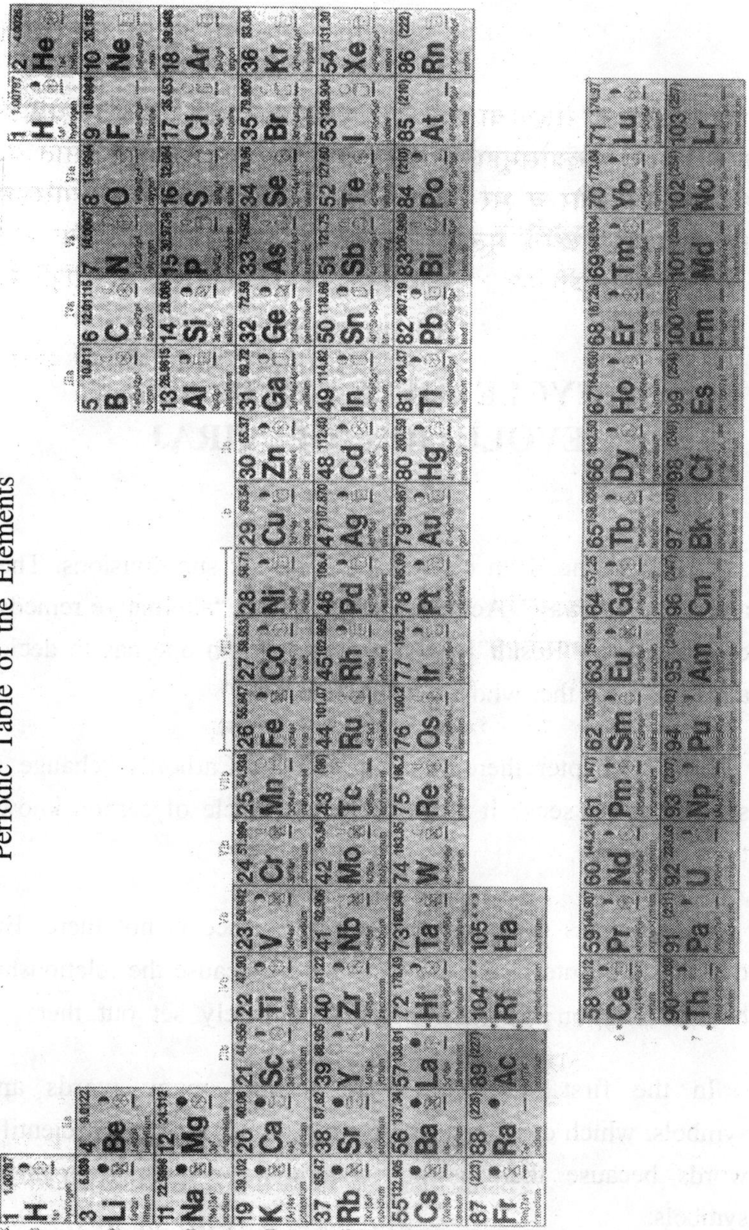

Periodic Table of the Elements

Chapter 18

CYCLE OF CARBON OR EVOLUTION OF VIRAJ

Of 8th Tome, 10th chapter there are six sub-divisions. They are called "Paryay". Actually Paryay means "alternative remedy" or "effect" or "Result" which meaning fits in one has to decide after reading the whole chapter.

In this chapter there is description of Carbon's "change in state". In one sense it is description of cycle of carbon known to Ved-author.

Evolution as spelt out by modern science is not there. But that does not interfere with our theory. Because the relationship between carbon has with life is completely set out there.

In the first sub-chapter, there are many words and symbols, which can't be elaborated in terms of modern scientific words because there is no modern way to interpret those symbols.

For example it is stated that after its evolution carbon merged with the following.

1. Garhya Patya Agni
2. Ahavaniya Agni
3. Dakshin Agni
4. Meeting place
5. At Samiti (Committee)
6. At Minister's meeting (Cabinet Minister)

We have seen how Agni (Fire) is connected with carbon.

Pandit Chitrav interpreted the words meeting etc. to mean various compounds of carbon. Hydrocarbon, Carbohydrates, Carbonil etc. and by this interpretation has deleted on evolution of carbon. This interpretations appears to be correct.

In the second sub-division (Paryay) we find that carbon evolved in space. Viraj (carbon) got divided in four ways for man and deities. They are 1. Bal Power 2. Stamina 3. Truth 4. Food. (Stamina is capacity for sustenance). Then it evolved in the form of medicinal herbs, and water.

It is as a result of carbon, that power, stamina, foods, herbal medicine, are created and carbon can be dissolved in pure water. This is the function of carbon.

Third division (Paryay) of the chapter is as mysterious as the first. In that carbon is linked with Time, Day, Month, Year. In this it is shown that carbon is killed by many. Table can be laid down as follows:

As per periodic table the elements corresponding with the aforesaid number are as follows:-

Viraj (carbon)	**Went to Whom**	**Killed by Consumed by**	**Effect**
Viraj (carbon)	Vegetable	Vegetable	Vegetable grows every Year
Viraj (carbon)	Ancestors	Ancestors	Vegetable grows every Month
Viraj (carbon)	Gods	Gods	Vegetable grows every fortnight
Viraj Men (carbon)	Human	Human	Instant need Human consumes Day and Night

The above cycle of evolution of carbon commences from herbs and ends with the food human beings consume day and night. Reference to 15 days month and year is related to the period covering production of herbs, food etc. In carbon cycle herbs are origin. Then come animals and then man. "Jivo Jivasya Jivanam" (One life feeds an another) is a principle which applies to Carbon. Herbs breath carbon in, and the process of carbohydrates starts. All carbohydrates, proteins, having become man's food make themselves available to man in milk, meat etc. and that is how time has a role to play in carbon cycle.

In the 4th sub-division of the chapter (Paryay) carbon goes to man as cow in various forms, many milk her, and many items of food grew out of milk. That order is as follows:-

Viraj or Carbon has created grain on earth. Viraj or Carbon created different fragnances, poisons when it got united with serpents and fermentation to create liquor.

Viraj (carbon)	Went to Whom	Who Milked	In What	What was created
Viraj (carbon)	Devils	Opposed	Iron Pot	Made (illusion) Maya
Viraj (carbon)	Ancestors	Yama	Silver Pot	Swadha
Viraj (carbon)	Human	Manu	Earth as pot	Cereals
Viraj (carbon)	Saptarshi	Brihaspati	Pot of chhand	Knowledge / Tapa

In the above evolutionary order Krushi and cereals were created on earth and for that the Vedas say carbon was responsible. Science says the same thing. There is no scientific basis in respect of Devils, Ancestors and Saptarshi.

Fifth sub-division and its evolutionary table is as follows:

Viraj (carbon)	Went to Whom	Who Milked	In What	What was created
Viraj (carbon)	Gods	Savita (Sun)	Chamas Pot	Power
Viraj (carbon)	Gandharva Apsara	Chitrarath Gandharva	Pushkara Purna	Chafa fragrance Smell
Viraj (carbon)	Others	Rajatanama Gandharva	Aampatra	Tirodha Power
Viraj (carbon)	Snake	Snake Gandharva	Alabu Patra (of Dudhi Bhopala Size)	Poison Power

In the above evolution carbon results in power, flower fragrance, Tirodha shakti (secret power), and poison. We have seen that carbon creates carbohydrates, proteins, herbs and vegetation and power in animals and human beings.

There are two kinds of compounds resulting from carbon, aliphatic and aromatic. In this the word Aroma signifies fragrance. Aromatic means all products that emit fragrance. Pushkar Parna means Lotus leaf. Pushakarni means the CREAPER of lotus. Pushkar-Parna Patra means blossomed lotus. Lotus is a flower and represents all flowers and is fragrant, and is referred to here symbolically as agent of fragrance. The fact that the Aromatic fragrance is derived from carbon is here symbolically stated by using words "Pushkarparna Patra" and "Pushpa Gandha" (fragrance of flower) and its evolution.

The fact that carbon's evolution reaches stage of snake-poison is also a scientific truth. In various types of snakes found in India like Cobra, Dhaman, Ghonas, the poison found falls under the category of "carbo-ecomolgnpeshatdetas". From the title of poison itself existence of poison origin viz. carbon is indicated.

The reference to Iterejan and the resultant evolution described in terms of "Aam-Patra" and "Tirodhashakti" is important and mysterious. Tirodhshakti means power that secretly resides. It appears that here the author of vedas have evinced most subtle and deep insight in their knowledge of scientific truth. And this secret is concealed in two terms "Aam Patra" and "Tirodhashakti". Tirodhashakti means Volatility. Aampatra means Fermentation plant. But before we answer the how of it, let us examine one more product of carbon.

Liquor, whether foreign or otherwise, contains either Alcohol or phenol or Ether. All these three are chemical compounds and are product of chain from other compounds because in their molecules one atom of oxygen and one atom of carbon are bonded together. Normally oxygen bearing carbon atoms, found in Alcohol, phenol and Ether, are part of hydro-carbon chain, in which hydrogen atoms are bonded.

Alcohol is divisible (on classification) in terms of atomic grouping. Like = C-CH, in which 3 atoms of carbon are bonded with 3 atoms of hydrogen. Phenol and Ether are also products of carbon chain.

Specific types of Alcohols are colourless, and are either in liquid or solid form. Original Alcohol in which there are less than 12 carbon atoms are ordinarily in liquid form under normal temperatures. But those in which there are more than 12 carbons atoms are in solid form.

In 1957 modern scientists discovered in Paris a method of classification and nomenclature that chart is as follows:

Name	(Carbon) numbers of Atoms
Methanol	1
Ethanol	2
1 Propanol	3
2 Propanol	3
3 Propanol	3
1 Bootanol	4
1 Pentanol	5
1 Dodekanol	12
1 Octadacanol	18

In manufacture of artificial Alcohol the process of fermentation is very important. In fact Alcohol cannot be manufactured without fermentation.

Any food stuff, e.g. Fruits, Sugarcane Juice, malt, Barley etc. in which there is starch and sugar can be fermented and alcohol manufactured. And in this process carbon has a very big role to play.

Alcohol, phenol and ether are volatile, meaning if they are exposed they evaporate in air.

The entire process of evolution of carbon described above relating to alcohol, was described by Authors of vedas in just two words i.e. by saying that carbon is responsible for evolution into Alcohol.

"Iterejan" (common people) referred to in Vedas, literally means those people who are not worthy of being specially mentioned, appear to have been consuming liquor. Therefore vedic authors showed skill in expression and also decency, by saying that carbon went to Iterejan (common people) in the 9th verse of Vth sub-division (Paryay). It takes plenty of money to install manufacturing plant of Alcohol. Hence there is reference to Vaishrevan (Kuber = Extremely rich person) or Kuber's son (This fluctuation is incidental and unrelated to scientific discussion, but is touched just to show that author or Vedas were highly knowledgeable about practical side of life also).

After carbon went to Kuber Vaishrevan, in the form of a Cow and if cow had to be milked, a pot would be required. That pot itself was mysterious, and one which had scientific foundation. That pot was called "Aam-Patra" in Vedas.

The term "Aam-Patra" was used to denote fermentation process. The word "Aam" is a root for the process of fermentation, which is signified by verb "Aambavine" which stands for fermentation. The word "Patra" does not here merely mean "A-cup" or "Pot", it stands for place where fermentation takes place. In other words "Aam-Patra" stands for fermentation plant, or plant where Alcohol is manufactured.

The product which is the result of fermentation is obviously Alcohol and this is described as "Tirodha" i.e. capable of disappearing i.e. Volatile. Thus this mysterious "Tirodha-Shakti" (power to disappear) is used in relation to volatile of Alcohol.

In the same sub-division a cautious advice is given to gentlemen, that they should keep away from people who prosper on this Volatile Milk. This advice is in the 12th Verse.

Whether intoxication arising out of Alcohol is worthy of indulgence or no is a personal matter, but there is intoxication arising out of imbibing knowledge, and that certainly is worthy of indulgence.

After the end of 5th sub-division dealing with evolution of carbon and ending with poison, authors of Vedas and the 6th sub-division by completing the topic in charming style. Here in a humorous strain it is observed that the reader (or Pandit) who realises the mystery of evolution of carbon (which ends with poison) should be showered with poison, so that they would develop immunity against the poison.

Is it not true that one who can enjoy fragrance (created by carbon), who can digest liquor (created by carbon) or who can digest poison (created by carbon); can such a person have enemies in this world? Poison and ignorance are equal killers.

Not accepting knowledge of Vedas amounts to resisting Vedas. Even if this book orientates the mind, not to resist knowledge imparted by Vedas, author would consider it to be a fulfilment of his effort.

Chapter 19

BRIHASPATI THE TEACHER OF ALL DEITIES = NITROGEN

Speciality of the "terms" (words) used in the Vedas is this, that the roots of those words without losing their original identity, expand or contract the meaning according to the context, because these words are used with a kind of elasticity. For example the word "Marut" in the context of earth are called "storms", but in context of sun are called "solar storms", and in the context of vast space of universe becomes "radiation of universal energy". Similarly "Ekadash Rudra" in the context of sun-earth relationship becomes cosmic cycle but in the context of earth alone becomes Sodium (We will examine this part in the next chapter).

Brihaspati is a similar term, whose meaning changes according to context. In relation to earth, in limited context it is the planet Jupiter. In the context of universe it is one of the stars in the galaxy. (Its identity in this context need not be probed there), but in the context of elements on the earth it is used by Vedas to denote Nitrogen.

Rigveda has devoted nine and Atharva Veda has devoted five chapters on "Brihaspati", and those chapters having treated

Brihaspati as nitrogen, have recited its properties and also indicated and identified places where it is available. These chapters are mysterious and moot, but are nonetheless expressed in a language which is easily understandable.

But before that let us see what is set out by modern science in relation to nitrogen.

In the periodical table of elements (cited earlier at page 107) in the column designated as Va, nitrogen leads to list of gases cited followed by Phosphorous, Arsenic, Antimony and Bismath. All these elements are called elements falling under the Genus Nitrogen. Among these are some important and some common features. They are similarities in chemical behaviour.

The order of the five elements as per the table is as follows:

Nitrogen	7
Phosphorous	15
Arsenic	33
Antimony	51
Bismath	83

In normal atmosphere both oxygen and nitrogen are present, but nitrogen does not assist in breathing. This discovery was reached in 1772 but discovery of Nitrogen was reached by Rutherford independently and since it was traced in a mineral called Niter, in 1790 it was labelled as nitrogen.

In dry weather its percentage is 75.5%. Nitrogen is found in the following and at following places.

1. In the meteors that drop from space on earth.
2. In the gases emitted by live volcanoes.

3. Sun, some stars.
4. Many bacteria stabilise nitrogen like hygobithum and Azotobaxter.
5. Besides bacteria Algae (Moss) also stabilise nitrogen.
6. Lightening in the sky creates nitrogen.
7. The supporter and creator of the earth (sun) is also creator of nitrogen.
8. In Guanos i.e. caves or places where there is heavy traffic of bats, nitrogen is plentiful.
9. In Eggs and egg shells.
10. In proteins of living beings its percentage is 17%.
11. Lightening in the sky, separates molecules of oxygen and nitrogen, and creates Nitric oxides and Nitric-dioxide.
12. Decaying of vegetation and dead bodies of living beings.

Just as there is Hydrogen cycle, Oxygen cycle, there is also Nitrogen cycle.

In atmosphere, and living enclosures (bodies) reaction process that is generated is called Nitrogen cycle. Vegetation, especially watery vegetation Algae or Moss absorb Nitrogen from the atmosphere, resulting in division of proteins, animals consume vegetation and nitrogen accumulates in their bodies. After death of animals & vegetation their bodies merge with earth. This results in oxidation and anti-nitrification, and process of Bacterial action takes place. Result is that nitrogen reaches the sea and from there is released in atmosphere. This includes the process of nitrogen coming out of shit of animals.

Construction of Nitrogen Atoms and their speciality.

From the category symbolised nitrogen is the most important element, although it is diatomic i.e. comprising of two atoms. It is a gas. Other elements from this group are solids. From the above category Nitrogen is one element which has the capacity to build multiple bonds. Hydrogen and Nitrogen can bond together, with other mineral elements.

There are five electrons in the outmost electric shell. They need to accept 3 electrons or lose five to attain stable configurations. Nitrogen accepts electrons. Nitrogen has a great tendency to form multiple bonds, and this tendency is absent in the lower down group.

After having examined some scientific data about nitrogen let us examine what Rigveda and Atharva Veda say about Nitrogen (otherwise called Brihaspati).

Rigveda :-

1. My body created out of Yadnya, which has in it seven deities, and which is support for Karma. 10.67
2. Brihaspati (Nitrogen) which is space-shaped and born in Aditya (or at Sun Frequency), which has seven mouths, and seven threads. 4.50
3. Light creator Brihaspati, has released from Dark Caves, Cows, from two doors of the lower side of the cave, and one from one door of upper side of the cave. 10.6.74
4. The space-filling roaring Brihaspati breaks clouds and liberates the Sun and Dawn.
5. With the aid of storms (Marut) which assault like wild-boars, Brihaspati killed vala.

6. Marut (storms) entertained in their minds the desire to make Brihaspati "Go-Pati" i.e. leader of Cows and their herds.
7. Brihaspati is capable of assuming different shapes and he has reached several rivers unto the sea.
8. Oh! (Brihaspati) love engendering. Bhag-like friendly, and causing union between Husband and Wife. (2)
9. Cows, released by Brihaspati have wonder lust are lustrous, and shapely. These cows were confined by Vala Brihaspati reached them to Deities with the fast speed possessed by Grain-Traders.
10. Mountain cows were liberated by Brihaspati, like meteoric-fall. This Brihaspati is cloud-breaker in the form of Meteorites and capable of causing water showers. At the time, with hooves of rain fall, dust-covered skin of earth was extracted.
11. Mountain Cows came out like young ones of chicken among out of egg-shells.
12. Brihaspati the tracer of Cows like fish from dry lake.
13. Newly born Dawn, with the aid of Sun-Fire, like muscles separated from bones.
14. Re-acquired Viraj Cows, like fallen leaves from trees during winter. (10)
15. Brihaspati gave cows to Deities which had adorned star constellations.
16. Brihaspati after expanding his muscles accepts food (8) (10.190)
17. Oh! loving friendly Brihaspati. (6.)

18. Sacred hymns run to Brihaspati, like rivers roaring to the seas. Brihaspati keeps a close watch on water-promotion and water-showers. 7

19. Brihaspati is born for multi-purpose activity. 8

20. Brihaspati who has several vehicles 7.97.7

Verses from Atharva Veda about Brihaspati:- 11.3

1. In this compound (Brihaspatistav) of phosphorous Brihaspati is the head.

2. If I consume phosphorous through the mouth I will die, therefore I am consuming it through Brihaspati's mouth.

3. Like the wind which carries watery moss, or Alage, Darkness destroyer Brihaspati, carried quickly cows like wind affected clouds 10.68.6

Modern science has listed nitrogen at No."7" because there are 7 protons at the centre of nitrogen. Vedas gave the same number to nitrogen. The body of Brihaspati is filled with 7 deities. He has seven mouths, and has seven strands. This is stated in various verses, clearly.

Just as nitrogen is in its own group (or class) chief of five elements, similarly Brihaspati also is head of herd of cows. "Odan" means phosphorous. The title of chapter 11.3 of Atharva-veda is "Brihastpatistavodan Sukta". "Sav" means together. The first verse of this chapter says "Brihaspati is the head of this odan (phosphorous) which means that in this compound between the two, nitrogen comes first and therefore is primary.

Chapter in Atharva Veda explains as to how phosphorous by itself is injurious, and while saying this it adds "I don't accept phosphorous by my own mouth, but I accept it indirectly through the mouth of nitrogen." This indicates that the compound of both becomes acceptable and would not be injurious to health.

Nitrogen in its own class of elements has a speciality, and that speciality is that this mineral element is capable of establishing multiple bonds. It is capable of establishing a bond with hydrogen, which others of its class cannot, and it is capable of giving its electrons to electrons of other elements, and in the same process it is capable of accepting electrons of other elements and creating compounds, and further capable of completing the cycle of 8.

This above scientific truth was disclosed by Vedas in figurative symbolic language. The reference to release of 3 cows, two through upper door and one from lower door, represents parting of 3 electrons in the process of creation of compound.

This capacity of exchanging and absorption of atoms of other elements and ability to create compounds, is symbolically expressed by calling Brihaspati (Nitrogen), capable of assuming various shapes; capable of causing union between husband and wife, friendly loving, capable of expanding his muscles and accepting food etc. Similarly inherent nature of nitrogen to run for union with other elements is expressed saying that Brihaspati has several vehicles, born for multipurpose activity etc.

All those places cited by modern science, relating to birth of nitrogen, are described by Vedas as follows:-

1. Nitrogen inhabits falling meteors, Nitrogen releases cows akin to falling meteors.
2. Nitrogen inhabits Sun and Stars. Similarly Nitrogen gave

cows to Deities among constellations. Created Dawn and Sun.

3. Lightening creates nitrogen. Lightening is variously described as Meghavidrak, Roaring, etc.
4. Nitrogen was born in the Sun (Aditya lok).
5. Cows of Nitrogen have wander lust, meaning electrons move and are eager to go and create compounds. That these cows (electrons) are shapely and lustrous.
6. That these cows are confined in "Val" meaning circuit or orbit.
7. Place where Nitrogen is abundantly available are caves of bats. They are also referred.
8. Existence of Nitrogen in eggs and its shell is also referred.
9. Reference to fish in waterless lake is also symbolised by dead bodies which create Nitrogen.
10. Decaying fallen leaves create Nitrogen is all referred to by talking of winter & falling leaves.
11. In 10.68.5 reference to moss, algae which creates Nitrogen is stunning. It is mentioned that they aid in stabilising Nitrogen.

अप ज्योतिषा तमो अन्तरिक्षा दुद्गः शीपालमिव वात आजत् ।
बृहस्पतिरनुमृश्या वलस्याऽभ्रमिव वात आ चक्र आ गाः ॥५॥

12. Cycle of Nitrogen is referred to as:- Animals and vegetation having decayed and Nitrogen is created. Then if reaches the sea, and through steam enters the atmosphere. Symbolism is clear. Like rivers running towards the sea hymns rush

to Nitrogen and Brihaspati keeps a close watch on promotion of water and Rain showers. One who merely watches is always neutral. This neutrality is also emphasized. Nitrogen does not help life or take part in fire. This is his neutrality.

13. Brihaspati reaching several rivers upto sea symbolises capacity of Nitrogen to merge with other elements.

Chapter 20

OXYGEN

Without atmosphere no life would either grow or survive on earth. Smallest of the small bacteria need oxygen to survive. Other more developed living beings like insects, worms, animals, fish, vegetation, and human beings cannot live without oxygen. Secondly without oxygen water itself can not come into existence.

Although oxygen is a number one necessity for life in the periodic table of elements it is listed at No.8.

In respect of categorising oxygen order in the table, modern scientists and sages of vedic age took identical view. The result was although chapters and verses were written about oxygen but while enlisting it the scales were held even and the number given to oxygen was No.8.

IVth chapter of 11th Tome of Atharva Veda oxygen is well known as "Pran-Sukta" (Life Chapter). Twenty second verse read follows:-

अष्टाचक्रं वर्तत एकनेमि सहस्राक्षरं प्र पुरो नि पश्चा ।
अर्धेन विश्वं भुवनं जजान यदस्यार्धं कतमः स केतुः ॥ ११.४.२२

This chariot of human body, having eight wheels and thousand axles and one Ring (Now Tyre) is running ahead of fire. This chariot which creates the whole earth with half of its body: where is the other half? How to identify it.

Oxygen is a known element to all. Therefore there is no need to set out its scientific side, nor any need to compare it with symbolic rendering. Besides this, both modern scientists and Vedas have set out its elemental order as eight. Eight wheeled chariot.

Wherever there is it is necessarily followed by carbon - dioxide. On this point Vedas do not lay behind. Viraj as we have already seen is carbon. Reference to it arises the following manner in Verse 12.

"प्राणो विराट् प्राणो" देष्ट्री प्राणं सर्व उपासते ।
प्राणो ह सूर्यश्चंद्रमाः प्राणमाहुः प्रजापतिम् ॥

Motive power of all living beings i.e. Pran (Oxygen) is praised by Sun, Moon and life which is nourisher of all people.

Oxygen is of course described by Vedas, but there is no need to amplify it. But the fact that its order was known to Vedas, and the fact that it was irrevocably connected with carbon, is very very important.

In verse No.22 the riddle that is put towards the end viz. where is the other half of the chariot, is a riddle which now is easily answered. The other half is carbon.

Chapter 21

EKADASH RUDRA VIZ. SODIUM

Ekadash Rudra had different meanings in relation to different context.

Its first meaning is (a) Solar cycle of 11 years (b) Universal cycle (c) And dark spots on the sun.

In view of these interpretations to call "Ekadash Rudra" as mere "Sodium" will create confusion and would need explanation. It will also raise doubts about author's clarity of mind.

Although prime-facie it is natural to be oriented as above, I may humbly assure that my mind is without any confusion?

However it is the practice of Vedas to use identical term to mean different things, when used in different context. Hence the need to probe scientifically into its symbolism under changed context.

We say that the term Ekadash Rudra is used to denote Sodium in view of its description in the chapter which we are about to examine. If we do not embark upon this probe, then important part of Sodium's description in the Vedas will come to be neglected. Hence the following analysis.

As per the discussion in Vedas Sodium (or Rudra) has 2 forms.

First form is horrifying and destructive and we will later examine it. Second form of Rudra, is peaceful, life giving, life promoting, and power-conferring. Not only this, but Sodium is called "Vaidya-Raj" or King of Doctors (Bhishgwar).

If Rudra is destructive but is still called Vaidya-Raj or life giver, then probe is necessary to find out if life giver Rudra or Ekadash Rudra is different from destructive Rudra. This chapter is devoted for that purpose.

In the "Yajurveda" Samhita entitled "Shatrudriy" Rudra is extensively described.

1. Budhiy :- One who is at the bottom of all things, or cause (Root) of Tree.
2. Vaman :- Very small in shape.
3. Vikshinik :- Which cures mild attack of rise in temperature.
4. Shiv :- Peace giving. That which promotes happiness.
5. Anna - Pati :- Controller of food, Preserver of forests.
6. Kshudrak :- Negligible in form.
7. Its skin colour is yellowish or Reddish or whiteish.
8. Vanya :- It is tree like, or resides in forest.
9. Verse 1.43.3 - Sukhopdhiyukta Rudra (Inherently happy)
10. Verse1.43.5 - Lustrous like gold.

11. Verse 1.114 - Let us sing in praise of Rudra to ensure health and happiness for inhabitants of our village.

12. Verse 2.33.2 - Give us special medicine to enable us to live for 100 years.

13. Verse 2.33.4 - Oh king of doctors give us medicine.

14. Verse 2.33.6 - Rudra has satisfied me by giving me medicine.

15. Verse2.33.13 - Oh! Maruts. Give us the effective rare medicines.

16. Verse5.42.11 - Oh! The king of medicines we worship Rudra.

As per the periodic table, the element Sodium has No.11. Rudra is also said as Ekadash Rudra. Ekadash means 10+1=11. Sodium, Sodium Chloride and other allied minerals are absolutely necessary for animals and human beings. The salt or sodium we take in food is necessary for fighting with diseases; it gives strength and power to the body. If percentage of sodium or salt in body goes nil, as like in, dehydration man can die. Therefore, repeatedly it is said. Oh! Rudra protect us, keep us healthy. Sodium, sodium chloride or salt is medicine in food, therefore, Rudra is called as Aushodhi Samrat (King of Medicines) by Vedas. Therefore, there is similarity in the terminology in Ekadash Rudra and sodium not only because of their similarity in number (eleven) but we must also see other similarity as we have done in case of Hydrogen, Carbon etc.

Atharva:- 7.87.1

We pray in reverence to Rudra who is fire like, creator of

Universe and residing in or having abode in, medicines, creepers etc.

All living creatures on earth are under Your control (10). You are controller of Northern Sea.

All living beings are at your mercy. You are controller of Northern seas.

6.57 I have prepared this medicine to cure injuries from the tips of thousands of sharp edged weapons made by Rudra (May be reference to acupuncture). Wash injuries with cows urine.

Oh Rudra cure us from all diseases.

From the above description the absolute need of sodium as medicine, and its role as preserver of life of vegetation, animals and man is indicated. Rudra's connection with sea is clear. As sodium is available amply in sea water, it is described as antidote against low rise in human temperature.

Sodium is essential element of life. Low intake of sodium causes loss of water, Sodium salts, particularly Sodium Chloride are found everywhere in biological material.

A number of similarities between sodium and Rudra can be shown, but since this has been extensively gone into; hence to avoid repetition the chapter is closed here.

Chapter 22

BRAHMODAN MEANS PHOSPHOROUS

Atharva-veda is a Veda on Chemistry, Physics and Astronomy. Besides Hydrogen and Carbon it considers problems in the area of magnetism, Gravity, Universe-creation etc. The topics so far dealt with by us are separately considered under independent chapters (Suktas). Terms and words used in Atharva-veda like Skambha, Viraj, Vratya (Mischievous), dont appear to have been used in other Vedas.

Brahmodan or Odan is a term, which belongs to the above order. In eleventh Tome, 3 chapters are devoted to it viz. 1st, 3rd and 7th. And among these 3 chapters there are 19 verses.

Phosphorous is an element and as per periodic table its order is cited as No.15, because in the Centre of Phosphorous there are 15 protons. Brahmodan, or odan, or specific Brahmodan means Phosphorous and nothing else. But before we show why and how, we will consider some salient properties, construction, creation method of Phosphorous as per modern science. the information is collected from Marathi Encyclopedia part 10, and from books on chemistry.

Phosphorous

1. One "Adhatiy" (non-metallic), Solid, element, found in two or more forms.

2. Chemical symbol is P. No. of Protons 15, In the periodic table is included as element in category 5-B.

3. Has various colours, but principally is white, Red, Black but yellow, violet, black but dark saffron Phosphorous is also available.

4. White Phosphorous is soft like butter and smells like garlic. It is poisonous. It is always kept in water, because the moment it comes into contact with atmosphere it catches fire.

5. Red Phosphorous is not poisonous. It does not catch fire in atmosphere. Its fire temperature is 260.

6. In darkness white Phosphorous shines with a green shade. If heated emits white flame.

7. To extract Phosphorous from ore extremely high temperature is necessary.

8. Crystal (Renu) of Phosphorous is four cornered at each corner there is one atom, and it is connected with other three. The Renu (Crystal) is made up of four atoms:-

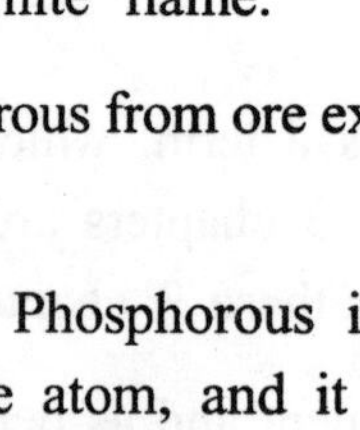

पांढऱ्या फॉस्फरसचा चतुष्फलकीय रेणू

9. The process of purification of Phosphorous requires plenty of water.
10. Phosphorous is found in white sand, dried urine, bones, ashes of bones, sea water, outer layer of earth, rocks of Phosphates. It is also found in all living beings, in their bones and teeth. It is found in milk and curd.
11. Phosphorous is necessary for development and sustenance of living beings and vegetation. To preserve contents of Phosphorous in fertile soil, fertilisers with Phosphorous are used.
12. Bones, Teeth and Proteins require Phosphorous as a necessary constituent. In very minute quantities it is found in brain and blood. It has some role to play in anatomy of humans, in their metabolism muscle functioning.
13. Yellow Phosphorous being poinsonous, it causes vomits, heat etc. in the stomach if consumed. If 0.1% of Phosphorous enters human system it results in Anemia, destruction of hunger and lessening of weight, and result in death.
14. As a result of smoke from yellow Phosphorous bones of human jaw can be affected and teeth can be dislodged.
15. The cycle of Phosphorous is as follows:-

    Phosphorous through rocks enters soil. This Phosphorous is absorbed by vegetation. Animals eat vegetation. From urine and excretion of animals, and also after their death from their dead bodies, it accumulates. It dissolves in water and from the rivers it reaches sea. It either accumulates there in layers, or is consumed by fish and that starts another cycle.
16. For preparing alloys Phosphorous is used.

17. There are many compounds of Phosphorous with or without carbon.
18. In the outer crust of the earth it is found in a low percentage viz. 0.13% in the form of various types of compounds. Being plentiful it is 11th in all materials. In one cubic mile of sea water 78 ton of Phosphorous is found.
19. Creation of Phosphorous:- Since the middle of 19th century, Phosphorous used to be manufactured, by using Sulphuric acid on bone ashes. After this wood chaff, common coal or coke used to be treated with it and dried. Then the mixture was put in a special pot and subjected to Ordhyapatan.
20. Nowadays electric heating plant is used. That heating plant has five to six exit outlets. From the top outlet gas and gaseous matter comes out. From one outlet (or inlet) mixture is put inside the plant. From the bottom pipe mixture is taken out. Iron phosphide being heavier than this mixture, it can be removed from below independently.

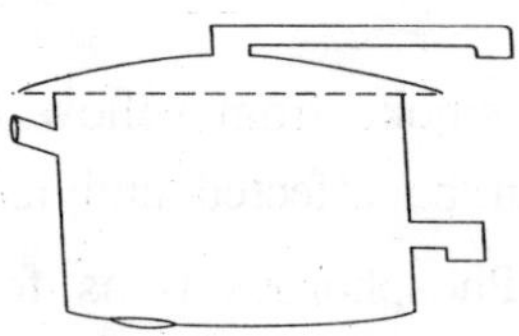

Plant creating Phosphorous having five outlets (or inlets)

After collecting the above necessary information about Phosphorous, we will now proceed to examine 1st, 3rd and 7th chapter of Atharva -Veda, to see how Brahmodan, odan have come to be discussed. The description in the Vedas is not couched in straight forward scientific terms. The language of the Vedas is involved in symbolic expressions. It is from these symbolic expressions that we have to filter truth. Therefore from

Nineteen verses on Phosphorous we are going to examine some important verses.

Order in which verses are set out here is changed. But the meaning of original verses is not changed.

1. Verse No.11.1.13:- Oh! Phosphorous (odan) from Great Great fathers downwards if we count the progeny, I have the honour to be the fifteenth from amongst.
2. Verse No.11.3.18:- Sun-shaped five mouthed plant (POT).
3. Verse No.11.3.19:- To stir, take wooden stirring implement or a piece of wood and Mali (either wash or mixture or heavy substance settling down at the bottom of the pot.)
4. Verse No.11.3.14:- Pot in which to boil and Fire.
5. Verse No.11.3.15:- The Chefs or Cooks Fire makers.
6. Verse No.11.3.13:- Canals and washing water is the water supply.
7. Verse No.11.3.12:- Cultivated land are ribs and sand is the place of mixture.
8. Verse No.11.3.13:- Earth is the storing pot, and Dyue Lok is the lid.
9. Verse No.11.3.14:-Yard (open space) is the pot, Isha (Ju) are the joints below the knees.
10. Verse No.11.3.5:- Horses are food particles, cow is the Tandul (Rice), Mashak is the chaff.
11. Verse No.11.3.3:- Musal (The wooden heavy rod with which one stamps on matter) = Eyes. Ukhal (The wooden enclosure in which Musal is used).
12. Verse No.11.3.4:- Sup = (wooden tray to separate chaff from grain) = Diti, Holder of tray. Aditi = chaff removed wind

13. Verse No.11.3.7:-Black Iron + meat, Red Iron = Blood
14. Verse No.11.3.8:-Trapu Ash = Lead, having flower fragrance.

Information about phosphorous is cited in Third chapter. But some principles are cited in the 1st chapter which are listed below:

1. Verse No.11.1.9:- With the aid of Musal & Ukhal (described above) you smash the grain and remove the chaff.
2. Verse No.11.1.10:-You will get 3 boons which you are seeking.
3. Verse No.11.1.11:- To purify (clean i.e. separate grain from chaff) use Sup or tray.
4. Verse No.11.1.12:- Oh! lady! after filtering the water bring it in a earthen pot (Jar).
5. Verse No.11.1.18:- Phosphorous will be prepared, by Ghrit-yukta Vrihi combined with water, and which is under spell of mantras.
6. Verse No.11.1.29:- Remove chaff from Vrihi.
7. Verse No.11.1.31:- After cleaning the upper part of phosphorous, and after processing mix butter milk in it.
8. Verse No.11.1.37:- This phosphorous, which confers Dyue-lok on deities by way of light.
9. Verse No.11.7.21:- Sugar, Sand, Rocks, Herbs, Grass, Lightening from clouds, Rain. All these are included in Brahmodan (Phosphorous).

The above details cited in various verses, and their interpretation applies to Phosphorous as follows:-

As per peridoic table, Phosphorous is listed at No.15 as element. This is symbolically expressed (Verse No.11.1.13) by saying that I get the honour to be the 15th descendant.

Phosphorous is listed at No.15, hydrogen at No.2, carbon at 6, oxygen at 8, lithium at 3, and this agreement between vedic nos., and nos. listed in periodic tables is not born out of accident or co-incident. Veda is the encyclopaedia of three sciences viz. Astronomy, Chemistry and Physics, and authors of Vedas were scientists par excellence. That is why this precision in comparative listing of number has arisen. Phosphorous primarily is white, red and black, is described by words Krishnaloha and Raktaloha. (Krishna is black and Rakta is red).

The fact that Phosphorous is soft like butter is expressed by the use of the word " Ghrut" (Butter).

The fact that Phosphorous smells like garlic is expressed by "Pushakargandha", Pushkar's current equivalent is lotus. But in vedic times it is not known whether it meant garlic. Garlic is white and has bud like constituents. Lotus also has similar construction.

In darkness white Phosphorous shines with greenish shade. At verse 11.3.25, we saw that Phosphorous is sun-like i.e. full of light, and green. If we combine these two adjectives we get "shinning with greenish shade".

As per verse 11.3.9 "Sphya" is yadnya implement, which, can't be described with precision. This word has similarity with two words "Sphuran" and Prasphuran". Yadnya sadhan means an implement utilised in manufacturing Phosphorous. Means the Rocks in which Phosphorous is found. It is noteworthy that greenish shine emitted by Phosphorous is called "Prashphuran" (Marathi Encylopaedia Part 10).

Phosphorous is primarily found in bones and sand. Reference to dug earth as ribs, and sand indicates the same. There is reference to Waluka, Sand and Rocks, which shows origin of Phosphorous.

Phosphorous is in herbs, medicine, grass and also animals. In 11.7.21 animal name of Kabu is referred to.

Phosphorous is in sea water. Similarly it is in earth. This truth is referred to in quoted verses where Prithvi is described as "Kanagi" and a statement is made that existence of sea and earth depends upon Phosphorous. (Kanagi means storing place made of mud and Bamboo).

Phosphorous and its compounds create oxides like germanium, Tin, lead. In verse 11.3.8 lead (Trup) is called ash of Phosphorous.

If white Phosphorous burns it emits white flame and white cloud is created. That is made up of Phosphorous Pento-oxide. Phosphorous is like a flame appears in verse 11.1.37 and in 11.3.6. Clouds are described as head of Phosphorous. Thus there is scientific agreement in descriptions.

As per science Renu (i.e. sub-atomic particle) of white Phosphorous resembles cubic triangle as sketched below.

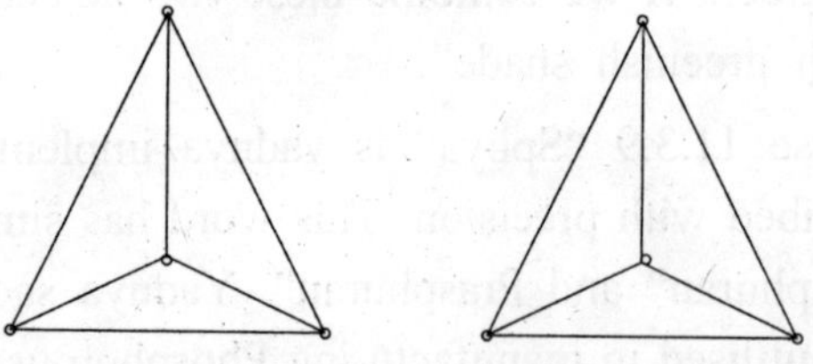

पांढऱ्या फॉस्फरसचा चतुष्फलकीय रेणू

Sketch described at figure is a triangle with three angles and 3 meeting points, but cubic triangle has four flaps and four meeting points. This is described at Verse 11.1.10 by use of word "Trayovar". Ordinary triangle has three sides but has only one surface area. Not three. In cubic triangle there are four meeting points, on which there is one atom on each meeting point. This, although not specifically mentioned any where, but either by design or accident, in the first verse the first chapter is divided under four heads (verse 1 to 10, 11 to 20, 21 to 30 and 31 to 37). The same practice was found in Viraj Sukta.

Viraj i.e. carbon has 6 protons and there are six divisions of viraj chapter.

In chapter 11.1 & 11.3 although process of creation of Phosphorous is not fully given, still some important hints and ideas are detectable. This process begins by collecting matter containing Phosphorous. It is as follows:-

1. Bones, sand, Rocks containing Sphya are collected, and stored in underground soils, where grain (then) is stocked.
2. This matter is to be washed with plenty of water, and needs water like flowing canals.
3. Then this matter is to be pounded in Ukhal (Wooden enclosure) with Musal (Heavy Wooden Rod) and reduced to size of rice particles.
4. In sup (Wooden tray) this material is cleansed by separating unwanted from wanted.
5. Wanted clean material is then to be poured upon by water. (Perhaps this matter was drenched either in Ghruta (butter) or fat of animals).
6. Then this material is to be put in five mouthed (outlets or inlets) Pot (Plant) and intensely heated. Heat had to be very very intense and hence special reference (11.1.17)

to "Agnipradipkarte" those who could ensure intense fire. Either it refers to human beings or to highly inflammable material.

Reference in Vedas to "Five-mouthed Pot" "Panchamuki Dera" to boil Phosphorous is extremely surprising as well as scientific. Panchamukhi Dera means a Huge Pot with five mouths (Inlets & Outlets) and sketched earlier, could be of metal or metals. Readers on their own are welcome to conceive of different types of constructions of this pot (one of which is sketched below). This pot must permit stirring of its contents from time to time with a wooden implement. Both water & butter (or fat) must be capable of being poured inside from time to time. This pot according to Vedic authors was like a Kanagi.

Since Phosphorous is derived by distillation following sketch is given by way of illustration.

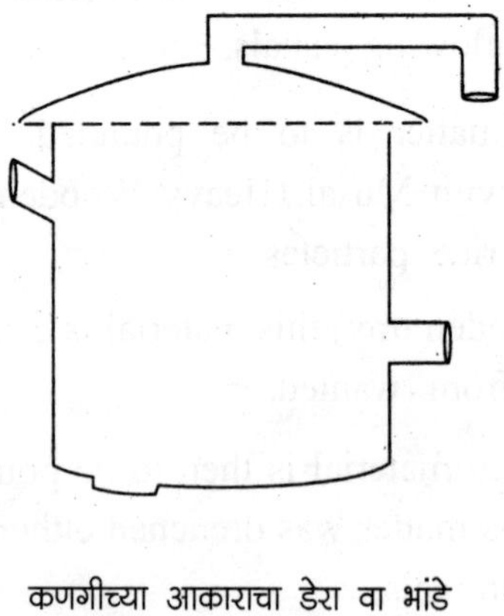

कणगीच्या आकाराचा डेरा वा भांडे

Chapter 23

BRAHMODAN (PHOSPHOROUS) AND PRECAUTIONS

Eleventh chapter has 3 parts. We have exhaustively dealt with the 1st part. In the second part there are 32 to 49 verses. Their distribution and classification is peculiar. Every verse is extensive and in addition there is a repetitive end, only some words in the repetitive end are changed.

Speciality of these verses is that while telling about the place where Phosphorous is available, and how to get it, they proceed to tell us the injurious consequences and loss that can ensure if proper precautions are not taken.

Since every verse is extensive, the thought is repetitive. We will deal with one verse as a sample, and examine other verses under the tabular form.

Verse No.32:- The aspirant says "the mouth through which ancient sages acquired Phosphorous, is the right mouth, and if Phosphorous is acquired through any other mouth my children will die. The Brahmavehktas (Sages) told me the aforesaid. Therefore I don't accept Phosphorous through my own mouth, but accept it through the mouth of "Brihaspati" (Nitrogen). The result was that my whole body reached perfection. Any one who knows this Phosphorous, fully and completely with all its pecularity, perfects himself."

Tabular Form

Verse Part of body (used	Consequence	How to consume (Through)
32. Mouth	Death of Children	Brihaspati
33. Ears	Deafness	Dyava Prithvi Era
34. Eyes	Blindness	Sun & Moon
35. Mouth	Death of Praja	Dnyan Marg
36. Tongue	Drop lifeless	Tongue of fire
37. Teeth	Will Split	Seasonal Teeth
38. Pranapan	Destruction	Pranapan of Sapotarshi
39. Space	Destruction by Disease	Space (Direction)
40. Surface	Death by lightening	Dyuelok Surface
41. Chest	Slimming	Prithvi Chest
42. Stomach	Dysentery	Truth
43. Kidney	Drowning	(Kidney) of Sea
44. Thighs	Destruction	By Varun Mitra
45. Knees	Lameness	By Twashta
46. Legs	Turing	Ashvini Kumar
47. Jaws	Snake Bite	Savitru
48. Hands	Brahma Hatya	Ruta
49. Earth	Supportlessness	Truth

The above verses ranging from 32 to 49 and its terminology is skilful and full of substance.

Phosphorous if consumed in improper ratio, results in adverse consequences. They also tell us as to where Phosphorous is in large quantities both in nature and in individuals.

Teeth, chest, thighs, knees, legs and hands are limbs that are "bony". And Phosphorous is more in bones and teeth, and if it is not in proper proportion diseases of bones and teeth set in.

Similarly kidney, urine and sea are references which show that Phosphorous is found there. This element was first discovered in 1669 by a German Scientist Henning Bront, by mixing sand & dried urine. In 1771 it was discovered that Phosphorous is found in bones.

Important discoveries in relation to Phosphorous range between 1669 to 1850. Sand, bones, urine and sea water contain Phosphorous was known to Vedas as already seen in various verses cited earlier.

We will consider the tabular form set out above from another point of view. It is well known that eyes, ears, surface of body, chest, kidney, thighs, knees, legs cannot act as agents of consumption.

Even then the aforesaid verses say that if Phosphorous is consumed by these organs, they will get destroyed. The word "consumed" cannot be taken as consumption of eatables.

In vedic times Phosphorous was prepared in five mouthed vessel and if the smoke or vapour emitted in the process goes in the body, then it can affect the health of man and his limbs and, therefore, these warnings were given in these verses.

As per science white Phosphorous is poisonous. Smoke of yellow Phosphorous is also poisonous. That is why workers working in plants manufacturing match sticks are affected by it, and their jaw bones, teeth soon get decayed. This experience compares well with the observation in the table showing that if teeth consume Phosphorous, they fall, and is perfectly scientific.

If yellow Phosphorous enters stomach vomiting, burning takes place, hence the observation that if stomach consumes Phosphorous it results in dysentery is scientific.

If 0.1% white Phosphorous enters the stomach, anemia, loss of appetite, reduction in weight results with possibility of death is a right alert signal.

Phosphorous is necessary for growth of body and good health. Bones, teeth and proteins require Phosphorous. Prayer in 11.1.22 "Oh! Brahmodan make the host healthy" is indicative of the same.

The fact that Phosphorous is in Milk and Curd is referred to in verse 11.1.25.

The extensiveness and importance of Phosphorous as referred to in 11.7.21 in which it is stated that breathing entities (vegetation and germs) and those with eyes (man and animals) are produced from Phosphorous.

We have seen cycle of Phosphorous. If we eliminate the part of decaying animals and vegetation from it, then that cycle is in verse 11.1.20 and 11.1.21 plus earlier reference to canals and sea.

Verse 20/21: Purified place, sand, Rocks, herbs, grass, rain with lightening, canal and sea are places related to the Phosphorous.

The above discussion will show that Phosphorous is a subject which was exhaustively and deeply dealt with by Vedas in aforementioned 3 chapters. Lastly in 11.3.56 it is observed that one who denigrates Phosphorous is destroyed. If we look at it humorlessly even than it is valid. Because no scientist treats any element as useless, defective or contemptible. One who sees only bad points, misses the benefits and suffers.

If this is right then, we must take necessary precautions against its over-use, ensure its consumption in right proportion, remain healthy and show respect for vedic sages who deserve it, and embark on further research.

Chapter 24

MATTER - ANTI MATTER AND INDRA-ASURA WAR

Birth and death are not different from each other. These are two wheels of chariot of life going in the same direction. There is no matter, element, entity which has birth but no death. Live entities die and lifeless get destroyed. Destruction does not mean total disappearance, it means division, or not remaining in same form or shape.

When universe was born, the forces of its destruction were also born. Their simultaneous birth is a necessity, because Time and Death is born with creation of universe. Space, Time and Motion, are Tri-dimensions of life as well as death.

Death is anti-matter of life. Poison is anti-matter of Necter. We don't know whether necter exists, but water, breath (oxygen) and food are necters only.

Matter that destroys these three into death is anti-matter of life.

In the beginning of 20th century scientists came with a hypothesis about existence of anti-matter which is at preliminary stage.

This theory came to be propogated while the study of atom was undergoing.

At the core of the atom there are positively charged protons and negatively charged neutrons and electrons are moving around the centre. If that is so, a thought occurred to scientist there must be anti-particles to protons, neutrons and electrons. Then after 1950 many particles and anti particles were discovered.

Electron	x	Positron
Proton	x	Anti-Proton
Neutron	x	Anti-Neutron

The theory further proceeded to the effect that in the atom of anti-matter, there must be similar types of protons and neutrons and, therefore, in all elements, there must be parallel anti-matter.

If the anti-matter is away from the original matter, then it can last forever. But if it comes in contact with matter, then the matter gets lost and converted into Meson. The life of which is very short. It will get again converted into ways which are very small penetrating Gamma waves and then in Neutron. In the Big Bay, according to this theory anti protons were less than one in million. But Scientist do not discard the theory that matter and anti-matter came into existence simultaneously. But they are puzzled as to how and by what process or what reason they got separated. In the existing world matter and anti matter cannot live together. But it cannot be recognized or identified from earth.

1. That if matter and anti-matter collide both are destroyed.
2. At the time of creation of universe both matter and anti-

matter must have come into existence. Simultaneously, but the principle separating them is unknown.

3. Anti-matter must pass anti-gravitational pull, but theory of relativity discards it.

In the context of above discussion, reference to Indra and Asura and their work in the Vedas would be relevant. Because Indra (matter) and Asura (devils) i.e. anti-matter, compare well with scientific concept of matter and anti-matter.

As per Vedic method of elaboration Indra is a Deity and a very important one. There are hundreds of verses relating to Indra, in the Vedas, and in Sama Veda they are maximum. But one important thing worthy of note is that in Vedas there is no reference to Swarga (Paradise or heaven).

In these hundreds of verses special virtues or qualities of Indra are given, his shape, face, his vehicle, his weapons, his extensiveness, broadness, and description of his achievements, his valour are also cited. Among these descriptions are names of Asur (satans, devils) or antisocial elements whom he killed. From these descriptions of battles, we are perhaps to pick up threads of our subject.

Those who were connected with Indra and got involved in war as per Vedas, these encounters have altogether different meaning and connotation. Those whom we consider as "Rakshashas described in Ramayana, Mahabharat and Puranas (legendary Tomes of ancient India), is inapplicable to the term Rakshasas used in Vedas with reference to war between Indra and Asuras. Asuras is not equivalent to Rakshasas.

It is noteworthy that Asuras described in Vedas are not physically lofty and horrible looking, they neither own any empire, nor have any state of their own, they are not drunkards, they have no family, or wives or children, they are also not power drunk, they are not experts in handling weapons, they are not among those who are after kidnapping beautiful damsels (Apsaras) from heavenly paradise (Swarga), and they are also not keen after putting Deities in conditions of poverty.

The above, which is normal feature of the word (Asura), is totally bereft in respect of those names as at war with Indra.

Without bearing in mind this, we will not understand true nature of Indra vs. Asura War.

Thereafter we must broadly consider the description of Indra. Classification of this description is set out below (as far as possible)

Indra Chariot

1. Verse 2.18.1:- Four horses, three whips, seven reins, and ten doors.
2. Verse 3.45.1:- Horses as beautiful as Peacock feathers.
3. Verse 4.246:- Horses having beautiful hair, which resemble peacock feathers.

Indra's appearance

1. Verse 1.3.4:- Multicoloured lustrous Indra.
2. Verse 1.3.6:- Red and green coloured Horses (Rider) Indra.
3. Verse 1.51.1:- Cloud coloured Indra.
4. Verse 1.51.7:- Indra, in whom all power in the world is centred.

5. Verse 1.51.9:-	Indra who basically is broad and great became wide enough to collide with Dyue-lok.
6. Verse 1.12.12:-	Powerful and one who has seven horses lustrous Indra, like negligible coral.
7. Verse 2.11.18:-	Killer of Vrithasur, opener of windows for light, for Aryas.
8. Verse 6.29.3:-	One who wears lustrous clothes.
9. Verse 6.29.5:-	Powerful like storehouse (lake or sea) of water.
10. Verse 1.51.11:-	Lightening shaped Horses (Rider of)
11. Verse 2.717:-	One who resides in Dyue-lok Lustrons in Dyue-lok.
12. Verse 2.728:-	Large handed, one whose hands are powerful.
13. Verse 2.142:-	Large necked Sam-Raudra
14. Verse 20.105.3:-	Indra who is water-promoter.
15. Verse 20.93.6:-	One who opened out space, and stabilised Dyue-Lok
16. Verse 1.51.10:-	One who separated worlds from each other.
17. Verse 11:-	Indra rode on curved, lightening sharped (on electrical horses).
18. Verse 1:-	Cloud shaped Indra.

19. Verse 8:- One who, in order to allow way to space water, took steel vajra (weapon) in his hands.

20. Verse 1.62.9:- One who created milk in immatured Black cows.

21. Verse 1.80.8:- Your vajras (weapon) are scattered on the banks of boat carrying rivers.

22. Verse 12:- Thousands edged (sharp) steel vajra (weapon).

23. Verse 3.39.6.7:- Indra in the company of Marut (storms) went to the entrance of mountains, and seeing this the mountain released the cows lodged in its core.

24. Verse 20:- Oh! Indra! Release us from the heavy mist surrounding us from four sides.

25. Verse 3.30.2:- Indra who makes distant lands closer.

26. Verse 17:- Oh Indra, destroy Rakshasas (Asuras) from the roots by cutting their middle and central parts.

27. Verse 3.39.6:- He removed the invisible fire (with his own hands) which were concealed in mountainous lake waters.

28. Verse 20.245.2A:- He stabilised moving mountains and unstable earth (Prithvi).

29. Verse 20.109.1:- The cows of Indra are various colours and in all his achievements they are in the front line.

30. Verse 30.34.11A:- After a period of (long) 40 years, Indra ultimately traced Shambar Asur who was in the mountains and with Vajra (weapon) defeated him.

31. Verse 2.15.6:- Indra re-routed river Sindhu from east to west.

32. Verse 2.15.3:- Indra fixed the routes of rivers and stretched them (made them longer with vajra.

33. Verse 2.12.12:- Directing all seven seas towards earth.

34. Verse 6.32.5:- Indra, who cut of his power causes rain in southern hemisphere.

After reaching above description of Indra, we have to get some idea about the trouble created by Asuras, and the nature of Asuras and then from it we can embark upon our scientific probe as to who these "Indra and Asura" were as per Vedas. Although the number of Auras slain by Indra are many, still, their (of Asura) nature, their aggression, and the nature of the trouble which Asuras created is same. We will first examine the above part, and thereafter proceed to find out their names, the weapons used to kill them, and the persons for whose sake they were killed.

Nature of trouble (calamities) created by Asuras:

Asura by name Vritta had created the problem of Jalstambhan (Stopped water flow). Ahir concealed himself both in space cave and at secret places in sea. Shambar had concealed himself in hundreds of castles. Nala had confined cows in prison. Rohit had caused aggression on Dyue-Lok. Asuras were denzies of water and were secret enemies of Indra. Mahankar Mountain who had imprisoned water supply was concealed in stomach of Vrittasur. Names of other Asuras are as follows-Shushna, Shambar, Valav, Sanak, Namuchi, Parnatra, Vrugandha.

All these Asuras were black in colour. They were extremely miser i.e. they were possessive in nature and were inclined to accumulate whatever they could get. They had confined cows. They had stopped water flow in universe. Some Asuras had created dark mist (fog) around themselves, they were inclined to destroy everything and were keen to establish themselves on soundly. Mostly they resided in dark caves, in mountains, or in castles. They had utilised prisons to confine cows and water.

The weapons used by Indra to kill Asuras were extra ordinary. For instance Indra used lustrous wheel (must be with sharpened edges) to kill Asuras like Karanjya. Some Asuras were killed by him by taking them far away.

Some Asuras were killed, by exhaling the air on them. Asura Namuchi was killed by foam of water. That verse is as follows (Samved 211.4)

"विश्वः स्पृदः अजयः इंद्रः अपां
फेनेन शिरः उदवर्तय

(Samved 211.4)

In the war between Indra and Asura and its description in the verse, there is frequent reference to rivers, seven-rivers, ninety-nine, ninety rivers. With the aid of Vajra (weapon) Indra fixed the routes of rivers, and created long winding rivers, east coasting Sindhu-river was made west coasting.

These rivers in the context of universe are Galaxies. As a result of tremendous powers of Asura, and their numbers, in the construction and orbits of these galaxies, Asuras created difficulties which were removed by Indra and Indra facilitated the process of universe pro-creation.

The weapon which destroyed Asuras is famous. This Vajra (weapon) was of either steel or gold having thousand sharped edges like thorns. This vajra is not one but are many. It is extremely speedy and has a long range. It is sharp like the horns of an ox. Vrittasur who was huge in size, and was extremely powerful was killed with the help of bones of sage Dadhichi. This Asura had started taking away all cows and water.

The killing of Asuras was done by Indra not merely with the aid of his huge strength and weaponry, but he had also sought the help of Indra +Marut, and the war fought against Asura.

The fact that, Indra had tremendous gravitational pull is seen by his foregoing description and especially verse No.3.30.2 which reads "Indra who had the power to bring distant lands closer". Earlier reference that Indra performs his function with the aid of lightening sharped curved body, reflects that Indra's power was manifested in Electro-magnetic highly potent waves.

Veda basically is a graph of moments at the stage of universe creation. Just as present astronomers seek to describe the condition of universe after Big Bang in terms of Time-divisions, like "after a million years" i.e., 1/1000th of second etc. The same universe, was described by Vedas with similar "Time-division" orientation.

"Krishna Sur" means "Krishna-drapsa" or "Krishna-Vivar" or "Black-Hole", has already been described in earlier chapters. The war which Indra waged was against these forces of "Black-Hole" and this will be clear from the various verses cited above. The forces of Black hole had imprisoned cows and stopped water flow, are the only two diabolic acts repeatedly referred to in the Vedas. These descriptions are patently symbolic. And this can never be over-emphasized.

The actions attributed to Asuras in the Vedas, and the Rakshasas in the Ramayana are clearly distinguishable. Asuras in the Vedas are not described as having thrown meat, blood, ashes in the sacred "Yadnya-Kund" to sully the spiritual rituals of sages; which acts were attributed to Rakshasas (Asuras) in the Ramayana.

Similarly the diabolic actions attributed in Vedas to Asuras are couched in precise terms, without needless long-winding descriptions.

Symbolically, confining of cows, and stopping of water flow are two natural nativities of "Anti matter". They are naturally called "diabolic" in Vedas because Vedas and all of us are on the side of creation, and Anti-matter represents destruction.

Immediately after the "Big-Bang", and universe creation, during the dirt initial moments, millions and trillions of actions and processes and reactions that characterised elements, energy and space, had to confront activities of Anti-matter also, because after the Big-Bang both matter and Anti-matter were born. This adverse activity of Anti-matter (which is natural to Anti-1) is described as "confining of cows" and "stopping of water flow".

Just as "black holes" attract elements, energy and space towards it with tremendous force, similarly all Huge sources of Anti-matter created during creation, all Anti-matters started attracting elements, gravitational pull of elements, magnetism of elements, rays and all kinds of radiation towards itself and this is symbolised in the verses by saying "through mountains (shapes) and Black dark caves or in impregnable castles" imprisoned cows. The same phenomena was expressed in two symbolic illustrations of "imprisoning cows and stopping water flow". It is noteworthy that during vedic period cow (the milk giver) represented food and other necessity of life was water.

We must bear in mind that cow is an animal evolved on earth. Scores of years after the earth was born, water, as we understood today, also is a speciality of earth only and it came into existence after the earth fully cooled down. Cow and water, therefore, could not be present at the time of creation of Universe and, hence we need to find out their real meaning in the verses referred to above, otherwise all the verses became totally senseless or worthless.

Asura means Anti-matter and Indra means the force destroying that Anti-matter. At the stage of universe creation, (whatever the time frame, small or big) Anti-matter was also born, but if force called Indra did not exist universe would not have been born. All matter and space and energy would have been imprisoned or destroyed by Anti-matter.

A small clarification is called for Indra does not represent matter. Asuras do not represent Black hole. Indra represents a force otherwise than matter. Asuras represent Anti-matter, but if matter and Anti-matter collides both get destroyed. Since universe exists, obviously this collision either has not taken place, or the possibility has been prevented.

Conclusion of modern science is that matter and Anti-matter have got to be equal, and must have come into existence simultaneously. But they can co-exist near each other. Therefore the modern science poses a problem viz. that by what mechanism anti-matter was kept away from matter is not known. This is an enigma for modern science. But if we understand correctly the vedic symbolism and concept of Indra vs. Asura war, we may perhaps be solving the enigma.

There is no need to repeat the description of Indra as given earlier. But Indra was the centre of all power in universe, and this power (Indra) who basically was indescribably huge widened itself to meet Dyue-lok and that power stabilised moving mountains (elements) and unstable earth (energy), and with the aid of Marut (storms) destroyed Asura. Thus we get the idea about the force which either destroyed or separated Anti-matter. That force obviously was Indra.

If Indra was one individual/entity or God, as is commonly understood, he would not have and could not have destroyed Asuras from 90 rivers.

The description in verse quoted above that Vajra of Indra are lying scattered round 90 rivers clearly show that Indra was a force acting at the every centre of creation of Universe which destroyed the anti-matter.

Modern scientists have concluded that there must be anti-gravitational pull (force) also, just as there is gravitational pull. This is a hypothesis. At the same time there is another school of thought that says that Anti-gravitational pull does not exist.

However if we examine the vedic concept of Indra and Marut, we find that as per Vedas both the above mentioned pulls did exist. In verse 1.37.8 of Rigveda it is said "The Maruts due to its intrinsic stormy force causes Earth to shiver". In verse 1.33.5 the description attributed to Indra "By just exhaling Indra caused Asura to fly way" is description of Indra's Anti-gravitational pull capacity. Similarly Indra's capacity (at verse

1.53) to kill Asura Nimuchi by just taking him away is descriptive of Anti-gravitational pull or some other similar power. Similarly (as per 1.33.7) Indra pushing the followers of Vritta beyond horizon and Dasyu below Swarga are indicative of anti-gravitational pull. From this it appears that all or some centres of Anti-matter were destroyed by Indra, like Vrittasur and krishnadrapsa, and some were thrown very very far away in universe across space.

According to modern science when matter and Anti-matter collide they mutually destroy each other creating energy (on this point science is at stage of infancy and no theory is set out).

Centres having tremendous gravitational pull cannot be destroyed without equally powerful anti-gravitational pull. If Black hole is to be destroyed, it can't be done with any power, element or energy known to science. Because Black holes has tremendous capacity to dissolve and destroy or neutralise any known, power, energy or element. And that is why a force which can counter Black-hole, or a similar power confining cows and withholding water (symbolic) must have tremendous anti-gravitational pull.

Either Indra possessed both kinds of contradictory gravitational pulls, or by an alliance with Marut the anti-gravitational pull used to be created.

Existences of universe shows that forces of anti-matter were destroyed. The modern scientific hypothesis that only proximity or collusion of anti-matter with matter destroys both, appears to be incorrect having regard to vedic recitals of Indra vs. Asura war.

Anti-matter can be destroyed by anti-gravitational pull also.

On this point verse (1.3.2.) from Rigveda is of stunning revelation. This relates to description of achievement of Indra. After describing destruction of Asuras like Vritra and Adi, verse 14 & 15 goes on to describe as to where Indra went, and what happened to him.

अहेर्यातारं कत्रपश्य इंद्र हदि यत् ते जघ्नुषो भीरगच्छत ।
नव च यन् नवतिं च स्रवंतीः इश्येनो न भीतो अतरो रजांसि ॥
इंद्रो यातोऽ वसितस्य राजा शमस्य च श्रृंगीणो वज्रबाहुः ।
सेदु राजा क्षयति चर्षणीना मरान न नेमिः परिनाबभूव ॥

Verse 14:- "Oh! Indra! After your triumph on Ahi lest ever-hating opponents took revenge, you have flown away like shen bird, beyond 99 rivers and space.

Verse 15:- Indra, the possessor of vajra, is the king or everything that is contained in it and all inhabitant of the whole universe. He encompasses the whole universe and protects it like the outer ring of a wheel.

The subject of Indra vs. Asura war deserves an independent treatment, in a separate book. The present chapter is the summary.

Just as Indra invoked alliance of Marut to defeat Asura, he also used a weapon called vajra, which in fact could be a subject matter of separate and independent research.

In the chapter (from which verse 14 and 15 are cited) there is a description of as to how rivers freely started flowing over the dead bodies of Vritasur after he was killed by Indra. His body collapsed in constantly flowing huge currents of rivers. This description is exceptionally scientific.

If Black holes are neutralised by Huge Anti-gravitational pull, and is destroyed, then the energy and elements condensed there, would freely flow out in liquid form like water or like gas streams in the whole universe.

"Indra in the company of Marut approached the mountains, and seeing him, the mountain threw out cow from its stomach" (Verse 30, 31,6/7). This Verse also is reflective of Indra's power of anti-gravitational pull. The mountain had through its own pull of gravity had attracted cows inside (i.e. elements, energy and space) but because of Indra+Maruts (Agaman and Nirgaman) coming and going i.e. pull of gravity the afore mentioned entites were sucked out. This reference also supports anti-pull of gravity thesis.

After creation of the universe, forces of destruction of universe also are born, and after destruction of one universe, another universe is born, is a thesis approved by modern science. This raised the hypothesis that anti-gravitational pull may develope inside Asura (Blackholes) itself and another universe can come out of it.

In fact the creation of universe through Big Bang is the result of anti-gravitational pull itself and perhaps that is why Vedas have stated that Indra was born when Aditya was born.

Because of fear of revenge by Asuras, Indra went beyond 99 rivers and now has encompassed the universe like outer ring of a wheel, perhaps means that after destroying "Anti-matter" Indra's anti-gravitational pull has stabilised itself beyond outer most space.

This thesis that matter and Anti-matter can't stay together, and the second thesis that anti-gravitational pull must be in existence, and yet is untraceable, are two hypothesis of modern science, which can be reconciled only in the and by the scientific analysis of verses in Vedas relating to Indra, Asur War.

The third thesis of modern science of expanding universe, wherein all galaxies are supposed to be moving out, could perhaps be explained by the fact that Indra's anti-gravitational pull encompasses the whole universe like outer ring of a wheel, and that therefore this pull of Indra itself may be responsible for expanding universe.

Chapter 25

SHAPE OF THE UNIVERSE VEDIC AND SCIENTIFIC VIEW

Till discovery of Copernicus (to the contrary) it was held that earth was at the centre of solar system. Therefore in this state of ignorance scientists (if any) did not apply their minds to the problem of shape of universe in the West, prior to Copernicus.

However, it appears that Vedas had applied their minds to this problem and had reached some conclusions. In the 10th Tome of Atharva-Veda there is a clear reference to this problem. But before we look into it, let us first check various conclusions or hypothesis reached by modern science on this subject.

Modern Science has so far not reached incontrovertible conclusion about the shape of universe. Various theories however have been set out. The first is that universe is isotropic i.e. equally extended on all sides. Some say that it is angular, and according to some it is flat.

To understand the problem scientifically space, time and elements have to be studied. As per Einstein space is four dimensional. If in space and time, elements are not included it becomes flat and infinite. But as a result of inclusion of elements four dimensional space-time attains curvature. Although this space-time is tremendously vast, it is not infinite. It is limited like sphere.

Inter planetary space, outer space, are species of spaces. But no space is elementless (matterless).

Euclid was born in 300 B.C. He set out principles of geometry scientifically. A point has no dimensions. A line has length but no breadth. Two points can be joined in various ways but the shortest distance between two points is a straight line. Through five scientific assumptions Euclid created his geometry which was universally accepted.

In the 10th century Euclid's geometry was rejected partially and Atoms oriented geometry was born. Later Eienstein's general and special theory of relativity came into existence. As per general theory of relativity elementless space-time is flat. But existence of elements (matter) makes it curved. In such space smallest straight line joining two points in space, would be different from a straight line in flat space. Its meaning is this that the rays can affect the straight line in a flat space, and the straight line so affected would be different. Existence of matter affects the straight line, and this effect lessen as matter goes away from this straight line. The force that affects this straight line is called gravitation.

The flat geometry of Euclid headed the field till 19th century. After Einstein it became out-dated.

The result was this, that scientists came to the established principle that space was curved and the universe is like a sphere.

This conclusion was strengthened by the fact, that scientists also discovered that all galaxies and every kind of entity in space was expanding and receeding.

Long before this conclusion was reached, and obviously long before Eucledean geometry came into existence, Vedas has propounded that space was curved. Let us see how and where?

In the Tenth Mandal (Tome) of Atharva-Veda there are many chapters dealing with the problem of universe-creation, and those chapters raise several problems about construction of the universe and solve them. Symbolically they seem to apply to individuals, but they relate to universe. Out of these chapters the second, seventh and eighth are very important.

Out of these 3 chapters, the questions raised in relation to universe are as follows:-

1. For this virat-purush (boundless) who created flowing water, morning, day, and evening? (in which there was light)
2. Who created this covered earth, and Dyue-lok upon it?
3. Give us information about the supporting pillar, of earth, space, Dyue, 3 worlds, fire, moon, sun and wind?

Many such questions were asked but since we are not considering them in this chapter, they are not quoted.

Twenty fourth and twenty fifth verse from 2nd chapter is very relevant for our subject.

"केनेयं भूमिर्विहिता केन द्यौरुत्तरा हिता
केनेदमूर्ध्वं तिर्यक् चान्तरिक्षं व्यचो हितम् ॥२४॥ १०.२.२४

ब्रह्मणा भूमिर्विहिता ब्रह्म द्यौरुत्तरा हिता ।
ब्रह्मेदमूर्ध्वं तिर्यक् चान्तरिक्षं व्यचो हितम् ॥२५॥ १०.२.२५

Who stabilised the earth? Dyue-lok (swarg)? was established by whom? Oblique (angular) space and other matter (of the universe) was created by whom?

In the first place, Brahma stabilised the earth, established Dyue-lok (Swarga), created oblique angular space and universal matter also was created by Brahma.

Twenty-fourth verse raises purely scientific problems, and twentiy-fifth verses answers them. The fact that space is oblique or angular is known to the querrist. It is known either as an established truth, or an assumption (a priori-Hypothesis). And twenty fifth verse merely repeats it.

The answer that Brahma created the stars etc, is an answer which we will eliminate, because science does not accept a creator.

But we are concerned with the answer that this universe is oblique or angular because it is scientific, and these two verses make it clear. It is rather astonishing that what was accepted as late as in the 19th century was already stated by Vedas some thousands of years ago.

In the tenth chapter of Atharva-veda the shape of the universe was referred to, and elaboration of the same was done in Ribhusukta of the Rigveda.

तिर्यग्बिलश्चमस ऊर्ध्वबुध्नस्तस्मिन् यशो निहितं विश्वरूपम् ।
तदासत ऋषयः सप्तसाकं ये अस्य गोपा महता बभूवुः ॥

Verse 10.8.9: In a reverse (upside down) cup, whose bottom is to the top and whose mouth is oblique or angular the power of the Great Brahma is centred and in the same Cup reside sapatrishis (seven sages) who protect him.

Thus this verse clearly states that the shape of the universe is like a cup with Oblique or angular mouth. The word "Chamas" (here translated as a cup) used in the Vedas, stood for what kind of receptacle is not quite clear, translators have translated it as a "cup".

A cup is a receptacle for drinking water. If cup is kept upside down, the shape which it assumes is the shape of the universe. This is the symbol used by Vedas.

Some shapes of up-side down cups could be as follows:

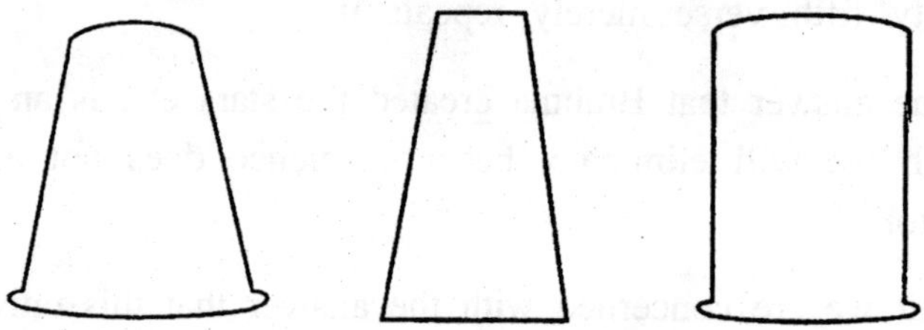

पालथे किंवा उपडे असलेल्या पात्राचे किंवा पेल्याचे विविध प्रकार

What is noteworthy is this. The cup is not oblique/angular. The shape of the mouth is oblique/angular. We shall try to see how this could be by examining shapes given below.

In the description "oblique/angular mouth" two sides of the cup, cannot be equal. If two sides are either equal or similar, the shape of the mouth cannot be "Oblique" or "angular". If two sides are equal the mouth of the cup or vessel will be straight. Straight mouthed (shaped) cup means a cup whose two sides or all sides are equal in height. Such a cup which occupies space, would be limited. But the space covered by a cup with oblique or angular mouth would be infinite but nonetheless limited. Following sketches would clarify the position:

१ ते ५ तिर्यंग्मुख अथवा तिरके तोंड असलेले चमसपात्र वा पेले

In the above sketches, cup No.1, is a cup with straight mouth. AB and CD are its sides. If they are extended upto E or F indefinitely, nonetheless they acquire limitation, and the concept of oblique/angular space becomes inapplicable. But cup No.2,3,4 and 5 are the cup with oblique/angular mouth. Maintaining the shape of the cup. But widening of the angular angle can result in covering area, any where below 180 degrees.

In Rigveda there are many chapters concerning the Deity Hribhu. This deity Hribhu represents which power, is going to be considered separately. However in this chapter some limited portion is considered.

Twashata is the giver of shape to the Universe and a sculpture or an architect. Hribhu is his disciple. He is equally expert in the field.

See verse No.6 from chapter 20 of tome (Mandal) one.

उत त्यं चमसं नवं त्वष्टुर्देवस्य निष्कृतम् ।
अकर्त चतुरः पुनः ॥ १.२०.६

Oh Hribhu! You created four vessels out of a single cup (Chamas) created by Deity Twashi.

In Rig veda (Mandal, chapter one, verse 161) Deities had ordered Hribhu to prepare four equal parts of Cup (Chamas).

Accordingly Hribhu created four parts of cup (or prepared four cups) which were lit like day light.

We have seen as to how shape of one cup (Chamas) looks, oblique/angular mouthed cup is an allegory used to describe oblique shaped space. Purpose of allegory is to clarify the concept. Hribhu divided the cup in four parts. We also saw as to how one cup and its oblique mouth, makes space curved.

If the same type of cup is divided into four parts, remembering that the mouth is oblique the following interesting position arises. It is best set out in sketches for clarity.

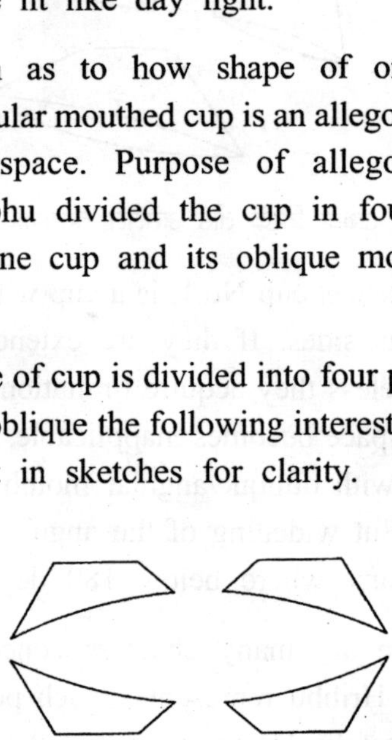

तिरक्या मुखाची चार चमसपात्रे या पद्धतीने लावली असता
विश्वाचा आकार किंवा "तिरके आकाश" दर्शविणारी आकृती

Unless the four parts of the Cup (Chamas) are juxtaposed as above, we will not be able to understand as to what was passing in the minds of vedic authors. We can well see that completions reached only by four parts. If 3 parts are taken, and juxtaposition is altered at random, original concept cannot be illustrated.

If we take a cube, or a cubic triangle, and divide it in four equal parts, every part resembles the original. If we remember this we find that if a cup with oblique shaped mouth, is divided in equal parts, the same result follows:-

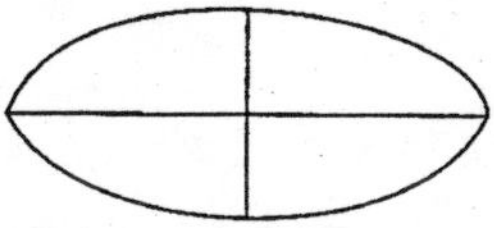

तिरक्या मुखाची चार चमसपात्रे अशा पद्धतीने
लावली तरी विश्वाचा आकाश बदलत नाही

If these four parts are fitted in as per figure No.Z, we get to know the shape of the universe, and if fitted in as per figure No.Z2, we get to know the universe. The above configuration and the concept of modern science about the shape of universe are not at all different.

Verse No.5 from chapter 33, Mandal 4, gives a particular description, and throws light on one more mystery.

ज्येष्ठ आह चमसा द्वा करेति कनीयान त्रीण कृणवामेत्याह ।
कनिष्ठ आह चतुरस्करेति त्वष्ट ऋभवस्तत् पनयद वचोवः ॥५॥

In all there were 3 Rhubhu brothers. Eldest proposed that he would construct two cups, the middle one proposed that he would construct 3 cups. The youngest suggested that only four cups should be made & as per his suggestion only 4 cups were made.

It was in the 20th century that the discovery that space is curved was reached. Vedic statement of oblique/angular space, the inverted cup with oblique shaped mouth, having four parts, is a concept, which totally tallies with modern research. In Yajurveda the following verse 13/14 also supports this concept.

अग्निर्मुर्धा दिवः ककुत्पत्तिः पृथिव्या अयम् ॥१३॥ ॥१४॥

The space is curved like shoulder of a bull.

Chapter 26

HRIBHU THE POWER THAT CREATES STARS

Hribhu is half-human Deity. Hribhu had 2 brothers Vaj and Vimbhan. They were disciples of God's architect "Twashta", and were sons of sage Angiras. Being disciples of Twashta they possessed enormous capacity for creation. On Hribhu, in all eleven chapters are written in Rig veda (1.20, 1.110 - 111, 17,3.60, 4.33 to 37, 7, 48, 10.176)

Hribhu in fact is a power behind creation of universe. But before we identify it, let us first see its qualities and characteristics as described in Vedas.

1. Verse 1.20.4: Straight forward and possessed of special powers. His creation is immortal.
2. Verse 1.111.4: It attained God-hood in one year having acquired radiance like Sun it became immortal.
3. Verse 1.111.5: He has extremely sharp weapons. He is an extremely competent artisan.
4. Verse 4.34.3: He is lustrous and has human form.

5. Verse 4.35.8:	He is resident of Dyue-lok.
6. Verse 4.37.4:	He has a steel helmet, a shining chariot.
7. Verse 5 :	They are co-habitants. They achieved the following.
8. Verse 1.167.7:	Created a live cow out of a hide of dead cow.
	Gave youth to parents who had become old like rotten sticks.
9. Verse 1.20.4 :	Gave youth to old parents whose bodies had disintegrated.
10. Verse 4.34.4:	For one year protected, cows, beef, and cow-lustre.
11. Verse 4.35.1:	Achieved the rare feat of establishing in space Horse, reins and chariot.
12. Verse 4.34.7:	Hribhu remained for 12 days as a guest of lustrous sun. He has a steel helmet and his chariot emits light, and its horses are powerful.

Prima facie achievements of Hribhu appear to be strange and improbable. To protect Beef for one year appears to be impossible and only play of imagination. Meat is perishable. It can't remain edible even for 24 hours. Even in deep freeze it can't remain fresh for one year. It is also not possible to say that sages and men of vedic times did not consume beef. We have also to consider as to why the term disintegrated bodies was used in respect of parents.

We have seen that Vibhu made four parts of a Cup (inverted) whose bottom was at the top whose mouth was oblique. This reference is symbolic of a certain occurrence. Similarly we have to see as to what mystery is concealed in the aforesaid verses.

Vedas are a graph of creation of universe. Wherever there is creation, there is also an end and destruction. This process of creation and destruction in endless. And hence Vedas refer to both creation and destruction.

In this universe there is no complete destruction of anything. Matter gets destroyed but turns into soma kind of energy. Before assessing the work of Hribhu, we shall consider scientifically this part of phenomena.

From creation of the universe following Big Bang 10 to 20 thousand million years have elapsed. During this period thousands of galaxies came into existence, Huge Stars came into existence. Numerous detectable and non-detectable phenomena took place in space. One very important force called gravitation was born and because of it Galaxies, clouds, comets, Nebulaes, etc. were created.

Every star is a huge Atomic plant, where atoms due to splitting, heat, explosions etc. releases tremendous heat and energy. Every second millions of tons of fuel is burnt, it results in disintegration of stars.

Ordinarily stars of same mass evolves along similar lines. But a huge star due to early consumption of fuel turns into Red or White and dwarf (white Dwarf). In space such Red (Huge) and white dwarfs are seen and they are close to each other. The result is that huge Red dwarf releases energy into white dwarf. Hydrogen consequently accumulates in white dwarf and its heat increases. It results in thermonuclear reaction and white dwarf flares up. It is called Nova and it happens in such twin stars.

Super Nova is one star phenomena. External cover of super nova and atmosphere flare up in space. In case of Super nova matter in the stars is thrown in space in huge qualities, and spreads. Liquified gas and gas proper due to extreme heat are characterised by deep blue rays and display of Red and blue rays is seen.

Super nova is nothing but explosion of an extremely huge star, resulting in formation of nebula. Nebula is nothing but ever expanding gaseous cloud which are remnants of disintegrated star. They are called inter steller medium. In our galaxy there are any number of such nebulas. The crab nebula in the constellation Taurus is an example.

Gravity in the clouds of nebula is very low. This gas travels at the speed of 50 kilometers per second. Density of these clouds is ten lakhs of atoms per one cubic centimeter. In such state, ions and electrons collide and this collision can result in course of time in the union.

In the achievements of Hribhu are included creation of live cow from hide of a dead cow, restoring disintegrated parents to fresh youth, are symbolic of creation of stars from nebula, or the dwarf star getting energised through Red giants Nova. Similarly preservation of beef for one year or preserving lustre of cows for one year are symboling of either energising of or recreation of stars from the nebulae. (1.161 Rigveda).

The constellation Sagittarius is symbolised by Deity half - horse and half - man. This constellation is in the southern hemisphere in the longitude 20 to 30 and lattitude 19.

In this constellation there are 3 known Nebulas. Omega (M17), Lagoon (MB) and Tripid (M.20)

Hribhu is called a deity which is half man. The constellation Sagittarius is half man and half horse. Hribhu is called co-habitant. In the twin stars (Binary stars) the star having greater density and having giant body, first transforms into a giant Nova or super nova, leaving the dwarf as it is which gathers all the matter from Nebula, and this space phenomena fits in with descriptions of achievements of Hribhu. Hribhu, Vibhu and Vaj are 3 brothers. (Vibhu means elder).

Hribhu is inhabitant of Dyue-lok (perhaps residence of stars) and hence is described as having light. He wears steel helmet, possesses sharp edged weapons and has limitless art.

See the description at 1.161.10 in Rigveda is as follows:-

"Oh! Hribhus two brothers out of you 3, took out a lame cow from water and her cuts were separated for ritualistic sacrifice then, one of you removed and cleaned her intestines. In what better way can devoted sons serve their parents?"

This description is mysterious and moot, and symbolically applies to Nebula acquiring stardom.

Hribhu like Indra should not be considered as a man. It is a description of certain process. It is energy.

Chapter 27

PLACE OF ASHWINIKUMAR IN SPACE

This chapter is devoted to showing that some of the Deities described in the Vedas, could be certain constellations or stars in space. Among them are Rudra, Ashwinikumar and Vrushakavi. This research conclusion is based on the descriptions specialities, and their characteristics set out in Vedas.

Ashwinikumar:

1. They are two, and they stay together. Out of these two, one is leader of Deities, and second is son of Dyue-lok. (1.181.4). Their vehicle is sometimes an Ass (1.11.6) and some time they sit in the chariot drawn by Ox, and crocodile l(1.116.8). Sometimes the animals pulling their chariot put on disguise of Ass and female wolf.
2. The chariot of Ashwinikumar is triangular with three wheels and having three spokes.
3. Along with Ashwinikumar their young wife, (daughter of sun), is sitting in the chariot.
4. They are consumers of sweet juice. That juice contains honey. From the wheels of their chariot their juice also comes out. They are carriers of sweet food.

5. They took in ocean, boats with wings, to liberate sons of Tugru, and with the aid of 4 boats liberated them.

6. 100 goats were slaughtered for their vehicle puller asses.

7. (1.116.12) Having offered sage (Dadhancha-Aharvana) head of a horse and after having pleased him, they learnt Madhu-Vidya (soma art) from him.

Constellations answering all the above descriptions are in space. Let us see how:- To the north of the central equatorial astronomical dividing line, within 0 to 10 degrees between 8 to 10 longitude, in the Constellation Cancer is a constellation "Praesepe". In this group of stars there are many binary stars and also triangles of stars. In the Mesiyar Catalogue classification of all group of stars is made, and they are numbered which are universally accepted. Thereafter a new general catalogue was prepared and numbers given. They are preceded by letters M and NGC. This constellation is identified by No.M.44

The binary stars in M44 and triangle of stars, tallies with description of Ashwinikumar as a binary combination, and to the accompanying star described as daughter of sun, and also three excelled chariot with 3 wheels. Normally all wheels are round but the chariot of Ashwinikumar has triangular wheels, 3 in number and with 3 axels. This description being special, this group of stars derives special attention.

The connection shown in respect of honey and sweet juice with Ashwinikumar, cannot be deciphred. But either accidentally or coincidentally or because of some unknown link between knowledge and concept this constellation has come to be described in English as "Bee-hive-store?"

Bee hive constellation is in terms astronomical calculations very close to earth (It takes only 5 - light years to reach) and is 650 millions year old, and is part of our own galaxy. Enc. Brit.volume 17 page 601.

Bee hive is a cluster in milky way is very very old.

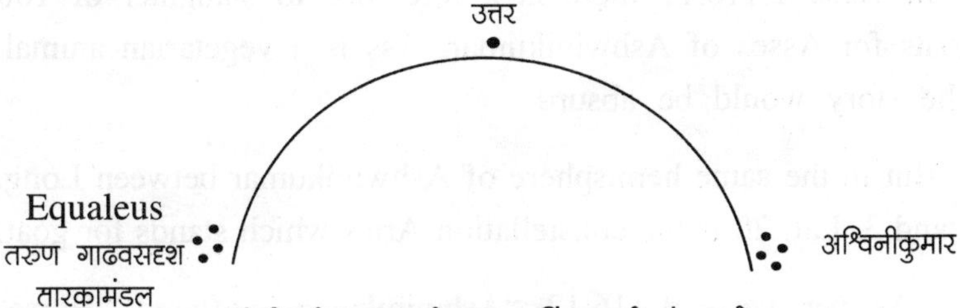

अंतरिक्षाचे मस्तक बैलाच्या वशिंडाप्रमाणे उंच आहे.
यजु. अ. १३/१४ अग्निर्मुर्धा दिवः ककुत्पत्तिः

It is described that sometimes asses drew the chariot of Ashwinikumar. In terms of astronomy distance between chariot, charioteer and the animals is bound to be astronomical.

To the north of equatorial dividing line of space at Longitude 10 and lattitude 21 to 22 there is a constellation "equalous". In common parlance it is called "Foal" means young horse (or Ass). Ashwinikumar and foal-like Ass constellation lies in the same plane as is seen in the above sketch.

Ashwinikumar are described as moving all over universe, and to rescue sons of Tugra they are supposed to have used boats with wings. Constellation answering this description is the constellation Carina in the southern hemisphere between 50 to 60 Long. and 8 Lat. Carina means KEEL or a skeleton of a ship. This constellation is to the south of Ashwinikumar.

Ashwinikumar some times travels in a chariot pulled by ox or crocodile. Constellation Taurus (Ox) and Capricon (crocodile). These constellations are respectively to the north and south of cosmic equatorial line, 1st being between 20 long. and 4 to 5 lat. and second being between 30 long. and 20 to 22 lat.

In the same hemisphere at 9 long. is Ashwinikumar constellation, with Bee-hive constellation closeby.

In verse 1.116.17 there is a reference to slaughter of 100 goats for Asses of Ashwinikumar. Ass is a vegetarian animal. The story would be absurd.

But in the same hemisphere of Ashwinikumar between Long. 2 and 3, Lat. 20 is the constellation Aries which stands for goat.

As per verse 1.116.12 "Ashwinikumar" offered "Horse-Mouth" to Sage "Dadhancha Athavarna" and acquired "Madhu-Vidya" (Art of sweetness). In this story offering of "Horse-Mouth" is important part. Emphasis is on "Horse-Mouth".

In space to the north of Astronomical equator from 0 to 12 long, upto 41/2 to 6 Lat, there is a nebula called "Horse-Head" which means "Horse-mouth" which is in the constellation "Orion", and it is spread. The "Horse Head" referred to there is made up of cold dust clouds, and hence appears dark and black. Around it are hot clouds of gases. Ashwinikumar situated in Longitude 9, this horse-head situated at 5 and 6 long. is close.

In verse 1.181.4 Ashwinikumar have prayed "drive away the atheists who are jealous". There is no reason for making a prayer of this type, and hence this symbol appears to have been used by Vedas to denote beasts (Atheists), because this whole chapter is devoted to description of achievements and characteristics of Ashwinikumar.

In the northern half hemisphere of constellations, there are two constellations which are in appearance beast like 1. Canes

Venatia which means a hunting dog 2. Canes minor which means puppy or small dog. In the southern hemisphere is the Canes major or the "Great Dog" i.e. huge dog.

Out of these "Canes minor" constellation is situated between 20 long and 8 lat, i.e. close to constellation of Ashwinikumar. And Canes Major is situated is the southern hemisphere between 20 to 30 long. and 6 to 8 lat. In the constellation Canes Major there are about 100 stars and they are at a distance of 1600 light years from earth. In this very group are "dog-star", "Beast-star", and "Sirus". It is binary star. They revolve around the same point of gravitational pull.

In the northern half of hemisphere between 40 to 50 long. And 13 lat. is situated Canic Venatic i.e. hunting dog.

This constellation is numbered as M/51. In fact it is a circular galaxy. This galaxy is at a distance of 20 million light years from earth.

The prayer attributed to Ashwinikumar constellation is obviously symbolic. This prayer perhaps relates to constellations described above.

Chapter 28

TRIT-APTA, WOLF, AND STAR CREATION

In Vedas in various chapters, prima-facie strange incidents are cited. These incidents don't fit in with the subject discussed and appear to be strange fluctuations. But if we probe into these mysteries, certain scientific truths surface from them.

Rigveda's 1st Mandal (Tome) chapter 105 is written in relation to Deity "Trit". As per some commentators "Trit-Apta" was a sage, but Rigveda has elevated him to the status of a Deity among the family members of Indra. Trit-Apta is a form of Fire, and cohabits with Deities Varun and Somdeo. Literal meaning of the word "Trit-Apta" is son of fire. As per Macdonald Trit-Deity represents electricity.

Sage Trit-Apta has fallen in a well, and he prayed to Brihaspati and Brihaspati saved him. Large part of this chapter is mysterious. After being rescued by Brihaspati he addressed Brihaspati as follows:- "Oh Universal Deity, while proceeding on a road a reddish coloured wolf obstructed my way and as he was crossing for a long time, he stood straight as if his back became stiff & immobile.(18)

In this chapter of 19 verses this 18th verse is extremely different. It does not fit in with the tales or subject of other verses. But in this patent disparity rare mysteries are concealed.

Wolf is a forest animal, but he is never of reddish colour. Forest (then) was full of wild animals, and they, it seems always obstructed the path of sages. Therefore there was no need to refer to such insignificant incident in the Vedas.

But by now, we must realise that Vedas are a graph of creation of the universe, and hence this incident refers to some event in universal creation. It is from this view point that we must examine it.

Modern Science has classified stars in space. From these, there is one group comparatively small, but have unusual special characteristics. They are termed as "Wolf-Rayet-class". In the coloured spectrum they show emission lines which are many times more than the ionised element. This shows that their shells are expanding. Many stars from this group are Binary stars.

"Trit-Apta" has described the wolf as reddish colour or of the colour of dawn.

The second half of the verse which describes the wolf as "Since he (wolf) appeared to be crossing for a long time he stood stiff as if his back became stiff and immobile". This description is description of ionisation of elements. It is speciality of group of stars called "Wolf Rayet".

Ions when in pairs make up the substance of many crystalines include table salt. When such an ionic substance is dissolved in water ions are freed to a considerable extent from restraints that hold them within the rigid array of crystals (En. Brita. Vol. IX)

Due to Ionisation atoms gets electrically charged and movement, motion or speed is created in them. Rigid ion in salt gets dissolved if salt is put in water, and ions get liberated. Ionisation is a separate and independent study in chemistry. Essence, is that ionisation creates activity in matter and elements. If ionisation does not take place matter becomes rigid and is dissolvable.

The wolf who met "Trit-Apta" sage, had a stiff back & neck, because of constant strain. This means that Trit-Apta sage is inviting our attention to those group of stars in which process of ionisation has not started, or has started at snail's pace.

If today's scientists find that process of ionisation has started in these group of stars, then it must have started after these verses were written.

As per Encyclopedia Britannica (Vol.I p.250) the stars in this group are extremely hot and are called white dwarfs. Hence these stars exhaust their fuel extremely fast. Their density is equal to sun but its size is equal to that of earth. Some 4 to 6 thousand years ago (vedic period) that star must have been red (wolf) and must have been on way to becoming white dwarf.

The first verse from this chapter is as follows: "Moon with beautiful wings, whose residence is unknown, is proceeding towards Dyue-lok through clouds whose borders are shining with golden light." Thereafter in the 11th verse it is stated "Golden Moon from "Dyuelok" is driving away the wolf moving in space."

Majority of stars from this group are binary. "Suparna" means one who has wings. Wings are always two. Therefore Binary stars are indicated by the winged Moon. Therefore it means that binary stars drove away the wolf "Trit-Apta" sages who were 3 brothers. Ekat, Dwit and Trit. Dyue-lok although part of space is charged with electro-magnetic power.

Reference to wolf in the 11th chapter, and reference to stiff necked wolf, may both signify same thing. They symbolise group of stars described as "Wolf-Rayet type".

But this may also be a symbol for another group of stars, because in space in the South hemisphere to the extreme south of the constellation "Libra" and to the east of the constellation "Scorpio" between 40 long. and 14 to 16 lat. is a group of stars called "Lupus" which also means wolf. In this group also there are many binary stars. Binary stars always revolve around each other.

"Trit Apta" sage were actually not sages but were a star, group of stars, Nebula, or some astronomical entity or part of entity, and this is reflected in chapter 105 and its construction.

Verse 8: Ribs of my back are torturing me, like other wife of my husband.

Verse 9: My Navel is tied very tight, by seven ropes, and hence I am praying for your help to liberate my brethern.

Sage "Trit-Apta" had fallen in a well. This condition of his described above, is mysterious and peculiar. Secondly Trit Apta is treated as Deity in the family of Indra. All Deities are luminaries, and are electrified, which means they are stars.

Diseased sage having fallen in well, and his nabhi (umbilicus) is tied with seven ropes tightly, and compare this with two winged moon coming out of dark clouds (sage was rescued) - is easily comparable.

All the above is completely scientific although symbolic.

In space there are innumerable nebulas, and they are lustrous because they are on fire. They are a part of our galaxy.

Lustrous clouds can be divided in two parts:

1. Dark lustrous, these appear like dark patches and their shape is not even and they absorb the light of stars beyond them.
2. Those emitting their own light, bright, or reflect the light falling on them from stars close to them.

There are four varieties of IInd type of clouds. 1. Diffused nebula. 2. Reflecting brightness 3. Planet like, sphere like, but bright 4. Super novas (self shining).

The well in which Trit-Apta falls is a well in space. Deep like well, there are some areas in the space. This is part of the 1st variety of dark lustrous clouds. It is cool like well, containing neutral non-affecting matter. (cold netural clouds of material)

In these types of clouds many important results occur in the inner core. e.g. construction of stars. Here it is assumed that such clouds do not have their own inherent motion, or speed. The matter contained therein on a small scale radiates. It is blue, because hydrogen or helium is not sufficiently ionised. This lack of radiation promotes construction of matter, which is necessary for creation of a star. Matter then becomes dense, because of internal gravitation.

This process is as follows:-

"The force of gravity in nebula constantly pulls it together working against disruptive collisions of any one nebula or cloud with its neighbours. But even if gravity can hold the cloud together against other forces, the cloud cannot collapse unless it can cool. Gravitational energy is released in a contraction and would heat gas cloud; thus increasing the outward pressure. A cloud therefore contracts under its own gravity.......

As it contracts the density and gravitional binding increases and finally the cloud's gravity so dominates the internal pressure that the material rushes almost in a free fall." (Enc.Brit.Vol.XII p. 926 to 934)

It is helpful to follow the process of creation of stars out of dark bright clouds. It is also helpful to note the use of words. The matter in these clouds have to confront three force viz. contraction, condensation and gravitation. Similarly these clouds have to protect themselves from external bright clouds and collision with them. We will make a mental note of the above and come back to the problem of "Trit-Apta". "Trit-Apta" having fallen in the well says "My umbilicus (Nabhi) is tied very tight with sevens ropes. My ribs (at the back) are torturing me intensely like my husband's co-wife."

Above observation, and description of process of black lustrous clouds turning into stars, has exceptional resemblance, and therefore the prayer of "Trit-Apt" is description of a scientific phenomena. It is only expressed symbolically.

Process of star creation takes place in the centre of lustrous clouds. Umbilicus is the centre of human system. And pressure of forces in the creation of stars (from all directions) - concentrates at the centre.

This process of creation has to face neighbouring lustrous clouds and their force. "Trit-Apta" who has fallen in the well, is also describing similar event .The description in the 1st verse of "Twin winged beautiful moon is coming out of golden bordered cloud" is description of "Bright nebula". And it affects the lustrous cloud emerging from the well in which "Trit-Apta" has fallen.

Just as falling of "Trit-Apt" in the well, is an allegory connected with creation of universe. Similarly, it is also connected with molecular binding i.e. chemical binding.

In the book "Chemical Bonding" chapter 4, author observes as follows:-

"When various types of atoms are bound together by chemical bonds, it creates a molecule. Molecule (Renu) is a very very small particle of an element, and can exist independently and can retain its properties .Just as hydrogen is a very small atom, similarly H2 is a simple molecule. To see what happens when bond is created between these two molecules, it is necessary for two atoms to come together with their electrons.

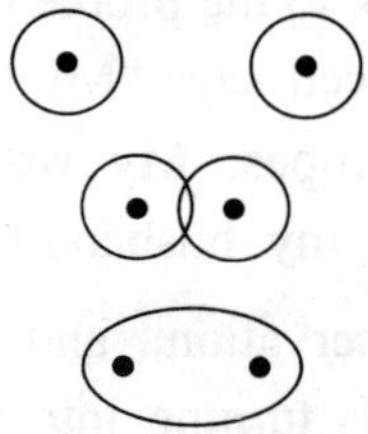

दोन वियुक्त अणू त्यांच्या कक्षांसह — अ

त्यांचे परस्परांवर आरोहण — ब

रेणूंच्या कक्षा एकमेकांत मिसळतात — क

In figure A, two atoms have come together and are yet to decide whether or not to mix. In figure "B" we find they have inter-crossed, with the result that orbits of electrons get mixed. In figure C we find complete union of electrons of two atoms. But both atoms preserve their independence, and one molecule is born.

The same process is explained in the following sketch:

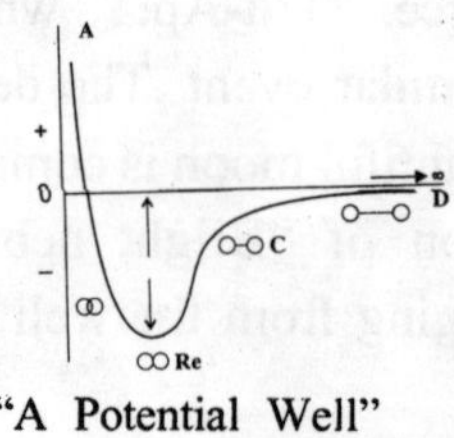

"A Potential Well"

This figure shows the energy changes which take place when molecules come together. An energy curve like this is sometimes called a potential well, because the behaviour of the system it describes, parallels the behaviour of a rubber ball a curved well of the same shape. If a ball is placed at point A in the figure, it will roll down to the bottom and stop at RE. An energy D would be required to lift the rubber ball out of the well.

Above the well at point C, the energy of the system is just that of isolated atoms; there is no bonding energy and the atoms may fly apart.

The above paragraph and the figure drawn, which scientists call a potential well, coincides with the story of "Trit-Apta" falling in a well, and both fit in like a glove. It creates a foundation of scientific truth. Thus the story of "Trit-Apta" and scientific thesis about two molecules and their union, or the scientific truth about creation or union of two stars, is one and the same.

"Trit-Apta" prayed to Brihaspati and the latter rescued him from the well. "Trit-Apta" then came to be regarded as one among the family of Indra (as a deity) is a story symbolic of the fact that the star was created which was self-luminary. During the process of creation of a star, sometimes a proto-star or a small star is created, or sometimes a star of the size of sun or even bigger star is created. Or even a star system can also be born. The result is that "Trit-Apta" is one out of the 3 described above. Around such a star a Nebula also can be born.

In the constellation Taurus, Proto-star with a nebula is found; and comparatively he is young. This star is classified a "T-Tauri" star. Similarly in the constellation "Orion" such stars exist, but they are not visible, because they are covered with clouds of dust.

Constellation "Taurus" is in the northern hemisphere between 20 Long. and 4 to 5 Lat. In this Crab Nebula M11, Pleiades M/45; Hydes, and RA04 exist. The constellation Orion is in the southern and northern hemisphere, between 10 long. and 5 to 6 Lat. from both sides in it are the "Horse-Head" nebula RA 05 and M5.

In the constellation Taurus, in the open clusturs pleiades, there are young hot stars. Around them are bright clouds and even now, the process of formation into stars from within is going on. Their age is only 60 lakhs years. "Trit-Apta" who were three brothers; could they be in Pleiades?

If we call for "Trit-Apta" by addressing the constellations "Taurus" or "Orion", will it be possible to obtain an answer? For Deities and sages nothing is impossible. Our call must cover a distance of thousands of light years.

Classification of stars as "T-Tauri" and the name "Trit" phonetically show some resemblance. Is this similarity an accident? Same applies to "Wolf-Rayet", and the name Rohit and Landga (wolf).

Chapter 29

AKASH GANGA (OUR GALAXY) MEANS "SARASWATI"

There are innumerable galaxies in the universe "Akash-Ganga", our galaxy is just one of them. It is spiral in shape, and in the centre is circular (quarter spherical) raised portion like upside down saucer. Its diameter is 30,000 Parseks. Its thickness is 5000 Parseks. (One Parsek = 3.6 Light Years). Sun is at a distance of 8300 Parseks from the centre (i.e. 29880 light years).

Our galaxy in the astronomical space stretched south-North, and in it there are millions of stars and groups of stars.

In Vedas many rivers are referred to. Among them is Saraswati. This river is our galaxy. It can be established beyond doubt.

Rig Veda describes it as under:-

1.7.15	City made up of iron which supports everything, Fast moving, full of water, full of currents, giver of milk and butter, wearing white clothes.
2. 7.96	Superior among all rivers, white coloured, full of sweet and powerful waves, visible.
3. 6.61	Destroyer of mountains peaks, comprising powerful waves, having golden wheel of chariot,

mover through the cosmos, visible because of powerful shining, speeding like a chariot, spread vast across, having bright noisy rapids.

4. 2.20.8 Destroyer of enemies with aid Maruts (Storms)

5. 1.3.12 Out of self-achievement capable of giving rapidity and speed to water flow.

6. 5.42.12 Following the pre-determine path Saraswati with full of light.

7. 5.42.11 Deity full of lustre like butter, let her come from Dyue-Lok and mountains to our place of worship (or Yadnya).

Atharva-Veda (and Verses)

1. 7.57.2 All dealings are going on well, because Maruts (Sons of water) have ensured free flow of seven currents for the sake of Gods.

2. 18.1.42. Pitaras from the south are worshipping Deity Saraswati. Pitaras means souls of the dead from a family.

Rig Veda

1. 10.17.9 Oh South-based Deity Saraswati.

Yajur Veda

If we look up and have a look at space we find that Dyue-lok is stretched South-North.

2. 6.1. Presiding Deity of Yadnya pined for southern Deity and ultimately had united with her, Indra came to know this and entered the body of the Deity and took birth as her son.

Note: Pitar means souls of the dead from a family.

3. 33.21. There is a river by name Rasa which beautifies supports of people of Dyue-lok and earth.

4. 34.11. River initially runs with the aid of 5 currents but later in the same country she merges into one current and becomes Saraswati.

("पंचनद्यः सरस्वतीमयी यंती सस्रोतसहः ।
सरस्वती तु पचंधा सो देशे भवत् सरितः ॥)

The above description fits in with our galaxy, otherwise called as "Milkyway" (or 'Akash-Ganga') by modern scientists.

Saraswati travels in a chariot which has wheels and body of gold. Wheel of chariot is circular with spokes and hub. It also denotes speed. By calling it golden, emphasis is on light. Our galaxy is circular. It has five twists (or arms). It has Nabhi (i.e. Navel). This centre is gold-like, and entire galaxy shines due to its inherent illumination.

Saraswati is wearer of white apparel, white coloured, illuminating, visible, giver of milk and butter. Butter like lustrous. The stripe of milky way visible during night, answers to all this description. The stripe of milky way is white, illuminating, beautiful. It is giver of milk, which means it is white like milk. That is precisely why it is called "Milky Way".

Saraswati also gives clarified butter besides milk. This symbolism is at once mysterious and scientific. "Ghrita" means clarified butter. Solid clarified butter is white in appearance, but as a result of "oilness" the bond between various molecules of clarified butter is tight. Similarly, clarified butter has a tendency to solidity early.

Clouds of hydrogen and helium in the milky way, and also of elements, if they were to be rarified (i.e. at a distance from each other), no bond could have been established between their atoms, with the result that no new stars could have been created.

The element (hydrogen & helium) which inhabits milky way has the capacity to create bonds, resulting in creation of stars, and hence Saraswati is described as giver not only of milk but also of clarified butter.

Saraswati is described as capable of covering the earth and Dyava the three worlds, space, travelling, luminary, coming from Dyue-lok. Dyue-lok is ever full of light and energy. Vedas have divided universe under 3 heads Earth, Dyue-lok, and space. Saraswati or milky way is ever shinning Dyue-lok. Saraswati is described as Dyava and Earth covering. If we treat earth as our planet then phrase Dyava-earth covering applies to us. During night time we find that milky way touches both north and south horizon. In this way also Dyava Earth covering is a valid interpretation.

"Three worlds covering" (Trailokya Gamini) also validly described vast expansion of milky way. Similarly "Ever space travelling also applies to milky way.

Even according to modern science the Milky way galaxy, is fast going towards the centre of the Universe, therefore, it is aptly described as space travelling.

Saraswati is described as enemy destroyer with aid of Marut. Marut means solar storms. But this concept is applicable to 3 positions. Earth life, solar system and in the universe. Because after the big bang in universal creation Marut's played a role in bringing elements and energy together.

Thus this description of Saraswati fits in with milky Way (Akash Ganga).

Not only in milky way but in outer space beyond milky way if maruts were not there, elements and energy could not have combined and no creation could have taken place.

With the aid of Maruts says Rig Veda, Saraswati destroyed enemies. How is subject matter of next chapter. Saraswati is described as "Giver of power, full of waves and full of powerful tides." This adjective waves is patently applicable to river .But it also applies to giving of power with aid of Marut in bringing elements and energy together.

The description "with self-achievement giver of speed to water currents" is not applicable to river. Because after big-bang during initial stages there was no water .That is why words water or current, or rapids used in context of river, symbolise elements and gaseous clouds in milky way. And these are given motion, speed and power.

Vedas have given a great similarity between milky way and river Saraswati by saying that Saraswati stretches South-North.

Author of Vedas did not stop here. They precisely located and identified the place where Saraswati (Milky way) was born.

"Oh! South born Saraswati" are the words used which means that milky way originated in South hemisphere, and spread to the north. Modern scientists ought to examine this "Origin" viz. South as the birth place of milky way. The basis of this hypothesis is set out below.

If we examine the "stretch" of South and North in universe, we find that galaxies or groups of stars in the South outnumber the galaxies in the north. Similarly the "stripe" of milky way in the South is more illuminating than the "stripe" in the north.

In Krishna Yajur Veda, in Taitriya Samhita, (Kand 6. Para Pathek 1). There is a verse as follows:

God of Yadnya (Sacrificial worship place) pined for Deity of South, and had sex with her. Indra came to know about this he entered the body of Dakshine Devi and was born as her son. This is an allegory. But from this one thing becomes clear that Yadnyadeo (Universal illumination and its origin took place in the South) scientists admit that out of a total of 88 groups of stars 52 are in the southern hemisphere and 36 are in northern hemisphere.

"युक्ता मातासीद् धुरि दक्षिणाया अतिष्ठन् गर्भोवृजनीष्वन्तः ॥"

In Shukla Yajur Veda (Kandika 33 sloka 2) there is a reference to a river Rasa who beautifies the habitations of Dyue-lok and Earth.

"आ सुते सिञ्चन श्रिय रोदस्योरभिश्रियम्."

In a book "Vedic Index" by R. Roy, the author says "the word Rasa originally means flavour of water" and hence its use is made to symbolise the river Saraswati. Hence the river Rasa symbolises river Saraswati.

In shukla Yajur Veda (Kandika 34 slok 11) "Saraswati originally flows in five currents, although she becomes one in the end."

"पंचनद्यः सरस्वतीमयी यंत्री सस्रोतसः ।
सरस्वती तु पंचधा सोदेशे भवत्सरित् ।

In Rig Veda also there is reference to seven rivers. If we closely observe Milky way stretching South North, or if we go through the charts, we find that there are five or seven fluctuations of Milky way or slight divisions.

In fact that river Saraswati referred to in the Vedas symbolises "Milky way galaxy" is strengthened by one more verse of Atharva-Veda quoted below:-

देवा इयं मधुना संयुतं यवं सरस्वत्यामधि यणावचर्कृषुः ।
इंद्र आसीत सीरपतिः शतक्रतुः कीनाशा आसन् मरुतः सुदाननः ॥

God created "Yav" a sweet cereal (grain) for human beings on the banks of the river Saraswati, when Marut became the "Krishival" i.e. Agriculturist and Indra became Haldhar, i.e. the holder of plough. Haldhar means wields the plough.

Besides our milky way there are innumerable galaxies in space. Some are spiral, some are elliptical, some are barred spiral, and some are irregular. Majority of galaxies are millions of light years away. But some are comparatively closer. They are called local group of galaxies. Among them are galaxies which are smaller than our own (Dwarf) but they are not less than a million light years away. They are supposed to be members of our group.

If seen from earth they appear to resemble grain (cereal) crumb of "Yav".

"Yav" Grain crumb of Yav is slightly enlarged at the centre and tapers at both ends, as in this figure.

This scientific truth regarding shape of adjacent galaxies was stated in verse quoted above. However the problem as to how Indra became wielder of plough (i.e. cultivator)? is a concept which deserves separate application of mind.

Chapter 30

VEDA'S SUBTLE KNOWLEDGE OF "MILKYWAY"

In the previous chapter we saw as to why "Saraswati" of Vedas stands for "Milky way". But Vedas don't stop here. They describe in details the secret mysteries of "milky way" also. That part comes in Mandal one chapter 164 of Rigveda. Verses are as follows:-

13. All establishments are located on the wandering chariot (of Aditya) which has 5 spokes and one Nabhi (centre) umbilicus.

14. The chariot of Aditya, joined to inverted yoke, and which has ten horses always wander by the same route. The eye of the sun covered with watery clouds, travels along with this chariot, the whole universe is founded on it.

30. This body-shaped matter, which never stays at one place and is always moving and alive, while breathing, rests in the centre of the house. Conversely immortal combination that is Jiva and Body (spirit and body) wanders due to its own force. In this, are described different states and the changes of sun and Aditya: For instance:

Verse (2) Sun-one wheeled chariot - Three umbilicuses, seven horses,

Note: Nabhi = Umbilicus

Verse (11) Aidtya - 12 spokes, wandering in Dyue-lok, 720 couples.

Verse (12) In the 1st Parardha (1st part of the 15000 million years of Big-Bang) Aditya - 12 different forms, five footed (12 suns whether they are 12 Adityas)

In the second Parardha Aditya, with six spokes, and seven wheeled chariot (7 horses).

Verse (13) Aditya - Five spokes +1 umbilicus (centre) + Inverted Dhurva (yoke) +10 horses + wandering by same route.

Verses 13, 14 and 30 of Rig Veda's 1st Mandal and 164 chapter, describe the centre or nucleus of milky way. In the IInd Verse is described the centre (Sun) of our solar system. Seven sun's rays. Chariot is one wheeled and has three Nabhis (centres or Umbilicus). This part is dealt with separately in the chapter dealing with three different motions of the Sun.

However Verse No. 13, 14, 30: - Show the route of Milky way and its structure and we have to see it.

In this chapter 1.164 the word Aditya is used in different senses, and every different meaning indicates different state, result, and its active power.

Just as Verse 2 describes Sun as having 3 Nabhis (centres), it also describes the wheel of his chariot as having 12 spokes. These 12 spokes represent 12 months, and in the chariot inhabit 720 couples which works to 360 days + 360 nights. A couple represents day and night.

In the 12th Verse "In the first Parardha of Dyue, is the Aditya i.e. Father who has five feet." There are two parts of Dyue's Parardha. These represent two parts of time cycle of universal creation. This division of time frame in two divisions is perfectly scientific.

We will see how: -

In "The Amateur Astronomic path finder" a scientific book on Astronomy, at page 20 the author makes following observation. "After the Big Bang (15000 million years ago) galaxies began to be formed and our galaxy (Milky way) was formed 10,000 million years ago; from the expanding gas which cooled down. But not all the original gas condensed into stars. In some places it was too thinly spread out for star formation to begin. So far billions of years, the first star in our galaxy started getting burnt out. Then as they ran out of fuel and started to die out, some of the larger ones erupted in massive explosion called Super-Nova and so started a new generation of star formation. We now believe that our sun and its planets were formed after just such a secondary event about four and a half thousand millions years ago."

The thesis of Vedas of two time divisions, fits in with thesis of modern science in respect of star formations.

The first was "Big Bang". The second was "Super Nova Bang".

The first event was described by Vedas by saying that in the first parardha Aditya assumed numerous forms, was five footed and showered extensively.

The words "showered extensively" refers to Big Bang and distribution of matter in space. But the shower does not refer to water.

The scientific theory that our sun was created in the 2nd Explosion Super Nova is stated in the Vedas when they say Aditya of 2nd Parardha i.e. time span.

Vedas do not stop here but give description of milky way in Verses 13, 14 & 30 of Vth chapter. But before we go into it is necessary to find out construction of our universe as per modern science.

Scientists use the word Galaxy in two different contexts. It stands as much for our own galaxy (Milky way) as for other galaxies.

Our galaxy is spiral. During festive days (Diwali) we light a kind of fire works (Top-like) on even ground. After it is lit, it goes on revolving around itself and the light coming out of it is thrown on all sides. Our galaxy resembles with that.

The spiral Galaxy is as under:-

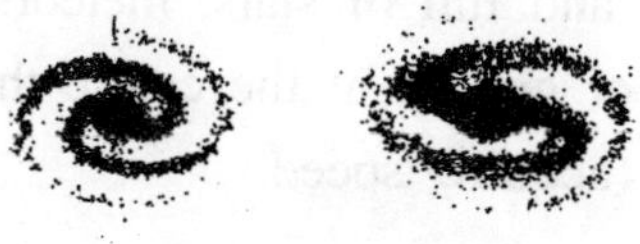

चक्राकार आकाशगंगा

The centre of milky way is called nucleus. From it spiral arms i.e. wheels with teeth or arms with teeth originate. These are fully shining dust clouds in which there are thousands and millions of stars. The teeth of the wheels or arms are attracted towards the centre which is like an extended glass on both sides at the centre but tapering at the ends. It is extremely hot, unimaginable in size (i.e. its diameter is one lakh 8 thousand light years in length). It pulsates. In one of its arms is our solar system. Distance between centre and the extreme end of our galaxy is one lakh light years.

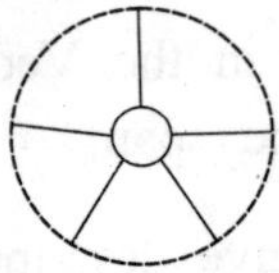

एकनाभियुक्त आकाशगंगेचे
केंद्रक व त्याला पाच आरे

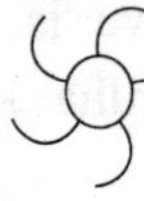

आकाशगंगेच्या केंद्रकाभोवती
वेगळ्या पद्धतीचे आरे

In the 13th Verse the centre of milky way is called "Aditya" and it has one Nabhi (centre). One Nabhi means one centre. It has five arms or spokes.

In the first figure five arms emerging from centre are shown. They are straight. When the centre moves around itself its five arms also move with the result that they become curved.

The curves near the centre of the milky way are gaseous and full of dust; and full of stars, meteors etc. As a result of tremendous pull of gravity at the centre the arms not only get curved but they acquire speed.

Our milky way has five arms according to verse No.13. Modern Scientists have not been able to photograph milky way from the top, because one will have to soar above the centre for 50,000 light years to be able to photograph (A.A.P. Page 19)

Therefore on the basis of photography of other spiral galaxies, our scientist have fixed the shape and size of our galaxy. The pictures shown in en. Britannica and other books on astronomy show curves or arms, emerging from centre and they are faint and their number appears to be 5, $5^{1}/_{2}$ or 6.

उताणा माणूस

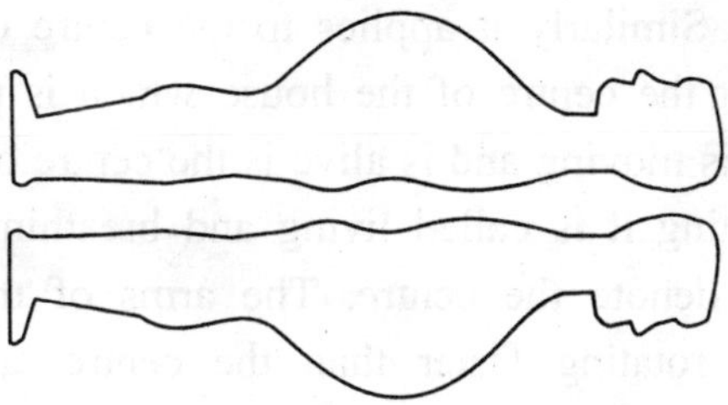

पालथा माणूस

In the 14th verse the description is that horses are tugged to supine contraption. In common parlance we use the words "Utana" (Supine) or Paltha (Upside down or facing Earth)

Tugged to supine contraption is a mysterious expression, but is scientific. This clearly shows that centre of milky way is curved at the centre like-an inflated belly. The same curvature is at the bottom picture. This is description of the centre (Nabhi) of milky way. The centre is like externally curved hence at the top and at the bottom.

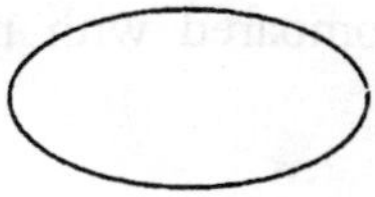

In the same verse the chariot of Aditya is described as moving constantly in the same route. Milky way has only one route. Milky way rotates once every quarter billion years (Karl Sagan cosmos page 205).

Our sun is part of this milky way and it revolves round the centre, and it is part of bright moving clouds, is a scientific truth and this was stated in the verse "Sun (Eye) which is in the midst of clouds is travelling along with this wheel of chariot, the whole universe (i.e. of our galaxy) is founded on it."

Description in the 30th verse also is applicable to the centre of milky-way. Similarly it applies to the centre of our galaxy. "The matter at the centre of the house which is pulsating with breath, which is moving and is alive is the centre of milky way." As it is pulsating it is called living and breathing. House is a term used to denote the centre. The arms of milky way are comparatively rotating faster than the centre, and hence the house is called stable. If the arms of milky way take a full turn around the centre in about a quarter billion years, then the movement of the centre rotating around itself must be called stable comparatively. In the same verse the reference "Immortal Being, rotates in the body with its own power" denotes the same.

Any galaxy in the universe have their rotating power, rotates because of its Dyue power, or gravitational power, or electro magnetic power. This power is called immortal Being by Vedas. Millions of stars in milky way which are dead (i.e. not alive) rotate round the centre with the aid of these powers.

And hence "Stable" condition of the centre is only a relative description, as compared with motion of arms of the galaxy.

Chapter 31

VRATYA DEVATA (MISCHIEVOUS DEITIES) MEANS COMETS

The 15th Mandal (Tome) of Atharva-Veda, and in its 1st chapter (Sukta) which has 18 sub-divisions are devoted to the description of only one Deity which is called "Vratya" viz. the Comets. No extensive Tome is devoted to the description of just one Deity on this scale in any of the Vedas.

M. M. Chitrav (commentator on Vedas) has extensively dealt with the problem of interpretation of the word "Vratya" with reference to various commentators, but has not set out any final theory about it. He has admitted it so openly.

The Sanskrit dictionary meaning of the word "Vratya" means, person without cultural education or spiritual orientation, and one who has not passed through the educative process resulting from ritual of "thread ceremony" and as per tradition one who has not acquired the cultural right of performing sacrificial ritual ("Yadnya Yagadhi" ceremony). The result is that such a person becomes contemptible and spoil. This variety of people are nomadic by nature, and consequently adopts wrong or bad path. Because of nomadic nature, they move in any direction of their choice. Hence their movements and acts are unpredictable. They have no fixed place of residence, nor do they belong to any fixed region.

Despite above meaning of the word "Vratya", Vedas have conferred on it the status of a "Guest" and also elevated him to the status of head of "Deities".

In fact in stellar context, Vratya i.e., mischievous could be no other than except the comet. Traditional notion about comet is that his visit, is a bad-omen, results in death of king, or visits earth with calamities. In this context, the elevation conferred on comet by Vedas is contradictory. Hence any attempt to rationalise this situation will appear to be futile.

In respect of the above two trends can be set out. First is that a scientific phenomena in the region of Stellar science, can never be contemptible. All elements and phenomena are worth studying.

So far we have seen as to how Vedas have studied universal phenomena with scientific attitude. Result was that Vedas studied "Comet" scientifically, and as per vedic tradition elevated it to the status of a Deity.

Similarly there is no proof since when we started treating comet as a Bad-Omen. There is also no proof that in the vedic times such disposition existed.

Vedic times are not less than 4 to 5 thousand years B.C., (despite any attempt made by any one to bring the period earlier). The period of production of other Books by Brahmins, may be perhaps capable of reflecting the "Bad-Omen" attitude of society. But this period is recent. We can't saddle vedic scientific attitude with this trend.

Thirdly during the time of Vedas "Guest" was treated with respect, and was worthy of worship as per the then tradition.

Guest can be defined as a visitor who comes without giving any advance notice. Other adjectives used by Vedas in respect of comet need not be considered. If in the fundamental features of "Vratya" (Mischievous), the answer "Comet" can be reached, then discussion of other adjectives is unnecessary. And this elevation done by Vedas must be construed to relate to comet only.

In Atharva Veda (19.1.20) and in Shukla Yajurveda, the word "Dhumketu" (Comet) is actually used. If this regular Sanskrit synonym for comet was available and was in fact used by Vedas, where was the need to become indirect and to call it "Vratya" (mischievous) "Devata" (Deity). To answer this problem the two relevant verses are discussed below:

Atharva-Veda

Verse : 18.1.30 :

"देवोदेवान परिभुंऋतेन वहाःनो हव्यं प्रथमस चिकित्वान् ।
धुमकेतः समिधाः भाऋजिको मंद्रो होता नित्यो वाचा यजियान ॥

Oh Dhumketu (Comet)! You who reaches Hay (......) to Gods with the aid of a Yadnya, similarly you who pleases Gods and are learned and aflame, reach Hayi (.....) to Gods.

Yajur Veda Kandika 2, Chapter 33

'हरयो धुमकेतहो वातजुता उपद्योती ।
यतंते वृथ गग्नयः । यजु. अध्याय ३३ कंडिका २

Oh Dhumketu (Comet) You who are yellowish and carrying smoke-like flag, and who is carried by quest of mind, which also carries fire, are attempting to reach Swarg (Heaven) by various ways.

Except the two verses above the word "Dhum-Ketu" is not used anywhere in the Vedas.

Neither the two scholars Mr.Chitrav or Mr.Bapat have offered any explanation to show that this word "Dhum Ketu" stood for comet, according to Vedas.

In Tomes (Kand) 15, possible reason for not using the known word Dhum Ketu (Comet), but describing it by using the adjective Vratya (Mischievous) could possibly be that the author of this Tome was sage Arthavan, and the author of Tome from Yajurveda was a different sage. Pandit Satawalekar in his Commentary has also not cited the name of the sage. There is also a possibility that the chapter using the word 'Vratya' was written in a different period (earlier or late) than the chapter which uses the word "Dhumketu"

The result is that interpretation of adjective Vratya to signify comet, is not affected. Because the central subject of Tome 15 itself is guest and Comet, which descriptions tally.

A small informative note may not be out of order here. Various chapters of various Vedas are written by various sages. And must all not have been written in one go. At least a period of 100 years must have needed. They were written on parchments. No printing machines, or xeroxing existed. Mostly the texts were passed on, from individual to individual by recitation and memory. No, research circulation of papers system existed. Authorship of some of the chapters is still unknown.

In 220 verse of 15th Tome, "Vratya" (Comet) is compared with all kinds of Deities. This comparison neither elevates his status, nor does it establish that comparison is suggestive of some other entity. M. M. Shri Chitrav also could not fix the identity through these verses.

It is positively stated that above verses relate to Comet only.

Majority of readers will not bother to read either the above verses of M. M. Shri Chitrav's translation. However the conclusion or the thesis reachable from them is stated here.

Vedas knew the object they were describing. And as stated earlier, they were dealing with, Stellar phenomena. Hence the conclusion that "Vratya-Deity" meant Comet.

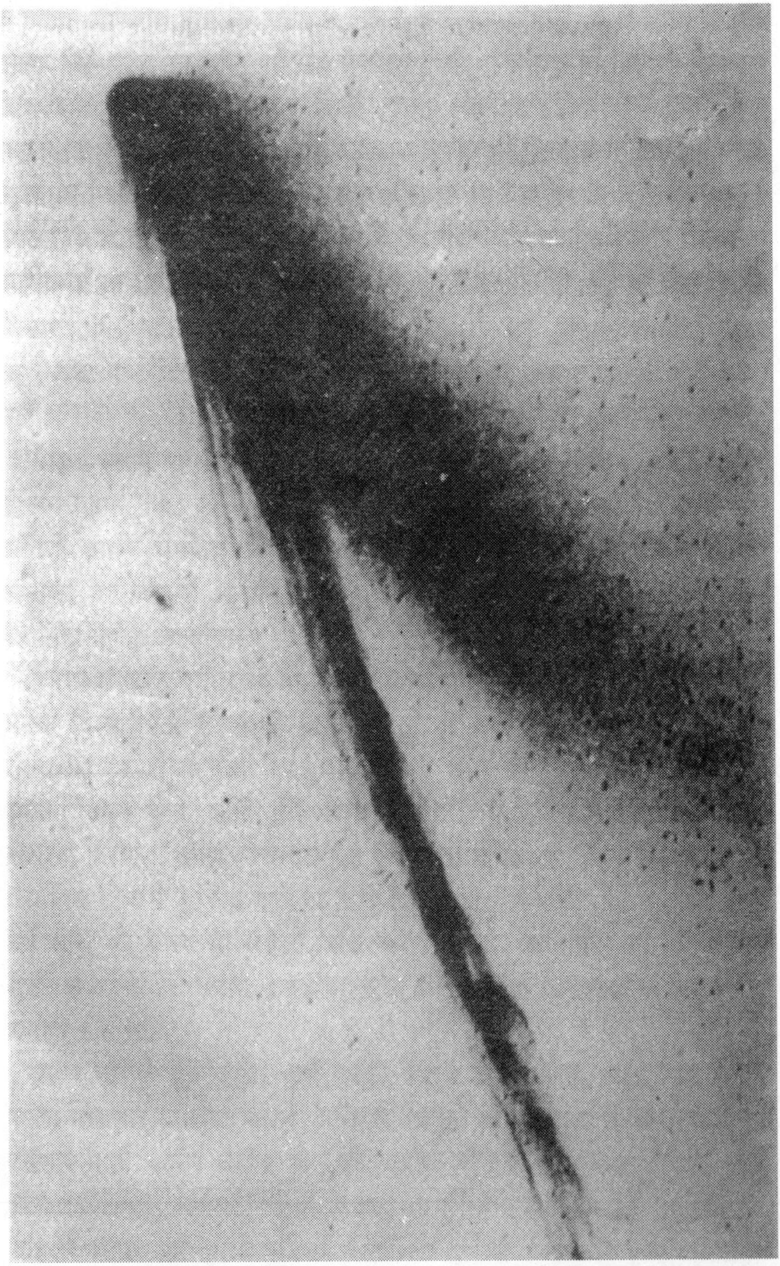

Chapter 32

VRATYA MEANS COMET "ONLY"

In the 15th Tome, and 18th sub-divisions, there are 220 verses. Out of these below mentioned verses are important. They are examined in detail, and the support of other sub-divisions is taken from its essential contents.

Sub-Divisions I : Out of 8 verses 1,2,6,7,8

- do - II : Out of 28 1, 5, 13

- do - III : 11, 1,2

- do - IV : 18 1

- do - V : 16 1 Only essence

- do - VI : 26

- do - VII, VIII, IX : - 11

- do - X : 1, 2, 4, 6, 9

XI, XII :-

XIII :- 13 9+ Essence (summary +9)

XV, XVI, XVII : 26 Essence

XVIII : 5 All five

Before we go into them, let us first see what modern scientists say about Comet.

Comet is a flame which belongs to solar system. If a star has a mica-like cover and a long tail, that would represent in miniature a Comet. Centre of the Comet is in its head which is star like (prima-facie): Its cover is called Coma. Together they constitute the head of the Comet.

From the head itself emerges its tail where the head begins and tail ends, is difficult to say.

Tail is divided in two parts. One part is straight, which is in line with the sun but is in opposite direction. This part is gaseous, and the other part is full of dust, is fanned out and is curved. At the head is the "atmosphere" of Comet. Sometimes from the head a fluctuation emerges in the direction of the Sun which is like a beak, and is also called anti-tail.

१९७३ साली दिसलेल्या कोहूटेक धूमकेतूचे चित्र. त्यात धूमकेतूची चोच दिसत आहे.

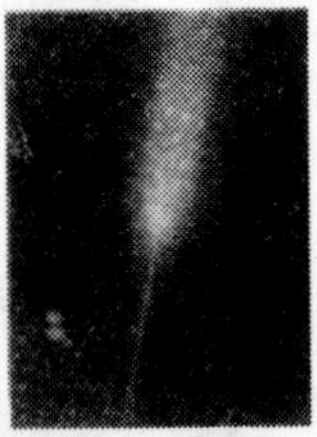

१९५७ साली दिसलेल्या अर्नेड रोलॅन्ड धूमकेतूमध्ये असलेला चोचीसारखा भाग

धूमकेतूची रेखाकृती

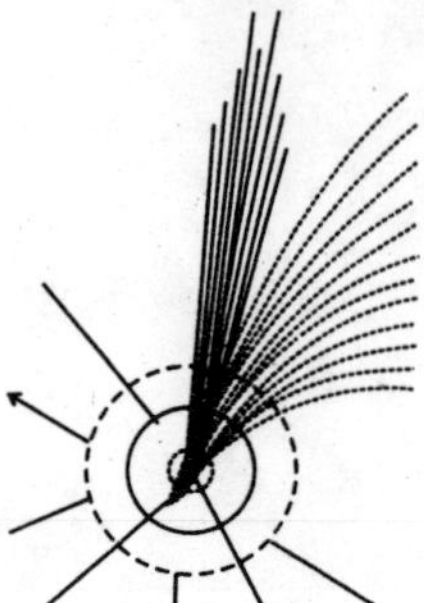

१. धूमकेतूचा गाभा.
२. धूमकेतूच्या गाभ्याभोवतीचे वेष्टन अथवा कोमा. गाभा आणि कोमा यांतून धूमकेतूचे शीर्ष तयार होते.
३. शीर्षापासून निघालेला लांबट अंधुक पिसारा किंवा केतू.
४. पुच्छाचे दोन भाग. एक सरळ सूर्याच्या विरुद्ध जाणारा व दुसरा वक्र धनुषाकार. हे दोन्ही भाग पिसाऱ्यासारखे असतात.
५. शिखेभोवतीचे धूमकेतूचे वातावरण.
६. शिखेपासून सूर्याच्या दिशेकडे जाणारा चोचीसारखा भाग.

While travelling in outer space; when Comets enter solar system, they get attracted to Sun due to gravity and, approach the Sun. At that time they become visible to us. In space they can manifest any point. Mostly Comets after sunset are visible in the West, and before Sun-rise, in the east.

The orbit of Comet in space is extremely complicated. Because during its journey it is sometimes affected strongly by gravity of planets and sometimes mildly. While describing the orbit of Comet we have to consider six items. The orbit of Comet is mostly elliptic, but can also become parabolic or Hyperbolic. For instance:

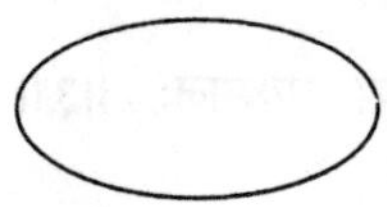

लंबवर्तुळाकार भ्रमणकक्षा

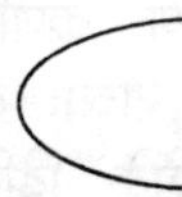

पॅराबोलिक भ्रमणकक्षा

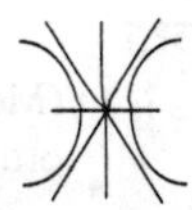

हायपरबोलिक भ्रमणकक्ष

The effect on orbit of Comet, of gravity of planet Jupiter, is called perturbation.

The head of Comet is full of light and illuminating. But it depends on the distance between Comet and the Sun. When Comet is between planets Jupiter and Saturn, its illumination ratio changes 6 to 8 times its normal light. In the spectrum of core of Comet, we find Hydrogen, Carbon, Nitrogen and Oxygen. Similarly it also contains frozen ice. Some Comets emit ultra-violet or Infra-red rays. When Comet approaches the Sun many colours are visible in its tail. Its tail has two parts. One is gaseous and other is full of dust. Comet is affected by energy waves (created by solar storm) of the Sun.

The aforesaid information of modern science about Comets was completely known to Vedas, as per verses on "Vratya" (Comet).

18th sub-division from 15th Kand (Tome) is important from this point of view. Out of them 5 verses and their meaning are set out below:-

तस्य व्रात्यस्य ॥१॥
यदस्य दक्षिणमक्ष्यसौ स आदित्यो,
यदस्य सव्यमक्ष्यसौ सचंद्रमाः ॥२॥
योऽस्य दक्षिणः कर्णोऽयं
अग्निर्योऽस्य सव्यः कर्णोऽस्य स पवमानः ॥३॥
अहोरात्रे नासिके दितिश्चादितिश्च
शीर्षकपाले संवत्सरः शिरः ॥४॥
अहा प्रत्यङ् व्रात्यो रात्र्या
प्राङ नमो व्रात्याय ॥५॥ (Meaning of the verses is not set out in order of Ruchas.)

The nose of this animal is night and day shaped, two parts of head is Diti and Aditi like, and head is like Samvatsar (4)

The south eye of this animal is like Aditya, and the other eye is like moon (1.2)

Left ear is like fire and right ear is like Pavman (3).

During day it is in the east and during night it is in the west. My salutation to Vratya (5).

The description of Comet fits in with these five verses completely.

En, Brita, Part 4.

"Comets" are often seen near the western horizon after sunset and or near the eastern horizon before sunrise." This description and description in the 5th verses fits in 100%. In fact it is this verse which is the key to the whole of the Tome dealing with Vratyas (Comet).

The figure which we saw at Figure B, in that Figure B is beak like portion of Comet, facing the sun. It is this which at Verse 4 is described as nose of Comet. Since this beak emerges from core of the Comet, its two parts were visualised and eye as well as ear (two each) were described. Southern was like Aditya, i.e. Fire, and other like moon. One part of the beak is called hot and other cold.

The head has two parts and it is from here that two tails emerge.

The tail of Comet is a very attractive phenomena. They are of two types. The first part is very active, full of fibres which resemble light, having clouds or beed-like. Second tail is curved, long, having smooth surface, but where fire rays and spirally twisted, can be seen.

There can be one or both types of tails to a Comet. The first type of tail is faint but sometimes illuminated and the second because of its reddish tinge appears to be impressive. The reddish tinge in the tail is reflection of the sun rays on dust. Tail No.1 has neutral Plasma, ions and electrons. Protons emerging from Solar storms enter into the tail of Comets.

The above scientific truth is denoted in many repetitive ends of several verses, of sub-division two:-

"मातरिश्वा च पवमानस्य विपथवाहौ वातः सारथी रेष्मा प्रतोदः ॥

Matirishva and Pavman are horses. Wind is driver and storm is whip. Rainbow has become leader of "Vratyas" and has held a bow in its hands. This has become famous as rainbow.

Second tail of Comet is Bow-like. Storm always brings dust with it. Here a connection is shown between the dust in the tail of Comet. First type of tail is gaseous and solar storms affect it hence, wind is called driver.

Horse means Rays. The Rays are not visible, and it combines all energy in it. It is called "Matrishav" and "Pavman". In the centre of comet elements like Hydrogen, Oxygen, Nitrogen, Carbon are found. All these are species of gases, barring carbon.

Scientists by now have located about 1000 comets. All of them, from construction point of view (electrons) are different. They have various colours like blue, yellow, golden, reddish. These colours have been visibly noticed. This truth is elected in the verse "The stomach of VRATYA is blue coloured, and its back is reddish."

The Comet's, figure at B, and the figure given below, if compared together we will examine, how Vedas have described them in poetic manner.

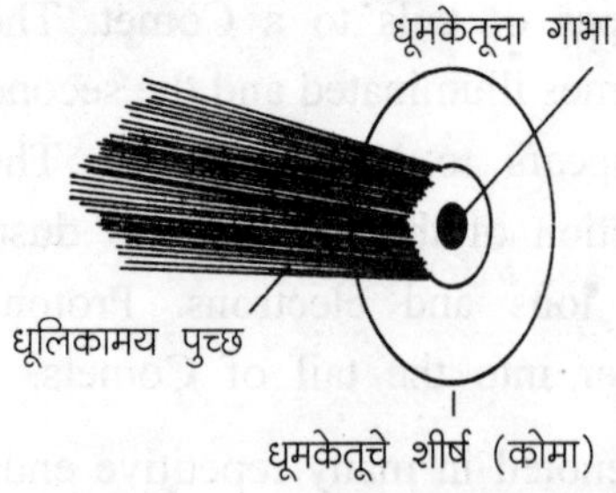

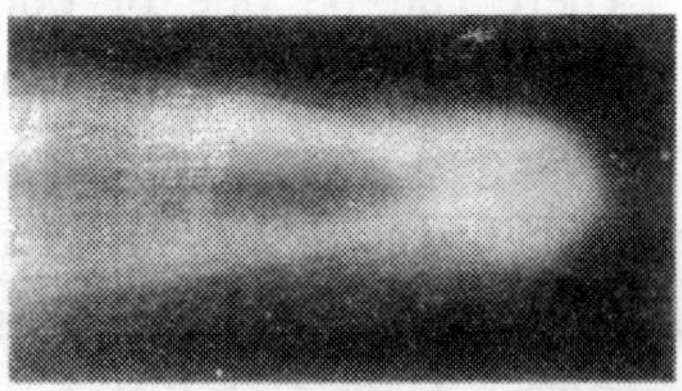

हॅलेच्या धूमकेतूचे १९१० मध्ये घेतलेले छायाचित्र

Vedas have described the head OR "COMA" as a helmet protecting Comet from heat. This description of Core and helmet, appears to fit in.

The same truth is set out in second sub-division as follows ;-

"It wears helmet of light (DAY-LIKE), Night-like (HAIR), ray like earrings, and star-like beeds". In this verse the Core is called star like beed, Head is called helmet of light, the illuminating tail is called ray-like ear-rings, and when Comet is seen during night, it is described as night-like HAIR."

Comet's colour blue and golden is stated (in 1st sub-division) by saying that Prajapati received gold gift.

Reference to "VRATYA" remaining as a guest, for one night, two nights, 3 nights, 4 nights, or for numerous nights ; is also related to Comet's proceeding and rotating around the sun for unpredictable duration.

Arrival and prolonged stay of Comet is referred to in strange and mysterious words in this sub-division. From this it is clear that during vedic times or during the time 15th Tome was written

Some Comet was visible in the sky for about a year.

"स संवत्सरमूर्ध्वातिष्ठत् तं देवा
अब्रुवन व्रात्य किंतु तिष्ठसीति ॥

After Vratya remained in a state of "SAMADHI" (Super-Consciousness) for about a year. Deity questioned him "Why are you standing?"

Karl Sagan in his book "COSMOS" states "In 66 A.D., a Comet remained in sky of Jerusalem for one year like a hanging sword. This description by Josephus relates to Comet "Halley".

It is clear from above description that in 66 A.D. Halley's Comet remained in sky for about a year. Today we are able to calculate Halley's earlier visits, and duration of visibility. On this basis, it may be possible to fix the time of writing of this 15th Tome of Veda. In view of the irregularity of visits of about 1000 Comets, Halley's Comet staying for a year would be a speciality. Therefore the description of stay for one year in 15th TOME can't be called as a freak of imagination.

The Comet Vratya is also described as "Manovipatham" i.e. moving as per the whim of the mind. This also supports the thesis that the Vratya is comet because comets were also unpredicatable in movement.

Chapter 33

SHOCKING SIMILARITY BETWEEN "VRATYA" AND COMET

As per En, Brita. Part IV page 972 "the orbit of some Comets is similar. Only difference is in their perihelion passage. These Comets fall under one class. Comets coming under this class were at one time united. Their splitting was the result of solar effects. Thereafter as a result of various forces working on them their speed differed. From this variety, there is a group of SEVEN Comets. It is titled under "Guty" class, which means sun grazing class, "IKEYASAKI" is one of them, all these Comets enter the CORONA of the sun."

The above discovery and above classification was done by Vedas in its fifth sub-division. The Deity of this sub-division is "RUDRA". In fact the number of "RUDRA" is eleven, but in some chapters it is given as eight. Therefore RUDRAS can total either eleven or eight. However strangely enough in the fifth sub-division only 7 Rudras are referred to, and also named; and it is further stated that these seven RUDRAS protect "VRATYA". This description fits in with the description with 7 Comets falling under the category of "CRUTZ". Names of these seven RUDRAS are "BHAV, SHAV, PASHUPATI, UGRA, RUDRA, MAHADEO AND ISHAN".

From chapter 15, out of 18 sub-divisions, five sub-divisions (2,4,5,6,14) set out 220 verses. Out of these 110 are in respect of the directions favouring "VRATYA". These directions not only include, EAST, WEST, NORTH, URDHAV (UP) and ADHAR (DOWN), but also to some new ones like UTTAMA, BRUHATI, PARAMA, ANADISHTHA, AND ANAVRITTA. Besides these new ones, there is one more viz. ANTARDISHA (INNER DIRECTION).

Devoting 110 verses to the subject of direction to which or in which comets go, appears to be that usual six directions or eight directions are insufficient to describe the directions where the comet will go or from where they will come.

More important than this is the fact that the orbit of comet is elliptical, parabolic, hyperbolic and therefore the study of Comet's entry and exit has to be done having regard to various directions. That is perhaps the reason why these additional orbits of Comets referred to above touches various direction in space. In order to find out various "TOUCH-POINTS" in space of the orbit of Comet, there could be many methods. Out of these Vedas must have followed its own.

Direction is a relative term with reference to a gross object in space. Directions are imaginary for fixing the location of the matter in space. For example, if earth is the centre then their aforesaid directions North, South, East and West plus two Above and Below. But the astronomical space is so huge that these directions are insufficient. Therefore, like earth, it has to be divided in longitude and latitude.

Therefore, which is meant by Uttama, Brihati, Parma, Anadishta, etc. cannot be said with certainty. But it is certain that in all 12 directions were considered by Vedas about the orbits of comets.

Perhaps Vedas did not consider earth as the fixed point, before citing additional directions. Or perhaps these new directions could be sub divisions of known directions. It must be candidly admitted that reference to these unknown directions and their analysis remains a problem that is unsolved. i.e. we cannot with confidence say what point of space is referred by the New Direction.

Vratya (COMET) is also described as "MANOVIPATHAM" which means one who does not follow a specific path. This description fits in with Comets.

A Comet once seen, may not go to the Sun at the same point. On his orbit huge planets like Jupiter and Saturn also have an effect. Despite this there is no guarantee that Comet will remain in its orbit within the solar system. Several Comets, come, visit and then disappear. They go outside solar system in inter-stellar medium. Once this happens then the Comet does not return.

While telling this truth the verse in the sixth sub-division says "The direction "ANAVRITTA" favoured "VRATYA" and he decided not to return.

Comets entering solar system are sometimes imprisoned by the gravity of Jupiter and such Comets remain in solar system. Out of known comets 100 have thus been imprisoned by Jupiter. There are 75 comets completely controlled by Jupiter they are regarded as his family. Their period of orbit is 12 years. If they approach Jupiter close enough they are severely affected. After approaching the earth go back in their orbit around Jupiter.

This relation between comets and Jupiter was known to Vedas. Essence of 11 verses from sub-division 10, is as follows:-

"If Vratya comes as a guest of king, the king should treat him as his superior and pay proper respects. There by king would not be undesignating his caste, or his kingdom. By conferring this honour both the families (of King & of Comet) become great. Then where should both of them go ? (sub-division 10/1, 2, 3). It was then decided that they should enter into Brihaspati (Jupiter). This earth (world) is Jupiter-like, (6). One who knows the Jupiter like nature of this world (9)......

Brihaspati is Guru (TEACHER) of Deities, and is an important Deity in Vedas. Many TOMES, and chapters of Vedas are written on Brihaspati. Normally this Deity is not to be identified with planet Jupiter because it is held to be a Deity having a role to play in creation of Universe. We have seen that Brihaspati in Nitrogen. But same term, acquires different meaning in different context. That method is the Vedic method. For example "MARUTI" stands for 3 kinds of storms, earthly, solar and inter-steller.

Similarly in the 10th Sub-division the word Brihaspati stands for planet Jupiter.

The verse from 10th sub division says the same thing "One who knows Brihaspati of this earth (world)" - meaning planet Jupiter. In the 6th verse world is called Brihaspati - like, i.e. a planet like Jupiter.

The reference in the verse that it was decided to enter Brihaspati (Jupiter) clearly means that VRATYA (COMET) should go back into its orbit around planet Jupiter. It means that as per scientists 75 Comets revolve in orbit around Jupiter. This is stated by saying that the guest VRATYA (COMET) taking the force of king decides to go into orbit around Jupiter, which has scientific basis.

As per scientific discovery, ice was found in the Core of Comets. In the 11th sub-division this reference is described in following words "Host should ask Guest (Comet) as to where he has put up, and then offer water to him'. In the next 4th verse it is stated that one who asks VRATYA (Comet) whether he needs water, are favoured by constellations of watery type.

Normally there is nothing scientific about asking such a question but recalling the status of guest conferred on Comet, asking such a question would relate it to existence of ice in the Core or not we cannot say for sure.

Chapter 34

KNOWLEDGE OF SUN'S MOTION IN VEDAS

Till 16th Century the West believed that Sun revolves around the earth. There was no scientific basis for it. It was a product of religious beliefs and traditions. In 1514 A.D. Astronomer Copernicus gave a shock to this notion, and established that all planets including earth revolved around the Sun. It similarly propounded that since earth rotates on its axis, it gives an impression that stars in the night sky are moving.

As Copernicus was employed in Cathedral Church, his theories were stiffly opposed by Christian religion's order. Since an old scientist Tolemy had opined to the contrary, the then group of scientists also opposed Copernicus. The result was, his book was proscribed and this ban was lifted only in 1835.

If we consider the Indian situation we find that after death of Ashok, degeneration in the area of science, art and allied branches set in. None had the impetus to discover anything with the result that during post-Ashok period there was atmosphere of intellectual stagnation.

But during Vedic period i.e. hundreds years before aforementioned stagnation, the Vedic sages were alive with the zeal or observation, verification and mental cognition of universal problems. Their capacities were scientifically oriented.

It is out of this that they had set out long before Tolemy and Copernicus, that earth revolves round the sun, and this was set out in all the four Vedas.

The verse in respect of the same in Rigveda is as follows:

आयं गौः पृश्निरक्रमीदसदन्मातरं पुरः ।
पितरं च प्रयन्स्वः ॥
ऋग्वेद १०-१८९-१
शुक्ल यजुर्वेद -३-६
सामवेद ६३०-१३७६
अथर्ववेद -६-३१-१
२०-४-४८
कृष्ण, यजु, तैत, संहिता - १.५.३.२

Other references of Vedas are as follows:

1. Rigveda	10.189.1
2. Shukla Yajurveda	3.6.
3. Samveda	630.1376
4. Atharvaveda	6.31.1, 20.4.48
5. Krishna, Yajurveda, Tait, Samhita	1.5.3.2

Meaning of this verse is as follows: this cow-like Pritvi (World) is revolving around its parents (Father and Mother) who are like Protectors. this world born out of water is rotating around the protector from all four sides (Protector is Sun).

Vedas not only knew that earth revolved around the Sun, but knew other details now proved by modern science, regarding the motions of the sun.

The verse from Atharva-Veda is as follows:

"सप्त युञ्जलि रथमेकचकृमेको अश्व-वहति सप्तनामा त्रिनाभि
चक्रमजर मनव यत्रेमा विश्वा भुवनाधितस्थुः ॥"

The Sun reaches his seven horsed one wheeled chariot, which wheel has 3 (Nabhis), Umbilicus and it is because of the support of the Sun that all life on earth is sustained.

Sun having a chariot is obviously a poetic idea. Chariot stands for motion or speed, and hence this is attributed to the Sun. This chariot has only one wheel, but has three Nabhis (axis). In this description itself the secret knowledge about the motion of the Sun is revealed.

Every wheel has ordinarily only one hub (Nabhi) and every wheel moves around its hub. Hub and Nabhi are synonyms. Nabhi is the centre of a thing. Just as umbilicus is the centre of human body.

In the light of above facts how can Sun's chariot have 3 Nabhis is a problem?

Axis is a word used in context of speed of earth. Earth moves around its axis. If earth is treated as a chariot it would have 2 axis (Dwi-Nabhi) because earth has 2 motions. It revolves around itself, and it also revolves around the Sun.

When chariot of Sun is said to have 3 Nabhis, it means that Sun has 3 motions. This compares well with conclusions of scientific astronomical truth.

Sun also revolves around itself, and to revolve once it takes 24 to 26 days time. Second motion of the Sun is around the centre of Milky way. Sun moves around the centre at the rate of roughly 200 kilometers per second. And its third motion is influenced by the movement of the entire galaxy (Milky way) which is revolving around the centre of the universe.

By describing the wheel as having three hubs, Vedas at once revealed and concealed its knowledge. But before this secret could be discovered, modern science had to advance a great till the 20th century.

Chapter 35

VEDIC KNOWLEDGE ABOUT SUN (SHOCKING DISCOVERY)

At the time of creation of universe out of 12 Suns that were born "Martand" (Sun) as per Rig Veda.

Our Sun was one of them. On Sun, there are many chapters in all Vedas, and characteristics of Sun are described. Most of the description is such that a layman can follow it. Hence only description which is very subtle and symbolic and scientific is now examined.

24th verse from chapter one, Tome Nine of Atharva Veda is as follows:

> यद वीघ्रे स्ततयति प्रजापतिरेव तत् प्रजाभ्याः प्रादुर्भवति ।
> तस्मात् प्राचीनोपवितः स्तिष्ठे प्रजापतेऽनु मा बुद्धस्वेति
> अन्वेनं प्रजा अनु प्रजापतिर्बुद्धयते य एवं वेद ॥२४॥

Prajapati who was born for benefit of living beings, and appeared in the sky in the form of roaring sound, was born with (Yadyanopavit) sacred thread. After wearing apparels and also my own sacred thread, I pray to him.

Prajapati is a name given to Sun, and is also an adjective. He protects all living beings. Immediately Sun was born, white fabriced apparel was also born with him, and he has put it on his right side.

Apparently this description may appear to be absurd.

In the above verse, construction of words is very important. This verse does not seek to make fun of the Sun by making him wear sacred thread like a Brahmin. The verse seeks to tell us that sacred thread was born when Sun was born. In other words they were born together; which means that Yadyanopavit was circular in shape like the Sun.

If Sun is photographed in red light of Hydrogen or blue light of calcium many minute details on the Sun become visible. Among them we find many white lines surrounding the Sun like small strips of grass. On the surface of the Sun they appear dark. But near edge of the Sun they are shining bright because of the dark background of the sky. Astro-scientists call these dark lines "Fibrils". The word "Fibrils" arises from the word Fibre, word fibre means thread or thread like item.

That which scientists called "Fibrils" was termed by Vedas as Yadyanopavit or sacred thread. If born along with the Sun, it obviously could not be a product of cotton. But it had got to be shining like the Sun, it had to go round the Sun, and it had to appear white like thread, all of which features the fibrils answer.

The photograph produced below will substantiate what is stated above.

(अ) (ब) (क)

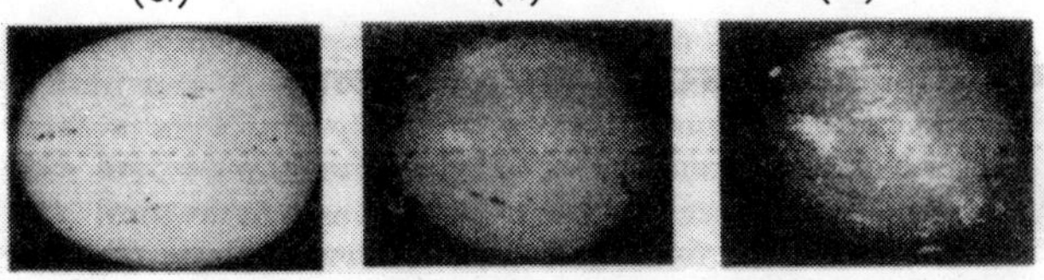

वेगवेगळे फिल्टर्स वापरून काढलेली सूर्याची चित्रे
(अ) पांढरा प्रकाश (ब) हायड्रोजन प्रकाश (क) कॅल्शियम प्रकाश ज्यांतून
सूर्याच्या अंगावरचे "जानवे", जे जन्मजात त्याला लाभले ते दिसते

The light strip seen above in the 3rd photograph is like Yadyanopavit. What scientists call Fibril is nothing but the sacred thread of the Vedas.

It is stated that Sun was born with it. Thus the verse is not a freak of imagination, but description of reality.

Chapter 36

VEDAS DISCOVERED BLACK HOLES (KRISHNA VIVAR)

In 1783 British Astronomer "John Mitchel" came up with the hypothesis of existence of "Black-Holes" in space. This hypothesis was contemporaneously rejected by scientists. Thereafter in the 20th Century (some 35 to 40 years ago) American Astronomers came with the thesis of existence of Black-Holes.

Black-Holes is a very strange and extra-ordinary phenomena of space. They are in fact stars having unimaginable pull of gravity. There are elements and matter, in it, but due to gravity their size has become small. If a star of the size of earth enters Black-Hole it would be reduced to a size hardly 2 to 3 inches.

If pull of gravity of earth is denoted as "X", then pull of gravity of Black-Hole is 1 crore. This pull of gravity affects not only matter but rays also. The net result is that rays are completely absorbed by Black-Holes, which ordinarily travel in space.

Existence of stars in space is deducted from the rays and energy emitted by them.

But since holes emit neither rays nor energy their location cannot be pin-pointed. But they were discovered with the aid of X rays.

In order to find out whether cosmic entities emit x-rays or not, a telescope was sent in space in 1971. This telescope discovered that in the Constellation Cygnus, there is a Black-Hole. It was classified as "Cyg x 1".

Around "Cygnus X_1", is a Huge star. When gases and dust emerging from this star collide with "Cygnus" they emit "X-rays". And their rate of pulsation is 1000 per second. Other Black-Holes like Cygnus were also discovered. They were named (1) V861 Scorgy; (2) GX 339-4; (3) 55-433; (4) Grainus X2. These Black-Holes are at the centre of various galaxies as per the scientists.

Black-Holes are like bottomless wells. Due to their inability to radiate light, they could not be located. Finally their location was done with the aid of X rays.

Despite all round development of science, discovery of Black-holes had to wait till 1960 to 1971.

The author of 137th chapter of 20th Tome of Atharva Veda is, sage Shirimbithi Bhardwaj. The credit of authorship of chapter 137 is obviously due to sage Bharadwaj whose inspiration and extra-ordinary talent, led him to the discovery of Black-Holes.

The verses describing Black-Holes are as follows:-

अव द्रप्सो अंशुमतीमनिष्ठा दियानः कृष्णो दशमिः सहस्रो आवत्
तमिन्द्रः शच्या श्वमन्तमपस्नेहितीर्नृमणा अध-तः ॥७॥

द्रप्समपश्यं विषुणे चरन्तमुपहरे वद्यो अंशुमत्थाः ।
नभो न कृष्णमवतीस्थवांसमिष्या मि वो वृषणो युद्दयजा तौ ॥८॥

अथ द्रप्सो अंशुमत्या उपस्थे धारयत् तत्त्वं तित्विषाणः ।
विशो अदेवीरभ्या ३ चरन्तीबृहिस्पतिना युजेन्दः ससाहे ॥९॥

1. Verse No7:- Indra (Benefactor of mankind) launched a sudden attack on Krishnasur who had stationed himself on the banks of river (Anshumati) with 10,000 troops, and destroyed both Krishnasur and his army.

2. Verse No. 8 :- Indra says "Oh! Powerful Marutas (Storms) help me to kill "Krishna-Drapsa", who has stationed himself in the non-tractable Caves on the bank of river (Anshumati), and who is moving in the caves like Sun in space.

3. Verse No. 9 :- Indra with the help of Brihaspati destroyed atheistic army of Drapsa, stationed on the banks of river (Anshumati).

4. Verse No. 10:- Oh! Indra, you are giver of happiness to 3 worlds (whole universe) and you have with aid of Sun enlightened this earth. You have benefited 3 worlds by killing seven un-conquerable Asuras (Enemies of life) whose names are 1. Krishna 2. Vritra 3. Namuchi 4. Shambar etc.

Apparently above verses appear to be one of the many verses descriptive of war between Indra and Asura. There could be attitude of treating them as legends. There is no historical proof of existence of Indra and Asuras.

Some commentators of past made an attempt to interpret them, and treated it as symbolic of actual war between Indra and Asura.

But let us examine the text of these verses under the light of discovery of Black-holes by modern science. Let us check up the meaning of the words used in the verse.

Essence of the description in the verses is set out below.

1. Asura named Krishnasur had stationed his army unit on the banks of the river Anshumati.

2. Krishnasur himself resided in the intractable caves on the banks of this river.

3. Krishnasur was illuminating like the Sun moving in space.

4. Army of Krishnasur was atheistic.

5. Indra with the aid of Brihaspati killed him.

6. Asuras like Krishnasur who were killed were seven in number including Vritra, Namuchi and Shambar.

7. Indra also took help of Marut.

In the Brihadevta there is a legend, that Brihaspati caught Krishnasur on the banks of river Anshumati, by tracing Krishnasur from the qualities or characteristics of Krishna-Drapsa (Black Drops) viz. of perspiration, on the banks of Anshumati.

Forgetting Indra and Asur we get following scientific data:-

1. Krishnasur = Krishna Drapsa = Black Drop = Krishna-Vivar = Black Hole.

Krishna means Black, Vivar means Hole

2. Anshumati river = Akash Ganga

3. Intractable Cave = Intractable portion of Milky Way.

4. Brihaspati = Male Scientist, Scholar or very powerful mass of gravitation.

5. Lupta Sam - Bindu = Light which is lost or Absorbed.

Now we will see how this story fits in with the properties of Black-hole.

If we check up the inherent vices of Asuras, we find that Greed, Lust etc. were their main vices. The result was wherever there was any prosperity, they chased it to acquire it.

Black-holes had the same property. Black-holes are acquisitive and possessive. They absorb all matter. Black-holes not only pull matter inside them, but they eat space and light rays also. Black-holes are black in colour and hence Sage Bhardwaj called them Krishna (Black) Vivar (Hole).

Krishna Drapsa means "Black Drop". This also fits in with Black-hole. It means an area which is dark, because all light is swallowed. Although no light comes out of Black-holes, originally they were infinitely larger in size than our Sun, and the intensity full of gravity made them black. Everything including light became over condensed. Their original nature which was that of Sun, was described by sage Bharadwaj by saying that in the cave Krishnasur moved like Sun moving in space.

The description that army of Krishnasur was atheist has altogether different meaning. Atheist is one who does not believe in God. But the original word in Sanskrit Nastik has two meanings one is Atheist, the second is "which is non-existent". Black-hole absorbs everything and makes it non-existent. It is in this sense that army of Krishnasur was non-existent (we can imagine the power of pull of gravity; where earth with diameter of 8000 miles becomes one Inch pill.)

Krishnasur (i.e. Black-hole) had his military camp on the banks of Anshumati river. The river stands for galaxy. Scientists have proved that Black-holes are at the centre of galaxy. Sage Bharadwaj called galaxy Anshumati river. Thus we know the scientific parallelism.

"With Ten Thousand warriors", the "Aggressive Krishnasur", are words which stand for "minor Black-holes" and "major Black-hole". During vedic period perhaps the major Black-hole (Krishnasur) must have been surrounded by numerous minor

Black-holes, hence reference to 10,000 warriors. But since the major Black-hole absorbed them, they were later called "Nastik" i.e. non-existent.

"Indra with aid of Brihaspati killed Krishnasur, means that the scholar or scientist discovered the Black-hole. Here killing is to be ignored.

This meaning fits in with the legend in "Brihadevata", that Brihaspati caught Krishnasur with the aid of "Luptasam Bindu" i.e. by noticing that light was being absorbed or turning into darkness. Caught means to "Trace".

Black-hole which originally is a star acquires the power to absorb its own light, and also all matter lit or otherwise, thereby causing full darkness. Black-hole thus destroys all stars that come within the range of its pull of gravity. Thus area of lakhs of miles around Black-hole is total and complete void. It absorbs everything. In universe this kind of area does not exist any where.

Thus we see that the light of other stars which earlier was visible, suddenly disappeared the moment the light or the star came within the range of pull of gravity of Black-hole. "Sambindu" means light of other stars. This phenomena studded Brihaspati (a scholar or scientist) and also Sage Bharadwaj which led them to the discovery of Krishnasur (Black-hole).

As per tenth verse not only one Black-hole was traced, but seven others including Vritra, Namuchi, Shambar & Shushna were traced.

We thus find that Sage Bharadwaj had in his own way described all features of existence of Black-hole, and traced it in the galaxy.

Chapter 37

DESTRUCTIVE EKADASH RUDRA AND SOLAR CYCLE

Since the time of Vedas Rudra is considered as a deity of destruction. Destruction on earth is the result of eruptions of nature. Hence the power that destroys is called Rudra. Although Deity of Death "Yama" and "Rudra" have parallel functions there is difference of degrees. Death is part of life. It can be natural, and straight forward. For that eruptions of nature is not necessary. And Rudra although a Natural eruption, and although could lead to misery, illness, pain and disease may not necessarily end in death.

Many deities, despite availability of verses which describe them appear to be un-knowable. Although here, we are not considering all deities, we are going to try to find out whether there is any scientific substance behind the concept of Deity Rudra.

Rudra

Creation of universe is a fact, and the elements, energy and space that was created has no end, although its state can be converted into another state. Death is only for animate world. And if one form of life is completely destroyed, then it is never re-created (e.g. Dinosaurs).

Therefore although "Rudra" is a power which stands for general destruction, still when it was discovered that it affects life on earth more, Vedas started probing into its nature and origin, and when they reached a certain conclusion, they started constructing verses in its eulogy.

Once we find that Rudra affects animate life, and we take into account forces that endanger life, we find among them, sun, moon, wind, storms, earth quakes, volcanoes, draught, floods, epidemics etc.

Vedas constructed verses as Sun, Moon, Fire, Winds, Storms (Marut), Rainfall (Varun); after probing their nature. Other destructive forces like earthquake, volcanoes etc. were events inside the earth and hence there was no need to construct verses for them i.e. epidemics, floods, storms, draught and excessive rainfall.

While trying to discover the cause of above; Vedas traced it to a power called "Ekadash Rudra". This destructive power of animate world on earth, must have some relationship with earth, must be on earth and yet somehow it must also be outside the earth.

When we consider above tests, Sun and Moon are the two entities that first strike us. As moon was not self-luminary, Vedas did not find any destructive power in it. The result was that the choice fell on sun; or sun-related power. Whether the hypothesis that Rudra equates with Sun or not has to be probed into.

There are many verses in Vedas which are descriptive of Rudra. Rudra has two forms destructive and peaceful. But its original state is of destruction. (By going through rituals of eulogy that power is sought to be pacified, but since it is part of spiritual practice, we will not examine it).

The root of the word "Rudra" is "Ru" which means to "painful weeping" "Roaring with infliction". Rudra also means red colour. Prishni is supposed to be wife of Rudra, and Marut (storms) as their sons. The word Prishni also means cow, or Pakhal. Some of the names of Rudras as per Atharva Veda are Ishan, Bhav, Shart (Archer), Pashupati, Ugra, Rudra, Mahadeo. Originally the number of Rudras were cited as 7, then 11, then 12, 100, and exceeding 100. In Vajasaney Samhita, besides the 7 names 1. Kapirdin (one with long hair, beard, and moustaches) 2. Bhav (encompassing the whole universe), 3. Shambu 4. Krutivasan are also cited.

Both indigenous and foreign scholars tried to decipher real nature of Vedic Deities. Since Rudra also means Red, Macdonald construed it to mean red-coloured stormy clouds or the thunder of storms, or the fall of lightening. Our own scholars also followed similar line of interpretation.

In the Taittiriya Samhita of Krishna Yajurdveda there is a collection of verses describing the nature or properties of Rudra, and this is entitled as "Rudra-Dhyay". "Namak" and "Chamak" are two parts of above and in the chapter Namak there is subtle and all-encompassing description of Rudra. Although 7, 11, 12 and 100 types of Rudras are cited, with universal acclaim to No.11 is linked with Rudra, calling him "Ekadash Rudra". And that is why each part of "Namak" and "Chamak" have eleven chapters. Saint Ramdas also accepted this No. as eleven. The scientific probe that we have conceived is confined to "Ekadash Rudra" (11 Rudras).

Note: 1. Pakhal is a huge leather bag to carry water or to irrigate lands from well water with help of oxes.

2. "Namak" means salutation

From this Rudra-Adhyay we will consider nature of Rudra. In Namak Adhyay the nature of Rudra is described as Horrible. His body is small (Vaman) he is hairless (clean patted) and has 1000 eyes. In his hands is a bow with arrows, a sword, and a contraption to keep hundreds of arrows. His residence is in Mountains or in islands. He always wanders.

In Rudra-chapter his hundreds of qualities are described. But we are going to consider only the following:

1.	Agravedha	- Killer from front.
2.	Apraj	- Born in second half of creation.
3.	Abhignan	- Hitter.
4.	Avarshya	- Like Sea
5.	Awatya	- Like a small well
6.	Urmya	- Like a wave
7.	Kumya	- Like river bank
8.	Khamya	- Like Halo of moon
9.	Guhya	- Cave dweller
10.	Durevadha	- Killer from distance
11.	Nipya	- Well constructed
12.	Pasankhya	- Like atom or dust particle.
13.	Vidhyutya	- Like lightening
14.	Vaishant	- Like Tatak i.e. Bank of river
15.	Hrudayya	- Dweller in deep lake
16.	Asyad	- Thrower of weapons

17. Prakrunt pati - Protector of violent thieves

18. Mrugayu - Killer of wild animals.

19. Vanchat-Parivanchat - Cheater by Betrayal

20. Srukavi Jidhansadu - Armed Killer Thief

21. Stayupati - Thief who mixes in crowds

From the above description of qualities of Rudra, the brief resume is set out below:-

Rudra is far away, but he kills from his front side. He is thrower of weapons as well as a hitter. He resembles a small pond, well, ocean, lake. He has banks like that of a river. He is like a Deep lake which is on the surface undisturbed, but its depth is unknown. He is a cave dweller. He is like Khale, i.e. halo round moon (which is a bad omen). He is dweller of Island.

Rudra is extremely cruel. A killer and thrower of weapons. He is killer of wild animals, protector of violent thieves, Betrayer, killer thief, and steals by mixing in crowds.

This description denotes that Rudra is heartless, and destruction is his creed. His destructive activity takes place (naturally) unknowingly because it is his nature.

In "Shat Rudriya" Rudra is described as follows: Dweller in mountains. Reddish, and yellowish in colour, like "Aditya", like having thousands of rays, space traveller, having lustrous skin, maker of universe, sword wielder, both hairless and full of hair, like the rising sun, like Krishna (when he was baby), foam like, cave dweller, having body which is Nilgriv and "Lohit".

Weapons and his appearance are as follows:

Bow with Arrows and sits pile, weapons that kill, helmet, full of weapons, thrower of weapons, wild animal killer, accompanied by a dog, having armour, sword, having thousands of weapons.

Rudra of size and his behavioral nature:

Rudra is very short tempered, horrible, enemy and killer of all life cattle, ladies on wells, beasts, cows, old and young human beings, fetus, children, horses etc.

He is mean-minded, living in organised set-up of like minded people, capable of assuming small form, pigmy, capable of assuming large form, fast mover, Atom like.

His destructive activity:

He terrorises every one and thereby sickens them. Makes them diseased. He injures every one; destroys cattle, by assuming the form of bacteria, in food and pots, makes people diseased. In space troubles every one by assuming gaseous from, by creating draughts and excessive rainfalls, troubles people, creates sand storms, rain storms and creates calamities.

Special description of Rudra's Bow and Arrow:

The first chapter begins by paying respect and compliments to Rudra's anger, arrows and bows - to earth destroying Bow & weapons, to his capacity to hold thousands of arrows, and prays to unwind chord of Bow and requesting him to keep away his weapons.

After checking up the above description of Rudra, and taking into account No.11 which designates their total No. and also taking into account No.11 as chapters of "Namak" and

"Chamak" each, totalling 22, and also after noting 11 names given at the end of "chamak", we find that No.11 has some close, and meaningful significance in the concept of Rudra. In the universe when we try to search whether this No.11 has any special significance with any entity in solar system we find that No.11 has some special significance so far as Sun is concerned.

Solar cycle is of 11 years. This solar cycle has been ascertained after close scrutiny of the sun and the changes that takes place within the sun. Sun's magnetic field contracts once within 11 years (winds up first) and then expands and is distributed. Thus Sun's magnetism switches every 11 years and its dynamo gets re-organised. The second event that takes place during these 11 years, is manifestation of sun spots, and their expansion. During 11th year the numbers of sun-spots is maximum.

Power, named Ekadash Rudra which is described variously as destructive in Vedas is connected with sun-spots and solar cycle. And description of Rudra in "Shat-Rudriya" given earlier tallies 100% with this phenomena.

The above will be clear after we check up description of solar cycle and solar spots.

The term solar cycle refers to the almost regular series of observed changes in Sun that accompany the winding up and subsequent release of magnetic field, solar magnetic field is formidably complicated. D. Star.

Sun spots number shows an 11 year period, but the time length is 22 years. The magnetic period of Sun is twice "year cycle, when account is taken" (The day time star.)

Solar cycle means regular series of internal changes that take place within the sun; which results in contracting or winding up of magnetic field and then is followed by its release i.e. expansion.

Solar magnetic field is a different complicated and involved subject. Earth's magnetic field is like a bar magnet. It reverses itself only after some thousands of years; But construction of sun is highly complicated and constantly changing. Its speciality is that every 11 years, suns magnetic fields slips over. The magnetic field at the north and south poles of the sun functions in strange fashion. This magnetic field is extended hundreds of miles beyond its poles on either side, with the result that the matter easily flows out of the sun.

High resolution will reveal that in the photosphere much of the magnetism is concentrated into filigree pattern that like the spiculas and fibrills clusters round the boundaries of the super-granule cell. The strength of Solar magnetism inside the small magnetic elements which measures 200-300 k.m. is about 1000. Most of solar magnetism is concentrated into cells of this type.

Highest magnetic field (in solar system) comprising of thousands of Gauss power is directly related to solar spots. In 1908 it was discovered that solar spots possess magnetic field, and is the active region of internal activity of the sun, Bi-polar magnetic field was discovered.

Solar spots exist in pairs, and in both spots opposite magnetic fields exist. In one specific solar cycle, and in one specific half portion of the sun, the spot travelling towards the equator of the sun, the magnetic poles of such spot are similar. At the same time spots in the other half of the sun, although have same speed and direction, their poles get reversed. In the next solar cycle precisely converse phenomena takes place.

Dark portion of solar spot is called Umbra; and semi-dark portion of the spot is called Penumbra. The depth of Umbra is about 7000 Km. In inner side of Umbra intense light points can be seen, and their diameter is 100 KM. Solar spots are of various shapes and sizes. Many are bigger than earth and during solar cycle sometime they are big enough to cover 1/5th of sun. Spots which are bigger than 40,000 KM are visible to naked eyes. In 1946/47, spots of the size of ten thousand million K.M. were noticed.

The action and reaction of solar spots takes place regularly. In 1843 Mr. H.Squab proved that the cycle of solar sports is of 11 years, and once during this cycle the spots reach their highest culmination point.

The area of solar spots is an area of extreme reactions; and activity, and in it are included the following:

1. Facules
2. Spicules
3. Flares
4. Prominances

Flares rises and falls in time with solar cycles as indicated by spotting of the disc. Flares take their birth at the tops of tight magnetic arches looping out of Sun. Flares are most important activity that affect earth. Scientist found temperature of flare of 17 million degrees.

The very speedy release of energy in a flare is puzzling to theorists. The energy so dissipated in one great splurge in which as much as 1025 joules get released. This is equivalent to total striking the earth in an entire year. Ejection of mass during such an event is 10 billion tons at a speed of 1000 KM per second.

Within the Sun spot zone a tube like magnetic field emerges from one spot and arches over to re-enter the sun at the other. About a day or so later then Sun Spot Pair itself emerges and an arching structure of filament connects the two spots. These arches can be 30000 KM. in length and 5000 KM high.

Solar spots are always in pairs. But some times the magnetic arch gets twisted while going from one spot to another. In the result obtuse angle is created and with the result that spot is enlarged and is created at wrong spot and both spots disappear.

During 11 years of solar cycle and period of sun spots, destructive power from sun to earth is thrown on a very large scale. Solar storms (Flares) are Electromagnetic storms (Facules) etc. are created. The region where these activities take place is called active region. This active region is in upper chromosphere and lower corona, and it is called arched magnetic tube, the responsible cause of the phenomena.

After seeing scientific information about solar cycle and solar spots, and after seeing pictures annexed to this chapter of solar sports, we will try to find out similarity points between description of Rudra and solar spots.

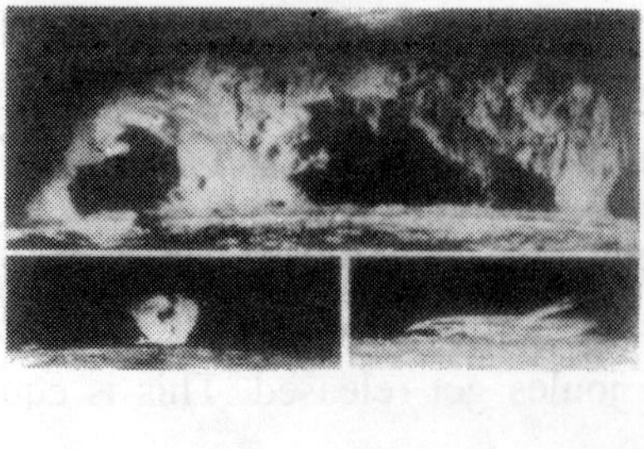

हायड्रोजन प्रकाशात घेतलेली सुर्याची छायाचित्रे ज्यांत solar prominances, streamers, arches 100ps इ. घडामोडी दिसतात.

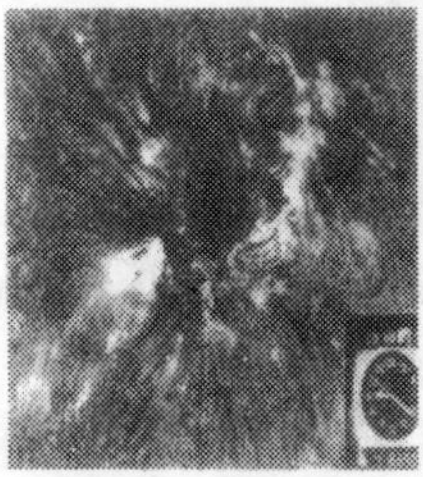
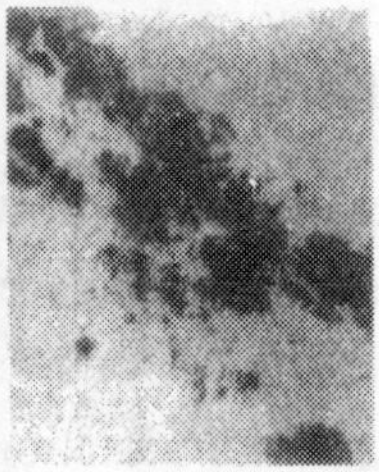

Rudra is lake-like, sea-like, like the two shores of river, ugly, like a stream, like an agressor. If we compare preceding description with pictures of sun-spots we find that they totally agree.

Similarly well-like, is a description which tallies 100% with pictures of solar spots, especially blackness of the well, its depth, its round type. Koop-Swaroop (Like-well) and Laghoo-Koop-Swarup (like a small well) tallies completely with "Pair-Concept" of solar spots. Solar spots are found to be as small as a well and as large as sea.

Solar spots are not only in pairs, but are parallel to the equator of the sun.

In the "Namak" of "Shat-Rudriya", the description of Rudras are invariably shown in pairs of qualities.

1. दूतायच प्रहितायच,
2. श्रुतायच श्रुतसेतायच,
3. वन्यायच कक्षायच,
4. दुन्दुभ्यायच चाहनन्यायच.

If we consider that solar spots are always in pairs, then we will realise the importance of this strategy.

"Agre Vadha", "Dure Vadha", respectively means killer from front, killer from distance, and giver of blow (Hitter). This description fits in with solar spots due to their destructive effects.

The beginning of "Shat-Rudra", is as follows:

"Oh Rudra, let me bow with respect to your anger, your bows and arrows". Having surrendered completely thereafter he goes on to say that his weapons can cause Deluge. In scientific description of a special situation of solar spots, the words used are "Archs of magnetism" or "Arching structure". This description is frequently repeated in verses. This "Arch of magnetism" is called "Rudra who causes deluge'" or, whose Bow is destrctive.

That Bow and Arrows of Rudra can cause deluge is also scientific; because it is through them that "Faculae", Flares, Prominances, (destructive events) take place on sun.

Rudra's arrows are sharp, and compare well with description of spicules. Spicules means a minute, slender, pointed hard body, and it applies to the arrows of Rudra, sky-lab saw at the north pole of sun giant spicules. They were about 40,000 KM in height.

In the 8th Anuwak Rudra, is called Baltrunswarup and Phen, Phen means Foam.

Following description of sun spot is worth reading: "Underneath the surface, the turbulent rumblings of the convection cells boil endlessly away. Creating the foamy structure of solar granulation."

"Wrinkles in the sun's battered skin, the Facules. Those are regions of great brightness, which look a bit like "mountains of gas" struggling above photosphere. Bright and well structured Facules quite often surround sun spot.

This is what Rudra is described in the Shat Rudriya as residing on mountain or peak-dweller or cave dweller. Sun spots are like caves and the description "mountain of gas" fits in properly.

In the seventh "Anuwak Rudra" is called carrier of a musical instrument called "Dundubti" and also like the "stick" or "trumpet" (instrument) which produces the sound.

The science describes sun spots as:-

"Within the sun spot zones a Tube like magnetic field emerges from open spot and arches over to re-enter the sun at the other."

As per "Shat Rudriya" and Vedas, Rudra despite being a deity is capable of cheating by betrayal, capable of stealing by mixing with crowds, like an opportunist pick pocketer, armed with dangerous weapons, and by nature violent. Even if Rudra were to be a Deity of destruction, aforesaid description was uncalled for. Because, creation existence and destruction is a known natural cycle. That is why precisely we have to find out as to why Vedas compared Rudra with a thief.

Sun is giver of life to this world. That is why he is called "Mitra" (friend). But Rudra the solar spots emerge from sun, and since sun is very far away the spots are not visible. But their bad effects were noticed by vedic authors and experienced and felt. That is why an entity concealed in another entity which is friendly, becomes entitled to epithet of "Betrayer" or "Thief". Otherwise, being called as Deity and described as thief and betrayer, does not fit in, in any logic.

Solar spots are in pairs. Calling them two shores of river fits in with "Shat Rudriya" description. Let us examine one more subtle description of solar spots, which fits in with description with the verse in "Dasham-Anuwak" (i.e. 10th part).

"Tiny sun spots form into a pair of rival sun spots. The pair lies in the direction of equator. The leading one (Sunspot) that leads relative to the rotation and will reach the limb first is usually more compact and it will move a little faster than the one following:- (Refer Day, Time, Star page 120.)

Having read the above, let us check up ("Dasham Anuwak" of Chamak) verse which relates to the items demanded from Rudra:

1. Oh Rudra give me cow-fetus, cow company.
2. One & half year old young one of cow & a cow.
3. Two years old young one of cow & a cow.
4. Two & half years old young one of cow & a cow.
5. Three years old young one of cow & a cow.
6. Four years old young one of cow & a cow.
7. Six years old young one of cow & a cow.

In this verse 6 pairs of male and female young ones of cows are demanded. Male is obviously more powerful then female and hence the leader in each pair. Hence female is follower.

This description talies with the fact that solar spots are in pairs, and one is always bigger than other.

Remaining part of above mentioned extract is as follows:-

"It is not unusual for the smaller spots to break through in the gap between two main spots. If this happens, the following spot may disappear leaving the leader which itself slowly subsides."

In the "10th Anuwak" itself after the demand for 6 items of pairs listed above, author of Vedas have demanded the following:

1. Barren cow and old ox

2. Cow which aborts and cart puller ox.

If bigger and leader spot cannot create another spot, or if it is not created, then it is called Barren Cow, Aborting Cow. Similarly, since behind the leader spot, the smaller spot follows, the bigger spot is named "cart-puller ox".

Effective pair of sun-spots are born out of small point "Pores or tiny spots are typically (but not always) form into a pair of Sun-spots.

The above truth is cited in 5th Anuwak.

"मीठुष्ठमायचेषुमतेच, न्हस्वायच वामनायच, बृहते च वर्षीयसेच."

"Assumer of subtle shape and size, or small easy size, and also assumer of vast shape and size and full of many qualities."

As per Vedas Pakhal (Prushni) is mother of Rudra. "Pakhal" means contraption (Bag) of leather in which water is stored. Pakhal is normally carried by "Bhisti" (water supplier to waterless regions). Mouth of "Pakhal" is small and its bottom is big. Once Pakhal is full its mouth has to be tied. If we have a look at solar spots in the picture, it looks like a Pakhal ("Prushni" in Sanskrit). Solar spots like Pakhal appear dark and small from outside; but are Big inside. Having regard to this tallying description, we have to admire inspirational talent of

Vedas in calling solar-spots, "Sons of Pakhal" or "Sons of Prushni".

Maruts are called sons of Rudra, i.e. solar spots. We have seen the nature of Marut. We have seen that solar spots are responsible for creating storms, and they affect earth. This is scientifically established.

As per Vedas when once in 11 year cycle the number of solar spots increase, the enormous internal activity in the sun, affects earth, resulting in huge storms, thunder and lightening and rain, increase in epidemics, and adversely affects living beings and vegetation. Food & pots get affected by bacteria. It also results excessive rainfall or draught.

We will proceed with science of solar-spots in the next chapter.

Chapter 38

STATISTICS OF RUDRA-SCIENCE AND EFFECTS OF SOLAR SPOTS

During cycle of sun-spots, or during culmination point of solar cycle we have seen enormous inner movements described as (Flares, Prominances or solar wind) which affect the earth, undoubtedly.

The magnitude of this effect, the nature of Rudra, its activity needs to be gone into and comparatively the mystery in the eleventh (11th) "Anuwak" of "Shat Rudriya" needs to be probed into.

Ionosphere starts at the height of 80 miles from earth; and it extends to about 1000 KMs (in height). In this area radiation emitting from sun and other sources in space collide with Atoms and molecules from our atmosphere. Ultra-Violate Rays, X rays, and high powered particles coming from foreign entities have the capacity, to separate electrons from atoms or molecules from our atmosphere. Hence this part of atmosphere becomes ionised. Here, percentage of oxygen is more hence temperature rises to 1000 C. Since however gases are rarified nothing burns or boils. This increased temperature is indicative of speed of Ions and electrons. (Day Time Star Page 160).

Since sun is principle source of ionising radiation, any main development within suns internal activity affects ionosphere invariably and results in change in construction of ionosphere.

We have seen how huge is the nature of solar "flares". As per Ency - Brit. Solar "flare" affects earth visible. In the light of hydrogen light, we find that Huge "flare" is constructed out of lighted filamentary structure emerging from solar spots. Following the "flare" gas from the sun is thrown at a high speed. (100 KM per second rising upto 1000 KM per second). From one Huge "Flare", huge energy, i.e. electricity is born on such a scale, that it can supply electricity to earth for a period ranging between a million to 100 million years. This can give us some idea about hugeness and capacity of "flare".

· As a result of sun spots, sun storms are born. This study is partly done in the chapter dealing with "Marut". Due to solar storms, the magnetic field of earth is affected. Ordinarily earth's magnetic field is extended upto 10 Raddi (i.e. ten times the earth) in Sun's direction and on the dark side upto 1000 Raddi, and thereafter there is an involved construction called "Magneto Sheath".

This magneto Sheath works as a barrier against energy and elements emerging from sun spots. In area in front of magnetic-sheath, (at extreme end of sun's confrontation) is another area like a "Stretched Bow". This area also protects earth from elements and energy coming from sun.

Following figure will illustrate:-

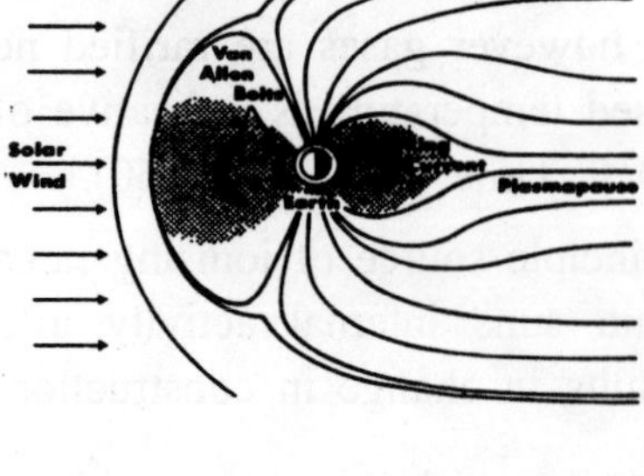

The flares emerging from sun-spots affect earth's magnetic field. If we consider the size of sun spots, their intensity, etc. we can well imagine the impact they could be making on earth's magnetic field.

Just as the explosions in the sun affect magnetic field of the earth, it also affects the atmosphere, water and life. Although modern science has not been able to find positive proof in respect of the same.

As this area of science is comparatively new, and despite study for 2 to 3 hundred years, science could not collect proof to show how solar spots affect life, it cannot be positively stated that solar spots do not adversely affect human life on earth.

Vedic Sages stated that they do affect, and in view of their scientific discussion and proof, we need not reject it.

As per "Shat-Rudriya" following effects result from solar spots:-

1. The rays (Alpha, Gama, Beta, X rays and other invisible radiation) affect those who move outside their houses e.g. cowherds, ladies collecting water from wells, cows and calfs, small children, servants, horses, etc.
2. Bacteria, (which are extremely minute) spaced in food and pots; or are created.
3. In atmosphere huge storms are generated and their results damage life.
4. Excessive rainfall destroys crops, floods damage crops and kill lives.
5. Draughts are created, resulting in unknown consequences.

6. Dust storms are created resulting in unknown consequences.

In view of the above, it will be seen that in the prayers to Rudra scientific truth was concealed.

The above type radiation from Sun will affect those working or wondering in open is most scientific. Those in houses or under roof are not likely to be affected by such radition. Therefore, Vedas have stated as above that cow-heard, women fetching water from wells, servants always moving outside for the work of masters, animals, horses, etc. should be protected by Rudra.

When the number of sun spots are maximum, naturally adverse effects are heightened. Radiation of all types is maximum. Among these are X rays, Alpha, Beta, Gama and Atinil (Ultra-violet) rays. Because sun is an ever active atomic power house and during the period of sun spots it is maximum.

During a flare sudden release of pent up magnetic energy leads to temporary local eating of plasma. Electrons, protons and other charged particles get whipped into a franzy as electro magnetic energy sparks off all around them. In next to no time the electrons are flying about at nearly speed of light and are stimulated to emit energy of every kind, from very long wave length, radio waves, right through energetic X-Rays. The ultra-violet and X-Ray radiation from Sun increases greatly. Gamma rays and ultra violet emission is also tremendous.

The total effect of the above is somewhat comparable (in lesser degrees) to the atmosphere created after explosion of Atomic Bomb. Its intensity will depend and vary, according to atmosphere, winds, constructions, buildings, or whether area is rocky or desert-like. Any living entity who is under shelter is less affected. Gama Rays affect blood cells, living cells, and they become powerless, and bacteria in the body are activated.

In sun's radiation, attack of neutrons can take place. They reach earth and dissolve in water. Vegetation absorb them, and through cows they enter human system.

Therefore the prayer made to Rudra for protecting exposed life of all kinds (described earlier) is understandable.

Alpha rays can be blocked by a simple paper; Beta rays penetrate paper, cloth, card board, but anything denser than this blocks them. But Gama rays and "X" rays can be blocked only by a screen made up of lead.

In the eleventh 'Anuwak' of "Chamak" Chapter of "Shat-Rudriya" following demand is made before "Rudra".

"Oh! Rudra please bless me to attain benefits from things which are designated by odd Nos, like 1, 3,5,7,9,11 upto 33 and even Nos. like 4, 8, 16 upto 48."

The things or entities for which aforesaid numbers stand is a riddle which is not solved. But nothing will be lost if an attempt is made to unravel it.

Scientists so far have discovered existence of 92 elements. Out of these most of elements are found in the sun. These elements have been classified and have been given numbers in the periodic table. And the order in which the numbers are given relate to the number of protons in the elements. For example uranium's no is 92 because there are 92 protons at its centre.

Vedic Rishis (Sages) knew this secret, and this has already been discussed in earlier chapters.

In view of this we will review the modern table of elements and their numbers, and try to find out the result.

Table of odds nos upto 44 (as per prayer in "Chamak") and names of elements:-

1. Hydrogen
3. Lithium
5. Boron
7. Nitrogen
9. Florin
11. Sodium
13. Alluminium
15. Phosphorous
17. Chlorine
19. Potassium
21. Skandium
23. Vanadium
25. Mangneese
27. Cobalt
29. Copper
31. Galium
33. Arsenic

Table of elements with even numbers:

4. Beryllium
8. Oxygen
12. Magnesium
16. Sulphur
20. Calcium
24. Chromium
28. Nickel
32. Germanium
36. Crypton
40. Zirconium
44. Rudhenium
48. Cadmium

We have listed some of the elements from those whose benefits were prayed for in the prayer.

The effect which solar spots create, (flares, prominances), whether gross, subtle, treatable, intractable, would need independent book and study.

All that can be said in the forum of tentative hypothesis, is that these Nos., relate to elements, and vedic Rishis knew about them.

If one who prayed to be benefited by them, then in same way they must be related to the likely effects of solar-spots, which at present may be intactable for our limited minds.

The prayer must have two sides (presumably) viz. to ask for beneficial effects of favourable elements and protection against damage from hostile elements.

Chapter 39

EXTREMELY SUBTLE SCIENTIFIC TRUTH ABOUT RUDRA AND MARUT

In the earlier chapters we have already discussed Sun, Rudra and Marut.

However this chapter spells out some special features.

In 9th verse of 52nd chapter in vth Mandal (Tome) of Rigveda, following verse is cited:

उत स्म पुरुष्ण्या पूर्णा वसत शुन्धवः ।
उत पव्या रथाना मद्रिं भिन्दत्योजसा ॥५.५२॥

The "Marut" clad in woolen clothes, and who by nature is a cloud-breaker, was roaring on the shores of river Purushani.

The scientific features of Marut which we studied in earlier chapters, and this verse does not fit in and appears to be meaningless. Because Maruts are illuminated, hot, and they get energy from sun spots.

Let us therefore try to probe into its concealed meaning if any.

Surface temperature of sun ranges between 6000 to 6500^0 C. But the temperature of inner part of solar spots is 2000^{0}C.

Why it is so less, is an enigma for scientists. However comparatively solar spots are cooler.

At page 130 of Day Time Star following para is cited:-

> "Without doubt a Giant refrigeration process is at work, carrying heat away from the spot so efficiently that the temperature drops by almost 2000°C. There are several explanations for this. One is that the strong magnetic field which is locked in with tumbling gas below the photosphere, can slow down convection (Transfer of heat by movement of heated substance) a great deal, and so form insulating lining under the spot. This is how fibre glass or mineral wool roof insulation works."

In Europe, as a protection from extreme cold, mineral wool roof is kept or used as house top. This roof causes delay in melting snow but that keeps warmth in the house.

Vedic authors in order to show comparative coolness of Maruts, and for showing comparative temperatures of solar spots and sun, used the metaphor of "woolen clothes wearer Marut" which was extra ordinary and yet 100% scientific. Strangely enough the metaphor used by vedic sages was also used by modern scientists.

In the tenth verse of same chapter there is description of ways utilised by Maruts to travel. Those four words descriptive of paths are set out below with English synonyms.

1. Anupths : - Path following, Following Path
2. Antpath :- Internal path.
3. Vipath :- Wrong Path
4. Aapath :- Multi directional paths.

One solar spot follows another. That is Marut's anupath. Marut can arise from within solar spot, that is its Ant-path, some time Marut departs from his path and goes astray, that is Vipath. And when they emerge from sun and spread all over that is Aapath.

Maruts are many times described as possessor of spear. (Bhaladhari) He resembles Spicules on sun. But Rudras are called "Helmet Wearing" in "Shat- Rudirya". Let us see whether it is scientific.

"During period of solar activity, we see that over the poles of the sun, there are polar Plumes, during the interval of minimum solar activity. These vertical columns of plasma are as much as 8000 KM across and may extend to the amazing altitude of half a million Kms. Structures named as Helmets are also seen over plague area." Helmet & Shirastran are synonyms:

In Rigveda at 10.61.8 the verse that touches special features is as follows:

"स ईं वृषा न फेनमत्स्यदाजौ स्मदापरैदपदभ्र चेताः ।
सरत् पदा न दक्षिणा परावृङ् न ता
नु मे पृशन्यौ जगृभ्रे ॥

This is famous as Vishve-Dev - Sukta

This Sukta describes Rudra, Ashwinikumar, Prajapati and Indra. In the 8th verse Rudra is addressed by "Nabhanedishta" as follows "Oh! Rudra! This Vastospati, who appears like sea-form, who is as powerful as Indra, has come in my way, and is not willing to return unless he gets the cows exiled in Dakshinapath, so help me."

Analysis:-

1. This verse is addressed to Rudra.

2. It is addressed by Nabhanedishta.
3. One Vastospati is obstructing person at No.2.
4. Vastospati looks like sea foam.
5. He is powerful like Indra.
6. He won't go unless he collects cows exiled in south region.

In the earlier chapter we saw that solar spots are in pairs. And they are always parallel to the equator. This pair is separated in two different and opposing half, south and north and they are connected by a magnetic tube. We also saw that if bigger spot does not get follower spot, it dissolves.

We must interpret above verse having regard to above scientific truth.

Enormous explosions that take place inside the sun, and the heat that travels from one place to another, in that process, solar granulation takes place and they are like foam. It is this "Foam granulation" who is called Vastospati it is part of inner core of sun and hence is turbulent and rumbling and hence is compared with Indra.

Cow is a word used to signify solar spot. Cow always follows the calf. Similarly one solar spot follows another. This Rudra or Vastospati is source of solar spots. Vastospati is born in North and he wants to create a companion in Southern half. This scientific truth is reflected here.

Chapter 40

GREEN COLOURED "SOMA" AND "PHOTOSYNTHESIS"

"Soma Juice" and "Soma-Art" (Or knowledge) is one of the most important topics in all four Vedas. Entire Sam Veda revolves around Indra and Soma. 144 verses in the IXth Mandal of Rigveda deal with this topic. There are other verses also. From this it is reasonable to conclude that concept of "Soma" was given an important place.

The discussion we had so far, makes it clear that Vedas were concerned with Astronomy, physics, chemistry, creation of universe and with life on earth. Vedas in other words can be said to revolve, around matter, liquid, elements and all the powers concerned therein.

Having appreciated the above, the concept of Soma, and its relation to earthly life has to be examined.

Although we propound that concept of "Soma" means photo-synthesis. But before we show as to how this conclusion is reached it is necessary to go into some introductory verse, and undertake some classification.

We must know that "Soma-yadnya" is a long time process going on in this Earth.

Food (Order No.1):- Vedas have called "Soma" ancient creator of food ("Prachin anna Nishpadak). Again "Soma" means "Food", or food shaped, or for the sake of food one who becomes fluid. He is great "Food-clothed". It is also said that this "Soma-Dev" (i.e. Deity of Soma) supplied food to two legged and four legged creatures. Food is sustainer of humanbeings, animals and vegetable kingdom. Soma is supposed to be running around to give good. He is in the place of parents to humanity. He exists in every part of the body. He distributes food from all four directions. He keeps human beings alive. One who keeps human race alive.

Enthusiasm and Power:- Soma gives power to all human beings. He creates permanent power and is Donor of enthusiasm. He is powerful. He gives power and lustre. He gives long life. He is nourishing. He gives support to life and gives fulfillment. Makes one dominating. Promotes intellect. He gives happiness without lust, and also strength. "Oh! Soma become my friend, and protect me indefinitely, and punish those who abuse the enthusiasm that you have conferred. (62.14)

Sweetness (Order No.3):- Soma is (Mad-Karak) creator of sweetness. He is delicious, tasty. He is Deity of all good and sweet things. He is inductor of enthusiasm and can also intoxicate.

Medicine (Order No.4):- He is creator of medicine (6.47.1.). he cures diseased, blind, and invalids. He is giver of nectar and enthusiasm. Soma is to be consumed as per rules. He makes you lustrous like lit fire.

Let Soma-Ras cure us from diseases (8.48.5). The Deities of earth, herbs, cows, are protected by him. (74.5). He is protector (75.4).

Herbs (Order No.5):- From all chapters on "Soma" one thing gets cleared explicitly that Soma and herbs are inseparably connected. Soma and herbs are connected like breath to man. Soma is green coloured and this itself shows it's direct link. It is Lord of herbs. He is promoter of herbs (9.12.7). Herbs are the area of Soma. (1.91.4). Soma is the cause of creation of herbs. (1.91.22)

Soma Jal (Order No.6):- Vedic description shows that water and Soma are more vitally linked than herbs. Hence water and Soma are frequently emphasized. Like "Oh Soma, lot of water is getting mixed up with you (9.2.4.). "Soma" is being mixed with water (9.2.2.). "Soma shaped, Yadnya (from Sacrificial fire), Havi (Product) water after being prepared, its sweet flow begins (9.9.7). Soma inhabits water waves (9.12.3). Flowing Soma floats on water. Water which enriches Soma, extracts all essence of Soma. Soma full of water was utilised by gandharvas (Divine beings) to create juice. (9.113.3). Soma is constantly described as juicy, full of juice (9.9.4) River altered (watery) juicy Soma (34.3). Creator of power in water (76.1). Ocean dweller, Yadnya worshipper beautiful girls taste Soma (78.3) (Here Jal = water. Sar = residents of water) Original word used for "beautiful girls" was "Apsara".

Soma and Sun (Order No.7):- Like herbs or water, soma is inseparably connected with sun. In fact the description makes it clear that without sun Soma can't be created. Like "Oh Soma daughter of sun creates permanent power in you." (9.10.6) Soma is created out of Yadnya. That means that he is created out of ever burning sun. "Soma" is crossing over sun-rays and going (9.15.6). Soma is "Saptavidh" (seven types i.e. seven colours of sun rays) Lustrous, full of rays, lighted (9.11.1). "He is sun-rays empowered" (9.111.3). He is Dyulokiya meaning ancient creator of food in Dyue-lok (9.110.8). He is also a protector with the help of hot Aditya. He is giver of inspiration to sun. He can expand like sun beams. (9.64.7). He emits light and lustrous (64). He is lustrous all around. Soma while collecting essence from all sides, merges with horses of Sun's chariot. In 54th chapter all four verses describe Sun-shaped Soma. Like "Ancient lustrous, light giving, Soma. Nature observer Soma who is like sun (2) Soma resides on top of the world like sun. Soma the possessor of seven bright rays (111.1).

Order No. Seven (Soma's Universal matters): Soma gets mixed up with several matters. He mixes with matter. He is flowing. Meaning he can mix with water. He is full of juice, and is juicy. Similarly he mixes with milk, curds, butter, flour (68.4). He is invariably present in Honey.

Order No.8 Colours of Soma:- Soma is multicolored. He is also green. He is like milk i.e. white. He is yellow (31.5). He is sallow complexioned (38.5). All the seven colours are part of the white colour of sun. He is shining. He is lustrous. He mixes with fire. He is golden. Soma is black (9.76.1). He is white in colour (74.7)

Order No.9 Place where Soma moves:- Although Soma is shown to be clearly connected with sun, still Vedas have described him variously in following terms. He soars in space, from Dyuelok he falls in pot. He flies and dives like bird. He comes with the speed of Falcon bird. He comes and flows speedily like river flowing over many things. (9.8.4). He is like war-going horses, or calf-searching cow. He has fast speed like horses of a chariot. He falls like rainfall on earth.

Order No.10 (Filtered Soma):- Soma falling from skies is filtered, is the peculiar description of Soma, as if he is filtered through actual filter and thereafter flows. (24.2) Soma who is without legs and is "Gravan that is filtered through a filter (24.5). Soma which is pored in a special pot (Dasha pavitra) and thereafter is put in copper pot (18.7). Soma which is filtered through woolen cloth, and like glorious rainfall is falling in powerful filter (16.7) The filter through which Soma is filtered is nabhi (umbilicus or centre) of universe. (12.4) Filtered Soma is attended to by Rutvij with ten fingers. (9.8.5)

This description, which is extensive and classified, is essence of description of Soma in Vedas. (Same description after repetition, is made throughout.) If we put this classification in some kind of rational order it would be as under:

Soma descends on earth from Dyue-Lok. He comes from great heights. He is created from sun. He comes through Sun's rays. He is filtered in space. He falls like rainfall. He gives sap to vegetation and herbs and enters into them. He spreads in rivers, lakes and oceans. He gives food to all animate life like human beings, animals, vegetation. He creates enthusiasm, power, strength, intellect, smartness. He mixes with milk, curds, flour. He destroys diseases.

If we see the above order we find concept of Soma and photosynthesis is the same. It is through sun that vegetation gets energy, from that food of vegetation viz. Glucose, Lactose, Carbohydrates, proteins etc. are created, and vegetation gets its green colour and it is these vegetation that give man grains, fruits, vegetables, etc. Animals feed on them and give men milk, butter etc.

In this process, the ultimate product is called "Soma" symbolically by Vedas. But this process of Soma process or "Yadnya" is related to creation of glucose or fructose in vegetation. Soma juice is sweet. Soma in a way means sugar. As per our earlier classification it is sugar that gives man force, strength, power etc. Those who are ill, and suffering are given sugar for strength, whether directly or indirectly or are given fruits containing glucose.

Although Soma is equivalent to photosynthesis, its details (of the thesis) are worked out in the next chapter.

Chapter 41

SOMA MEANS PHOTOSYNTHESIS

The fact that Soma is Photosynthesis was seen by us in earlier chapter. But some subtle similarities and other scientific part deserves to be probed into.

Sun and sun rays are creators of process of Soma, or are original parents. In Photosynthesis also sun rays are extremely important and are originators.

Before sun rays reach the earth they have to travel through atmosphere around the earth. This atmosphere is composed of various materials and ranges upto 1000 miles up. At the top is ozone a gas created out of effect of electricity on oxygen. Ozone, if it increases on earth is harmful. But as a belt at the top it is extremely useful.

Light is white but its spectrum is divisible in seven colours. On either side of this spectrum are ultra-violet and infra-red rays, besides x rays, gama rays, Alpha rays, and Beta rays. All these come to earth from universe. Out of these ultra violet rays are most damaging to human constitution and can be responsible for causing incurable diseases.

That is why "Ozone belt" at the top is useful which filters those rays before reaching on earth.

This ozone belt at the top is extremely beneficial. If it disappears, whole world and humanity will be endangered. Scientists lately are disturbed because they have found some holes in this belt over north pole.

In the vedic description this filtering process occurs twice. Once in space. The other on earth. The filtering of ultra violet rays is equivalent to Vedas saying that it is filtered in space. This process is emphasized as having taken place in space by use of words the "umbilicus of space" is itself the filter. (9.12.4).

"Space filters like umbilicus" is a phrase which fits in with Ozone belt. This belt is about 1000 miles up in space. Umbilicus is the place where all muscles are concentrated because it is from that child is born. Hence that belt becomes comparable to umbilicus. It is this belt which filters all damaging rays.

After Ozone "belt" filters it, sun rays come down and vegetation absorb sun rays through its leaves. The same is described by Vedas by saying "Soma visits good persons on his own" (8.48.11). Soma enters society (9.32.3). Like a lover going after his beloved, or bridegroom going with his bride. Soma goes to his pot. (9.103.14). This is indicative of sun rays going to vegetation and Vedas took the trouble of describing this pot (viz. Leaves). Like two lips of a board (9.73.3). Leaves of trees are like two lips (if we consider the central line of a leaf). And Soma enters it, (9.107.14) that is vegetation. This shows that what was meant was leaves.

When sun rays enter leaves, its rays of seven colours have a role to play in Photosynthesis.

The Soma's colours, Vedas have referred to various colours. As per the description Soma can be white (original colour of light) green, yellowish, reddish. The need to refer to it, by itself shows (if we read preceeding para) that Vedas were talking of Photosynthesis. Soma's one colour is red (Arun-varna). This is very scientific description. The importance of red colour was referred to in Marathi Encyclopedia Part 10 page 215:-

> "After describing chemical composition of "Chlorophyll it is stated in the colours spectrum of chlorophyll where, different colours are absorbed, it is found that absorption of blue and red waves or vibrations is more. In the reflected light the extract or essence of chlorophyll looks red."

Colours of Soma, as seen in the earlier chapter, is an important aspect. But one has to find out why Soma is called black or dark complexion. This is more necessary because no where in the sun light there is any black colour. The following passage from Enc. Brita. Throws light upon this aspect.

After years of study and controversy the quantum of requirement for Photosynthesis has been reliably established as about nine Einstein absorbed per mole of oxygen formed. The energy efficiency for glucose production with red light is 31%: this value coincides with the theoretical one calculated from the mechanism of photosynthesis, as the product of the efficiencies of the "light stage" (38%) and the "dark stage" (83%).

"The so-called "light stage" includes not only the photochemical steps but also some dark reactions that occur in or on chloroplast memberances. These dark reactions involve breaking the bonds of the water molecule (i.e. the oxidation of water), forming oxygen gas, transferring hydrogen (as electrons and protons), and storing chemical energy in the energy=rich molecule adenosine triphosphate (ATP). The maximum efficiency of the photochemical steps, which have an upper limit imposed by the second law of thermodynamics, is about 75%. The remaining steps of the light stage have an overall efficiency of about 54%.

> The optimal efficiency of the light stage of Photosynthesis has been measured only under carefully selected laboratory conditions, usually with algae such as Chlorela pyrenoidosa or Scenedesmus. These aquatic single celled plants have fever energy-requiring functions and can be supplied with the most desirable conditions more easily than can higher plants. The energy efficiency of the light stage in higher plants generally is much less than 54% for several reasons; the variation in the amount of light that reaches the leaves, the possibility of low concentrations of carbon dioxide in regions with many growing plants the energy requirements for synthesizing non-photosynthetic issues (e.g. stems, roots, fruit), and the other physiological functions that require energy. If agricultural productions (e.g. fruit) along are considered as the end product of the energy conversion process of Photosynthesis, the efficiency may decrease to 1% or less.

In the above analysis of light there are two stages "Light stage" and "Dark stage". In view of this we will appreciate why Vedas called Soma dark, or grey and also illuminating. The fact that both in science and Vedas, precisely identical synonyms should be used is not an accident. We have seen this in the context of description of seven comets in earlier chapter.

Soma was described as:

"Kandikyukta Soma" Kandik means a part of a bamboo stick.

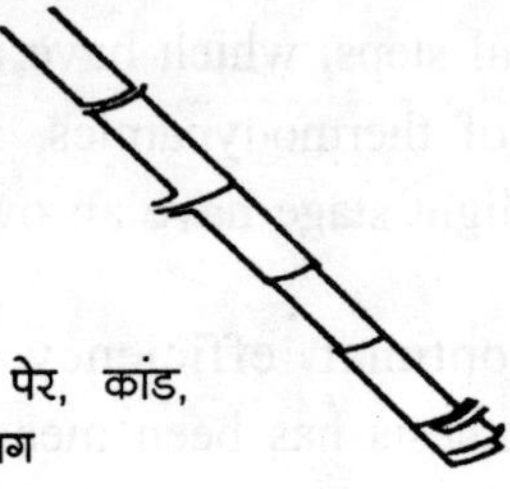

There are seven colours in sun ray. All these colours have different wave length, if we see a sun ray through a spectrum.

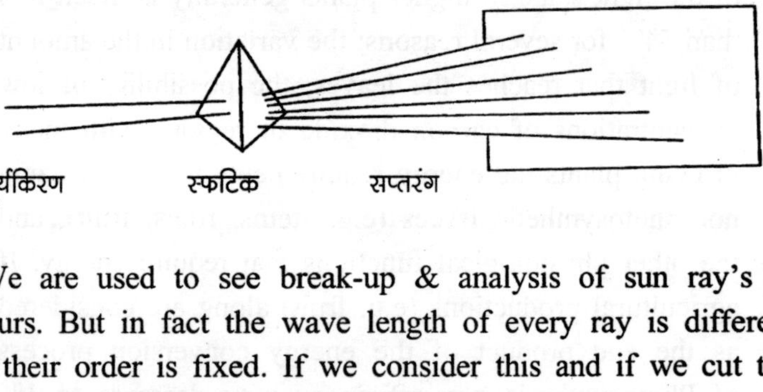

We are used to see break-up & analysis of sun ray's in colours. But in fact the wave length of every ray is different and their order is fixed. If we consider this and if we cut the sun ray vertically we get following result:

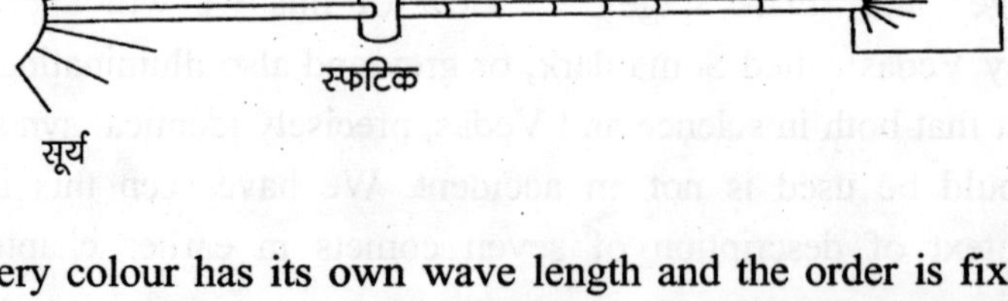

Every colour has its own wave length and the order is fixed, and hence the break up of sun ray into seven divisions will be as follows:

We will now be able to see that result appears like a part of a bamboo stick kept horizontally i.e. like, "Kandika" which was the vedic word used.

Vedas have revealed another great secret of Soma by calling it "Dwibhagjanma Soma" (having two origins or two places of birth).

"Oh, Dwibhagjanma Soma, you are the leader of all living beings and this world." (ताभ्यां विश्वस्य राजसि ये) In En. Brita. Part 14 page 370 it is observed. "In Photosynthesis 2 light reactions occur. During the transfer of electron from water to carbon dioxide ...... Evidence in support of the above scheme of the light reactions during the light stage of Photosynthesis has been obtained."

Entire quotation is not cited as it is lengthy. All that it proves is that this double light process and the observation "Dwibhagjanma Soma" means one and the same thing.

Vedas however did not stop here, in disclosing the secrets of Photosynthesis they added (9.33.5) Soma has 3 heads, i.e. 3 parts. One who is established in 3 parts (9.108.12). In the sacrificial ritual of "Trit Apt" sage Soma is established in 3 pots (9.102). And his 3 heads are named "Yava-Shir", "Gava-Shir" and "Dadhya-Shir" are the words used and 3 different pots are named ass "Adyavaniya", "put, bhrut". "Kalash" (9.103.2)

These 3 numbers have a close connection with Photosynthesis. It is inseparable connection. This connection is with carbon reduction cycle.

"The reduction cycle in which carbon dioxide is fixed, reduced and utilised involves the formation of intermediate compounds called "Sugar phosphates" and during a complete carbon reduction cycle 3 molecules of CO2 are added to 3 molecules of "Rebulose" Five "Diphoshpate and (RuDP L. C.) is carbo - acted and 6 molecules of phosphoglyceric acid are formed." The reduction of one molecule of CO2 to sugar therefore requires the energy contained in 3 molecules of A.T.P. and 2 molecules of reduce NEDP."

Verse 9.62.17 of Rigveda

तं त्रिपृष्ठे त्रिबन्धूरे रथे युंजन्ती यातवे ।
ऋषिणां सप्तथीतिभिः

The meaning is as per Shri Chitrav Shastri, Threefold light shaped Soma was established on 3 fold seats which were of Yadnya shape and Veda shape". Maharshi Dayanand has translated it as follows:

> "That, among other descriptions (which are not relevant), which is 3 fold, and for whose sake 3 seats are kept."

The meaning of this verse is mysterious but appears to be related to the process involving carbon, and ultimately clearly bound with the process of Photosynthesis. At least this required further probe.

अभिप्रियाणी पवते चतो हितो नामानी यहवो अधि येजू वर्धते ।
आसूर्यस्य बृहतो बृहन्मधि रथं विषश्च मरुहद्विचक्षणः ॥
ऋतस्य जिव्हा पवते मधुत्रियम वक्ता पतिर्धियो अस्या अदाभ्यहः ॥
ददाति पुत्र पित्रो रविच्योनांम त्रृतियमधि रोचने दिवः ॥९.७५. १ व २

(9.75.1) "A One who is born in water, body protector, and intelligence given Soma, rides the chariot of sun as a sacrifice to God of Yadnya (Sun).

(9.75.2) : Soma The inspirer of eloquence, promoter of vitality who is immortal and who is very life of yadnya, such soma who gives heavenly juices to his devotees, also confers following advantages (1) Earthly gains (2) Nakshatra (3) Somayaji".

In both the above Verses, and especially in the second, there is reference to 3 states or names of Soma, and in the 3rd verse there is reference to Soma attending all the 3 rituals of sacrifice (yadnya).

In Vedas we have seen that wherever any entity is linked with any number,or figure that is the place of scientific thesis or probe. Hence Soma getting linked with 3 names, 3 forms, 3 seats, is related to the concept of 3 carbons and their involvement in Photosynthesis.

Just as carbon dioxide is in atmosphere, it is also in water, and water being represented by ponds, rivers, seas, and hence water is involved in Photosynthesis. And Vedas have emphatically shown this relationship. One who is born in water, and in whom there is plenty of water, and yet it is water which absorbs Soma further it is described that Soma is relaxing in sea liked a child (9.86.19) surrounded by sea. It is also said that Soma is relaxing like a forest queen in water (9.12.6)

Photosynthesis is a name given by science to a prolonged and involved natural scientific process. To the same process Vedas have given a different name viz. Som or Somayag. Since however the whole process involves sun's rays it is called Somayadnya (Sun's sacrifice), which is an apt name,

Vedas have already said Soma is filtered. It is already stated that this filtering process takes place at two points. 1. Ozone filters it 2. The second is when Soma (Rays) enter vegetation.

And when the process of creation of sugar, carbohydrates etc. begins, filtering starts.

At (9.44.5) Vedas have called Soma as Gas and also Bhag - gami (entering through small pores). Leaves have pores and they are easily detectable if we see dried leaf of "Pipal" Tree. The word "Dasha" is descriptive of a old cloth piece which can act as a "strainer" or "filter".

Sun rays enter through thousands of pores of leafs and that is why it is compared with rainfall. That is why it is said that Soma resides in water, waves (9.12.3) indicating its residence (entry) in leaves (which is both pot and strainer or filter). Similarly Veda which is like foam goes to filter (9.17.3). Foam is full of bubbles. The reaction of sunlight on leaves is on oxygen and carbon-di-oxide is described here. For identical reasons Soma is called "Thousand edged" (9.2.26). As per Marathi Ency. (Part 10 pa. 219) it is easy to measure oxygen emanating in Photosynthesis, because it comes out in the form of bubbles.

As a result of Soma (Sun rays) sugar is created, hence "Soma" is frequently described as "Sweet" and as per various products emanating from its action on vegetation, it is respectively described as juicy, full of juice, etc. Juice is essence of food. Similarly it creates taste, sweetness, and is digestive and sustainer of life.

It is in this context that Vedas call upon Soma to remain in stomach (9.45). Sugar consumed by us creates power and energy. As a result of burning of sugar we have to frequently consume it through various medicines. But fat created out of Soma resides in stomach for a longer time, hence this prayer to "Soma" to reside in the stomach because that dispenses with the need to consume other forms for burning sugar. Hence this prayer is scientific.

Vedas have called Soma "Dashanguli Nishpadit" means extracted by ten fingers. In the creation of Soma as a process in the atmosphere, ten fingers have no relevance. But still it is indicative of something-else. The atmosphere around the earth is divided into five main and five sub-parts as under:-

1. Exosphere
2. Meso Pause
3. Mesosphere
4. Ozonsphere
5. Strato Pause
6. Stratosphere
7. Thermo Pause
8. Thermosphere
9. Thropo Pause
10. Troposphere

This atmosphere is extending thousands of miles above surface of earth. It contains all gases. Sun rays pass through these ten divisions and, therefore, perhaps it is said that Soma is extracted from ten fingers. Such a conclusion cannot be wholly ill-logical.

Vedas have called Soma "Nishpadit" (without legs) and "Dashamukhi". The need to explain this takes as to the following:- Chapter 9.5 is "Aapri-Sukta". "Aap" means "acquiring". Then Ten "Aapri" deities are as follows

1. Susmidha
2. Tanu-napat
3. eel
4. Barhi
5. Dwar
6. Ushasanakta
7. Daivyo Hautaro
8. Vistro Devya
9. Twashta
10. Swaha

"Dashanguti Nishpadit" is a mysterious phrase and it described in general way. The total work, process of Photosynthesis and the ten deities citied have an inseparable connection with atmosphere. Eleventh "Apri" Deity are herbs. Even science accepts that vegetation and living beings are related hence eleventh deity need not be explained.

In 9.8.4 (Verse) Mr. Chitrav has described the term "मृन्जन्ति त्वा दशक्षियो" to mean, "eaten by 10 fingers". But Mr. Dayanand has interpreted it to mean "Five gross five subtle element make Soma affiment". Mr. Dayanand's interpretation fits in with our scientific theory and since Dayanand's reference relates to 10 elements and joins them with atmosphere it becomes meaningful.

At various places in Vedas in the context of Soma, the word water is used and this is perfectly scientific because the Soma entering vegetation results in a product which is 90% water.

For breathing and for breathing of steam, the vegetation has pores in its leaves. CO2 which plays its role in photosynthesis, enters leaves through these pores. These pores open in light. In humid climate the pores don't open. From these pores steam molecules permanently keep coming out. Out of seven colours in spectrum of a Ray, the blue & red colour are conducive to the opening of pores. That is why it is said that this process goes on through "Harit Dravya" (Green matter viz. leaves).

The process of absorption of water by vegetation through its roots, and reaching of water upto its leaves is an independent subject in Botany. It's essence also is irrelevant here.

But the simile of different motions described, like, speed of falcon bird, speed of horse (9.82.1, 9.82.2) or reference to attraction of water of seven rivers (9.87.8) etc., relate to the function of either absorption or circulation of water.

In verse 9.97.1. two sides of Photosynthesis are referred to viz. the dark side and the bright side. The passage quoted earlier of En.Britannica is self explanatory and tallies fully with this verse.

Through Photosynthesis, vegetation converts light into water, CO_2, and minerals into oxygen, and compounds of oxygen. The result is that the percentage of oxygen in air is preserved and atmosphere remains purified. Absorption of CO_2 from atmosphere by vegetation also purifies the air. These scientific facts were stated by Veda in verse (9.97.17).

"वृष्टीं नो अर्ष दिव्यां जिगत् नु मिळावतीं शंगयीं जिरदानु ।
स्तुकेव विता धन्वा विचिनवन् बंधूं रिमाँ अवराँम इंदो वायून् । ९.९७.१७

Oh! Soma who through paternal love, absorbs, gas from air, please also create divine rain which creates food and happiness.

The words "absorbs gas from air" are indicative of absorption of CO_2.

Photosynthesis is affected by several factors but top constituent is light. This was shown by Vedas in verse 9.114.3.

"सप्त दिशो नानासुर्याः सप्त होतार ...
देवा आदित्या ये सप्त ते थिः सोमाभि रक्ष न इंद्रा येंदो परिस्रव ॥ ९.११४.३.

Oh Soma, protect us with the help of seven directions, seven seasons, seven Rutivaj and seven Adityas.

In verse 9.111.1 the description of Soma as possessor of seven types of rays, is given.

Veda have described Soma as "Madkarak" (intoxicating) and hence king of intoxicating drink. How carbon creates Alcohol has been seen by us in earlier chapters.

As per Marathi Encyclopedia, alcohol is created out of carbohydrates naturally available from vegetables. This truth was told by calling Soma a king of intoxicants. Soma gives sugar proteins, etc., which are not intoxicants. And hence in (8.79.7) Veda is called "Giver of strength and happiness without intoxication."

In expressing truth reached through research both Vedas and science have used terms, similes, of identical nature, and this we saw in chapters dealing with Marut, Rudra and Comets. In Photosynthesis also Vedic Rishis and scientists show parallelism.

Vedas have described light as Soma travelling like bird falcon, like arrow discharged from a bow. At page 291 Vol.14. En.Brita. following extract says "Light may act as a trigger imitating a reaction that once started can proceed spontaneously."

Trigger is a mechanism which when pressed releases the bullet. During vedic times guns were absent, hence simile of bird and arrow was used.

Chapter 42

FROM SHAD-DARSHANAS TO "SCIENCE"

"Shad-Darshanas" referred to six branches of knowledge with reference to ancient Indian thought. They are:-

1. Mimamansa	2. Vedant
3. Nyaya	4. Vaisheshika
5. Sankhya	6. Yoga

In fact "Shad-Darshanas" tried to go to the causes of creation of Universe. But the tradition bound interpreters converted them to certain aspects of human life. That approach limited the scope and interpretation of "Shad-Darshanas" and created obstacles in looking at them in proper perspective.

Among six Darshanas, Vaisheshika is special because it goes into fundamentals of creation of Universe referred to. This Darshana was born in 6th Century A.D. and Maharshi (Sage) Kanad was its author. This Darshana and its origin is comparatively recent as compared with "Sankhya" and "Yoga" which are more than 5000 years old.

Since Vaisheshika Darshana could not isolate itself from its main motivation of alleviating human miseries, the critics lost sight of the fact that in Vaisheshikha Darshana one could see the foundation and elaboration of two modern Sciences viz. Chemistry and Physics.

Foundation of Chemistry in Vaisheshika Darshana:-

It was laid down in this "Darshana" that nine Dravya elements were involved and they had 24 characteristics.

Elements were set out as follows:-

1. Prithvi (Atom)
2. Water (Aap)
3. Fire
4. Vayu (Gases)
5. Space
6. Time
7. Soul
8. Directions
9. Mind

The 24 features were set out as follows:-

1. Shape (Rup)
2. Ras
3. Fragrance
4. Touch
5. Numbers
6. Quantity (Pariman)
7. Quality of Splitability (Pruthakatva)
8. Union (Sanyoga)
9. Division (Vibhag)
10. Separation (Paratva)
11. Non-separation (Aparatva)
12. Gravity
13. Liquidity
14. Affection
15. Words
16. Intellect
17. Happiness
18. Misery
19. Desire
20. Hatred
21. Effort
22. Duty
23. Absence of duty
24. Traditional impressions

We are going to eliminate from our discussion 7th and 9th elements viz. soul and mind. Similarly from list of 24 characteristics we are going to eliminate characteristics listed between Nos. 14 to 24, because they deal with human problems, and are unrelated to Science proper, although their inclusion was motivated with elimination of human misery around which the Darshanas had initially centred.

The word "Dravya" used by Vaisheshikas was broader than the word "element" used by modern Science which says that universe is made up of 105 (or whatever the number) elements. By using the word "Dravya", we don't mean to show that they impliedly denote inclusion of 105 elements. Unfortunately, use of the word "Dravya" by Vaisheshikas was not probed into by scientists with open mind. If that were to happen the inevitable conclusion could have been that Vaisheshikas had probed intensively enough to reach, to the conclusion that Vaisheshikas could be called fathers of modern chemistry.

However right from the period of Emperor Ashok upto 1947, India lived in a state of slavery and hostile conditions, which destroyed all the attempts and urged to go to the root.

Modern Science got a lift after discovery of Atom. But it appears that this discovery of existence of Atom was reached by Maharshi Kanad 1400 years ago. It appears that subject of sub-atomic particles was dealt with Vaisheshika and Nyaya Schools.

Vaisheshikas by setting out 9 "Dravyas", and 24 characteristics 5 activities or Karma established basis of modern chemistry.

Unfortunately no Indian probed into this aspect or angle.

Present Science of chemistry discovered 105 elements. Two out of them belonged to liquids, 11 to gases, and rest to metals.

The word "Prithvi" cited as the first Dravya or element, does not mean earth, but it means that metal which has shape, mass, density etc. In other words it stands for "Atom". Similarly in the word "Aap" is included water steam, fire, humidity and liquidity ice. In the element "Vayu" (wind) all kind gases including Oxygen, Nitrogen etc. are there.

Similarly Agni (Fire), Akash (Space), Time and directions, these four elements have a big role to play in creation of Universe. However we will consider them later. However reference to "Time" is at once most surprising and shocking because the Greater Albert Einstein treated "time" as new dimension and coined the word "Space-Time-Speed.".

The modern theory of minimum space and minimum time is worthy of being referred to. It explains how "Time" goes into creation of atom. For example if without an electron taking a circuit around a nucleus atom is not born. Assuming that for an electron it takes "X" time to take a circuit, then any time less than "X" would not create atom.

For Vaisheshikas to cite time as an element going into creation of Universe, is a marvel of scientific imagination.

When Vaisheshikas referred to 24 characteristics of elements, and out of these 24 if we apply 14 to three elements viz. Prithvi (Atom), Jal (water) and Vayu (gases), we will find entire Science of chemistry fitting into it. This will exhibit peerless inspiration and insight of Maharshi (Sage) Kanad into Science of chemistry.

Analysis of table of these three elements combined with listed characteristics reveals the following:-

Prithvi (Atom)	= Atom + Numbers (Sankhya)
Do	= Do + Quantity (Pariman)
Do	= Do + Analysis (Pruthaktva)
Do	= Do + Sanyog (Compound)
Do	= Do + Division (Vibhag)
Do	= Do + Specific Gravity (Gurutva)
Do	= Do + Paratva
Do	= Do + Aparatva (Distinguishing Factors)

Do = Do + Liquidity (Dravatva)

Do = Do + Sanskar (Traditional Impression)

Jal (Water)

Jal = Atom + Numbers

Do = Do + Quantity (Pariman)

Do = Do + Analysis (Pruthaktva)

Do = Do + Sanyog (Compound)

Do = Do + Division (Vibhag)

Do = Do + Specific Gravity (Gurutva)

Do = Do + Paratva

Do = Do + Aparatva (Distinguishing Factors)

Do = Do + Liquidity (Dravatva)

Do = Do + Sanskar (Traditional Impression)

Vayu (Gases)

Vayu = Do +Numbers

Do = Do + Quantity (Pariman)

Do = Do + Analysis (Pruthaktva)

Do = Do + Sanyog (Compound)

Do = Do + Division (Vibhag)

Do = Do + Specific Gravity (Gurutva)

Do = Do + Paratva

Do = Do + Aparatva (Distinguishing Factors)

Do = Do + Liquidity (Dravatva)

Do = Do + Sanskar (Traditional Impression)

Scientists who went into deep research in chemistry, had examined the aspects mentioned above. The difference in atom of one element and atom of another element, is attributed to the difference caused by difference in above qualities.

Characteristics cited by Vaisheshikas, if tallied with English equivalents would show that there is no difference in thoughts of Vaisheshikas and modern scientists.

Chracteristics

Sankhya	= Number
Pariman	= Quantity
Pruthaktva	= Analysis
Sanyog	= Compound
Vibhag	= Division
Gurutva	= Specific Gravity
Dravatva	= Liquidity
Paratva and Aparatva	= Distinguishing Factors

"Number" plays an important role in chemistry. Periodic table gives different numbers to the elements. These numbers referred to electrons moving around the core of atom. One element can be distinguished from the other only because of the number. Therefore, taking "Sankhya" or "Number" as an important factor by Vaisheshikas is astonishing.

Second characteristics is "Pariman" meaning "Quantity". As per Vaisheshikas there are four kinds of quantities 1. Mahatva 2. Anutva 3. Dirghatva d. Matratva and 5. Rhasatva.

To complete two elements or their atoms this concept of quantity (Pariman) is an absolute must.

Thirdly every element or its atom is distinguishable from another atom. This analysis is facilitated by numbers, as well as by other qualities.

Sanyog (Compound) is the essence of construction of Atom. In compound a union between element and energy is implied. According to Vaisheshikas, compounds (Sanyog) is of three types. 1. That which is the outcome of another's action, e.g. where one entity is stable but another comes and inhabits it, like a bird inhabiting a stable mountain. 2. That which is the outcome of actions of two entities e.g. where two tigers get together. 3.Where Sanyog is the outcome of accidental act, e.g. where one reads a book and book and hands come together.

If we study the word Sanyog (compound) under the light of above discussion in chemistry we find the central scheme of construction of Atom, where we get to know about the nucleus, as well as electrons and protons, coming together.

Next characteristic is "Vibhag" or "Division". This principle is "anti-sanyog" or anti-compound. It connotes separation of sub-atomic principles from each other.

"Gurutva" or specific gravity has an important role to play in construction of an atom. Every atom has its distinguishing specific gravity.

Vaisheshikas have laid down that 8th quality of Dravya is Sanyog of three types. First is speed. It relates to speed of Atom (Prithvi), water and gases and it springs out of motion (Karma) and this speed generates other reactions. Motions of elements are of five types:

१) उत्क्षेपण, २) अवक्षेपण, ३) आकुंचन, ४) प्रसरण, ५) गमन

In the above discussion if we apply right meaning of the word, which means motion, we reach a conclusion that in respect of Atoms, water and gases, their motion determines their speed, and any one type of motion from amongst the five, generates other motions and speed.

Around the centre of every atom, electrons and protons move with unimaginable speed and this speed in its own turn generates any one or more of five types of motions mentioned above.

This movement of electrons and protons preserves existence of atom. It therefore appears that to preserve the basic feature of an atom which inherits the qualities of that element, two fundamental qualities are necessary and they are the speed on one hand and motion on another. Motion (as applied to innate matter) is called karma in this sense. Speed is called Sanskar, which means a traditional impression. When "Sanskar" as a term is applied to human conduct it means good traditional impressions passed on from one generation to another.

If elements had been brought in existence without speed and motion of atoms as described above, they would have disappeared and creation of universe would have been an impossibility.

Out of the nine elements cited by Vaisheshikas, we did not take into account Tej (Fire), Space, Time and "Direction", because modern science has not treated "Tej" (Fire) as an element. But as per Vaisheshikas Tej or Fire has a unique place in creation of the universe and in construction of atom. Similarly space, Time and Direction have a very important place as per Vaisheshikas and that cannot be disputed by Modern Science.

Every item of existence is subject to space, Time and Speed; Einstein's theory of relativity is based on these three items.

Every existence occupies space, it has its own motion resulting in speed, and in process covering space, time is needed. If we take into consideration the above, the analytical powers displayed by Vaisheshikas in analyzing forces of the universe, is indeed awe-inspiring. Vaisheshikas treated space and motion as a Sanskar (Traditional Impression).

Difference between speed of motion is perhaps one of quantity and not quality. But this again has to be a guarded observation in view of conclusions reached by "Quantum theory" in physics. The conclusions reached by quantum theory broadly speaking are as follows. More than half a dozen finest brains in particle physics directly or indirectly endorsed these conclusions set out below. Among them were Albert Einstein, Maxplane, Heisenbery, Scoondinger, Neil Bohr and Fermi.

The conclusions were as follows:-

1. Electron is a kind of energy.
2. This energy travels discontinuously (in capsules).
3. It sometimes behaves as particle and some time as a wave (exploding Aristotelian logic that A is B and A is not B both can't be true at the same time.)
4. Therefore the Brick (Atom) out of which the universe is made is uncertain.

If we take into conclusions reached by modern Physics, it is most shocking that some of the secrets that puzzled modern scientists were explained by Vaisheshikas when they described five qualities of motion. Contraction is one where electron becomes a particle, and expansion is another where electron becomes a wave.

It is astounding that where as Why? of this double nature could not be explained by Modern Science, Vaisheshika had explained it clearly by saying that it is the nature of motion to contract and to expand. The principle that governed the riddle in quantum physics was already solved by Vaisheshikas.

Although Vasisheshika Darshan was born in 600 A.D. it had drawn its inspiration from Vedas and it only reflects that scientific orientation that charcterised oldest hoary books was developed to unbelievable heights as shown in Vaisheshika research.

Time was treated as an element. We have seen earlier time does go as a Constituent, while studying theory of minimum time. We can well imagine the heights the Author Kanad reached when he treated "Time" as an element.

Annexure

Other works by the Author

1]	Kimidin	– A novel on 'Aghori vidya'
2]	Sankarshagni	– A novel on Saint Dnyaneshwar
3]	Vajrakamal Ghananeel	_ A novel on Lord Shrikrishna
4]	Vedateel Vigyan (Modern Sciences in Vedas)	_ A Research on Significance of Vedas in Modern Science. This book has received two awards one from Lokmanya Seva Sangh, Vile Parle, Mumbai and another from Government of Maharashtra and now being translated in other languages.
5]	Mahayogshakig Kundalin..	- A book giving a totally new approach to the "Science of Kundalini."
6]	Divyasparshi	- A biography of an outstanding personality called Dr. Ram Bhosale who was the famous masseur.
7]	Chinmaylila Vilas	- A book dealing with Yoga, the seceet of Omkar and the Basics of Indian Philosophy
8]	Operation Hiroshima	– A suspense novel.
9]	Rajasatta, Dharmasatta-Aani Dnyaneshwar	A book of probing and analysing the cause of creation of Dnyaneshwar.